The Future of Children

PRINCETON-BROOKINGS

VOLUME 21   NUMBER 2   FALL 2011

Work and Family

Work and Family: Introducing the Issue

Jane Waldfogel and Sara McLanahan

This issue of *The Future of Children* describes the challenges parents face in taking care of family responsibilities while also holding down a job and explores the implications of those challenges for child and family well-being. As children grow and develop, parents are the hub in a system of care to meet their needs, a system that includes extended family, preschools, schools, health care providers, community organizations, and others, but in which parents play the lead role. Often these same working parents have additional care responsibilities for other family members—in particular, the elderly—and are, for them too, the hub around which other caregivers, services, and programs revolve.

Work-family challenges are as varied as the families that must deal with them, and they change in nature over time. Some working parents are better positioned than others to meet their family's care needs because they have higher incomes, more access to informal support from family members and others, or more support from employers or public policies. But no families, even middle- and high-income families, are immune from the challenge of balancing work and family obligations. Employers' needs and capacities are tremendously varied as well, particularly

given the large role in the U.S. labor market of small, often family-owned businesses. Such wide variation suggests that meeting the work-family challenge will require flexibility and an array of options, rather than a one-size-fits-all approach.

The rising shares of women in the workforce and of families headed by single parents have made work-family issues especially prominent and challenging, as more employees, both men and women, face care responsibilities at home and fewer have a stay-at-home spouse to manage them. The work-family challenge has also been heightened by an increase in longevity that has boosted the share of the population that is elderly. Although many elderly Americans are healthy (and indeed provide assistance to their adult children and grandchildren), others require care and support from their family members.

Although these demographic trends have been observed to some extent in every modern economy, the challenges of meeting work and family obligations are particularly problematic in the United States. Simply put, U.S. work and family policies have not been updated to reflect the new reality of American family life. The social welfare system in the

Jane Waldfogel is a professor of social work and public affairs at Columbia University. Sara McLanahan is the editor-in-chief of *The Future of Children*, as well as the director of the Center for Research on Child Wellbeing and the William S. Tod Professor of Sociology and Public Affairs at Princeton University.

United States, more so than in other countries, is designed around the idea that government assistance is a last resort, provided only after families have first used available family, community, and employer supports, or in cases where such supports do not exist. Economists generally endorse limited government involvement but identify several types of situations where government may need to step in. For example, in cases where the benefits of a policy would accrue not just to the individual family or employer but to society more generally, it is in the public's interest for government to provide those benefits. That principle is the rationale for universal public education, where the United States has historically been a world leader, although its edge in higher education is eroding and it has fallen behind other countries in preschool education. In other situations, private insurance markets may not be able to cover a particular risk, necessitating public provision of social insurance. Social Security, for example, helps ensure that elders have adequate incomes; Medicare (and Medicaid) ensures that elders have health insurance coverage; and the Older Americans Act provides in-home services such as Meals on Wheels. These federal programs recognize the limits of family, community, or employer support for the elderly and fill in the gaps.

The U.S. system of public supports for families with children or families with elderly relatives who need more care is typically less well developed than the systems in other advanced countries, and U.S. parents continue to rely primarily on their families, communities, and employers for support. The advantage of this approach is that the United States has a larger community-based volunteer sector and a better-developed system of employer supports than do many other countries; the disadvantage is that these supports do not reach all workers, particularly those of low socioeconomic status. Employer policies tend to be inequitably distributed, with the highest-paid workers receiving the best packages of benefits. In short, the employees who may most need family-support assistance from their employer may be least likely to receive it.

A further consequence of relying heavily on employer supports is that work-family policies are seen—often quite rightly—as imposing costs on employers, costs that may be particularly onerous for small businesses. At the same time, the extensive U.S. reliance on employer supports has caused public policies in this area to be underdeveloped compared with those in other peer nations. The United States, for example, is the only advanced country without paid maternity leave and one of the few without paid paternity leave, sick leave, or annual leave. It is also unique among peer nations in not providing universal public access to preschool in the year or two before school entry.

In thinking about policy solutions to the work-family challenge, it is important to keep the American context in mind and to focus on policies that are consistent with American values as well as with the best economic evidence. At the same time, it may be useful to rethink some common assumptions that may be interfering with progress in this area. One such assumption is that work-family issues necessarily represent an area where employer and employee interests collide. The need to meet both work and family responsibilities may well pose a conflict for the individual employee who is trying to be in two places at once, but addressing work-family issues does not necessarily pit the interests of employers against those of employees. In particular, a good deal of evidence shows that greater

The challenges of meeting work and family obligations are particularly problematic in the United States. Simply put, U.S. work and family policies have not been updated to reflect the new reality of American family life.

workplace flexibility benefits both employers and employees. Allowing employees more control over their work hours and more flexibility to adjust hours or work location when family demands arise can lead to increased employee productivity, satisfaction, and retention. Far from representing a cost to employers, such policies, if well designed to take into account the needs of both employers and employees, can yield benefits.

Another questionable assumption is that work-family issues are of concern to women only. Although women are more likely than men to have care responsibilities, and to spend more time on them, the gender gap in caring has narrowed significantly. Substantial numbers of male employees have family obligations, and they too face conflicts between managing those obligations and their responsibilities at work. The landmark U.S. legislation in the work-family area, the 1993 Family and Medical Leave Act, recognized this new reality by adopting a gender-neutral approach, providing a period of leave for all new parents, both mothers and fathers, and for all employees, both male and female, who need leave because of their own health or the health of a family member. The approach is promising and researchers should keep it in mind in considering other policies.

A third assumption that bears rethinking is that work-family challenges are problems that only families and employers need address. As noted, it may be appropriate for government to take on an expanded role in some situations. But other sectors may also have a role to play. The family members for whom employees are providing care are typically receiving care in other systems, such as preschools, schools, health care providers, and other community organizations. Could these other providers do more to help address work-family challenges, by, for example, changing their opening hours or providing more coordination of care or more transportation? Fifty years ago, when most children had a stay-at-home mom, preschools and kindergartens could reasonably operate on a two-hour-a-day schedule, schools could expect parents to come in for parent-teacher conferences after school or to take care of children during teacher training days and snow days, and doctors' offices could expect a parent to spend an hour or two at a child's routine checkup. But with most children no longer having a stay-at-home parent, it would be a great relief for both parents and employers if schools and doctors' offices were to modify these expectations to correspond to today's family and workplace realities. Although such changes are often difficult to make and cannot eliminate all, or even most, sources of work-family conflict, they could certainly help reduce it.

The Findings

To understand the extent to which work-family conflicts may be affecting the well-being of American employees and their families as well as the productivity of American employers, it is necessary to answer several questions. First, what share of employees has care responsibilities, and for what types of family members do they care? To what extent are their work hours and work conditions compatible with their being able to meet those responsibilities? Can employees adjust their employment, on either an ongoing or an ad hoc basis, to meet family needs? Second, when obligations to employment and family come into conflict, what are the consequences, both at the workplace and in the family? What is the business case for providing employees with more flexibility? What does the evidence show about the consequences for child and family well-being? Third, what policy options might help employees better meet their obligations to work and family? What is the role of employers? What role might other organizations and systems play? What is the role of government? And what lessons do other countries offer? What policies have they adopted to address these issues, and what have researchers learned about the costs, benefits, and implementation of those policies? Should the United States consider adopting some of the policies that peer nations have?

To answer these questions, we commissioned a group of experts to write eight articles. The first article provides an overview of the demographic changes that set the stage for the current situation. The next four articles consider the challenges of employees who have care responsibilities for particular types of family members—young children, school-aged children, children with special health care needs, and elderly relatives. The final three articles consider possible policy responses, focusing, respectively, on the role of employers, the role of government, and what other countries do.

Demographic Changes

Suzanne Bianchi, of the University of California–Los Angeles, documents the dramatic changes in the American family and workplace over the past fifty years. The share of married mothers in the labor force has risen from a little over a quarter in 1960 to more than 70 percent today. During the 1960s, only 10 percent of mothers were at work within three months of giving birth; by the early years of the twenty-first century that figure had risen to over 40 percent, with 64 percent of women back at work within twelve months after a birth. Labor force participation rates are now nearly as high among women with preschool-aged children as they are among those with school-aged children. Over the same period, the share of children living with a single parent has grown sharply. Today about one-quarter of families with children are headed by single parents; the majority are single mothers, but single fathers represent about 15 percent of this group. Employment rates among single parents have always been high relative to those of married mothers and are particularly high now in the wake of welfare reforms that have promoted work. In 2009 single mothers had an overall labor force participation rate of 76 percent.

Bianchi notes one further demographic change—the aging of the population—that is likely to have a dramatic impact on work-family issues. The large baby boom generation raised much smaller families than the ones they were born into—with families averaging two children rather than three or four. As the baby boom generation ages, increasing elder care responsibilities will therefore fall to fewer siblings. Although it is difficult to find reliable estimates for both the number of older individuals who need care and the number of working adults who have elder care responsibilities, overall, the numbers for both seem to be rising steadily. Elder care demands will play an increasingly central role in work-family balance, often compounding already challenging demands associated with child care.

Workplaces are also changing. Bianchi documents increases both in nonstandard work schedules and in job insecurity and earnings inequality. For high-income families, often the problem is too many hours of work, although the long workdays give these families enough private resources to purchase care needed for family members. For low-income families, the problem is often too few hours of work, too little control over those hours, and insufficient income, although these families may be eligible for public programs that help meet some of their needs. Families in the middle not only face insecurity about their jobs and financial situation, but also have limited resources to meet their family's needs; their incomes are too low to purchase high-quality care for their dependents but too high to qualify for help from public programs.

Bianchi stresses that these demographic and workplace changes have increased work-family conflicts across the board but that the dilemmas they pose vary across the income distribution. That families with differing income face differing types of issues reinforces the point that work-family problems are highly varied and unlikely to be amenable to a one-size-fits-all solution.

Families with Young Children
Taking care of young children while holding down a job is challenging in the best of times. But Christopher Ruhm, of the University of Virginia, explains that it is particularly difficult in the United States, where policies involving the care of children between birth and school entry are less comprehensive than the early child care policies in many other developed countries.

Two principal types of policies help parents take care of young children: one is parental leave; and the other, early childhood education and care. Ruhm reviews current provisions in each of these policy domains in the United States and compares them with those in Western Europe and Canada. In both domains, he concludes that U.S. parents face particular challenges, because of the limited reach of public policies and the unequal array and distribution of private policies. He describes how European countries provide a more integrated set of supports that combine provisions for parental leave and child care. Despite tremendous variation across these countries, all provide at least some job-protected and paid parental leave followed by support for early childhood education and care, including, in most countries, universal preschool in the year or two before school entry.

Ruhm then reviews the evidence on the consequences of such policies, in terms both of economic outcomes and of child and family well-being. He concludes that short to moderate periods of parental leave (ranging from three to twelve months) are unlikely to have negative repercussions in the labor market and are likely to have benefits for child and family well-being. Periods of leave in excess of a year have less clear-cut benefits for children and families and pose some risks in terms of employment and earnings. These findings are relevant for U.S. policy, where current federal law provides just under three months of unpaid leave to about half the workforce and where only a handful of states provide a short period of paid leave to new mothers and, in some instances, fathers.

With regard to early childhood education and care, Ruhm's review of the evidence points to substantial benefits, particularly for disadvantaged children for whom preschool promotes sizable gains in school readiness. He notes that an important question for U.S. policy is whether child-care expansions should be universal, and available to all children, or targeted to disadvantaged groups. As he observes, most European countries have moved to universal preschool in the year or two before school entry, a model that both promotes public support and improves preschool quality. But given limited resources, and the larger documented benefits for disadvantaged children, a case can also be made for targeting program expansions. Another issue for policy makers to grapple with, Ruhm contends, is the quality of child care, particularly for children under three. Measures to raise quality will also raise the costs of care, straining family and public budgets.

Although the comparative evidence is not entirely conclusive, Ruhm suggests that it does indicate that moderate extensions of U.S. leave entitlements (up to several months) would improve child and family well-being by increasing mothers' time at home with infants and could also improve mothers' job continuity. He also suggests that the leave be paid to facilitate its use, particularly by low-income parents, and recommends improving both the quality of and access to early childhood education and care.

Families with School-Aged Children and Adolescents

Although it is often thought that family demands diminish when children start school, in fact, as Kathleen Christensen of the Alfred P. Sloan Foundation, Barbara Schneider of Michigan State University, and Donnell Butler of Educational Testing Service point

Periods of parental leave are unlikely to have negative repercussions in the labor market and are likely to have benefits for child and family well-being.

out, schools are open only 6.6 hours a day, on average, for only 180 days a year. That schedule leaves many hours and days during which parents must arrange care and supervision. And although school-aged children and adolescents may require less hands-on care than younger children, parents continue to have important roles in their lives. The authors describe the kinds of support that parents provide to older children, explain why that support is important for child health and development, and show how overly rigid work demands interfere with it.

The authors observe that many aspects of school design and policies reflect outdated notions of families and parental availability and that work-family conflicts could be reduced through school reforms that take into account the changed nature of families. Such reforms could include scheduling parent-teacher meetings outside of work hours, providing more services at schools, and providing child care before school, after school, and during school vacations. The authors note, however, that schools are not likely to implement such changes in the current economic climate and conclude that for the time being schools can play only a limited role in meeting families' needs. Workplaces, they argue, may be the better place for reform.

And, in fact, workplace flexibility is the strategy parents prefer for balancing work and family obligations. Christensen, Schneider, and Butler recommend two types of flexible work practices: flextime arrangements that allow parents to coordinate their work schedules with their children's school schedules, and policies that allow workers to take short periods of time off for either planned or unplanned occasions. Many companies that have implemented such policies, the authors say, have benefited through employee retention and higher job satisfaction.

Despite their benefits, however, flexible work practices are the exception, not the rule, in U.S. workplaces. And even when such practices are available, employees often hesitate to take advantage of them. The authors conclude by examining the factors that contribute to a culture of workplace flexibility that supports both employers and employees.

Families with Children with Special Health Care Needs

All families have children who are sick from time to time and who in addition require regular preventive and routine medical care such as checkups and immunizations. In addition, roughly 15 percent of families have children with ongoing special health care needs. Mark Schuster of Harvard Medical School and Children's Hospital Boston, Paul Chung of the University of California–Los Angeles, and Katherine Vestal of Children's Hospital Boston describe the burdens that these health care needs place on parents, who are central to the health care their children receive. In addition to providing a good deal of care directly, parents also coordinate and facilitate the often complex care their children receive.

Taking care of a child with special health care needs while also holding down a job presents

difficulties for both the employee and the employer. Neither benefits when employees come to work distracted and stressed because they need to be with an ill child, but employees who take time off on short notice or for extended periods can create problems as well.

The authors recognize that policy solutions are not straightforward. They review the existing policy framework and suggest a variety of changes that might make the workplace more responsive to the needs of families without placing an undue burden on employers. Virtually all employees, for instance, could benefit from access to discretionary leave to allow them to respond to routine, acute, or short-term health care needs of a child. This and other types of leave could be funded through employer-employee cost sharing and include protections against fraud as well as financial protections against the costs of employee absences. Such policies might substantially improve employees' ability to respond and care for children with health care needs, but would not necessarily address more challenging longer-term health care situations.

The authors suggest the health care system might be able to help ease the burden on parents by adapting its practices to reflect the new reality of American families. They detail some of the ways in which the system now makes demands on families, and they provide examples of ways in which the burden might be alleviated. For example, studies have shown that poor communication and coordination of care can have negative consequences for patients and their families. Enhancing comprehensive primary care through patient-centered medical homes might relieve parents of some of the difficulty of coordinating care and reduce their odds of work loss. Coordinating care with community-based resources, such as schools (where children already spend much of their time), might also provide parents with more convenient options for more routine care.

Caring for the Elderly

One of the most striking aspects of the changing demography of the American population is its increased longevity. People are living, and staying healthy, longer. But, as Ann Bookman and Delia Kimbrel of Brandeis University point out in their article, most elderly Americans will eventually become frail and require extensive support and care, and even the nonfrail elderly typically receive a good deal of support and care from extended family members. Social Security benefits provide an income platform for the elderly, while Medicare provides health insurance coverage. Medicaid covers all nursing home care, but only for those with low income and minimal assets. In addition, the Older Americans Act provides services such as Meals on Wheels and day-to-day assistance with household chores and shopping. Although these services are helpful, they are subsidized only for the poor.

As is the case when children have special health care needs, employees who are caring for elderly relatives with special health care needs may require time off from work on short notice, or for extended periods of time. Experiences of elder care also vary by gender, race, and socioeconomic status. In this area as in others, families would benefit from government and employer policies that allow flexibility, provisions for care, and access to health care. Although government policies address some elder care needs, the authors note that they do not provide adequate support for chronic illnesses, home care services, or long-term care. Just as with child care, adult caregivers are at the hub of care

coordination, managing multiple systems to provide care for their elderly relatives.

As the population ages, an increasing share of employees will be involved with elder care, which will likely shape understandings of work-family balance. The political coalition behind the Family and Medical Leave Act of 1993 recognized that employees with care responsibilities are caring not only for young children, but also for adult relatives and elderly relatives. As more Americans age and require care, the constituency for better work-family supports will grow ever larger.

The Role of Employers in Providing More Flexibility

A recurring theme in the articles in this volume—the need for flexibility—is the central focus of the article by Ellen Galinsky, Kelly Sakai, and Tyler Wigton, of the Families and Work Institute. For much of the twentieth century, they note, research on work-family programs in the workplace concentrated on a small set of specific policies to help employees better meet their work-family obligations —policies such as allowing time off for new parents or providing information on, or financial assistance with, child care or elder care. But more recently researchers have zeroed in on the promise of workplace flexibility.

As the authors document, surveys of employees consistently show strong demand for flexibility. But these same surveys find that many employees, particularly those who are less advantaged, have no access at all to flexible work arrangements and that some who in principle do have such access hesitate to use it.

Although some employers are skeptical of the value and wary of the costs of workplace flexibility, the authors show that flexibility offers several advantages to employers, including greater employee engagement, satisfaction, retention, and better health. A significant body of research shows that adopting flexibility in the workplace enhances productivity and is good for companies' "bottom line." It also shows that when employees are offered workplace flexibility, they tend to use it conservatively, minimizing costs to employers.

Even for employers who show interest in moving to more flexible workplaces, changing the culture of work can be difficult. The authors describe an extensive intervention they carried out that engages employers, employees, and their community to encourage and support employers in implementing more flexible workplace practices and to facilitate employees' use of these policies. The results of the intervention thus far are encouraging, with participating employers providing significantly more flexible options than the average nationwide.

The authors conclude by discussing the implications of their research for broader workplace change. They include a detailed list of "lessons learned," which they say are informing replications of their project in communities across the country.

The Role of Government

Another recurring theme in articles in this volume is the potentially important role of government in the work-family arena. Government at all levels—local, state, and federal—plays multiple roles here, as an employer, as a source of data and information, and, most important, as a source of policy. Heather Boushey, of the Center for American Progress, focuses specifically on the policy-making role and in particular discusses the evolution of three main types of

policies: those that address workplace hours and flexibility; those that provide paid time off for family responsibilities; and those that cover the costs of care when potential caregivers are at work or school.

Tracing the history of these policies since the 1930s, Boushey shows that policy developments have not kept pace with the changes in the American family and workplace. She also stresses that because policies have developed unevenly, their benefits have not been equitably distributed. She then discusses recent and current policy activity at the local, state, and federal levels and identifies what she sees as the most promising avenues for future policy action. For example, Boushey looks at a variety of pilot and experimental programs implemented by private employers and governments to provide workplace flexibility. Careful evaluations of these programs reveal that flexibility can be increased without adversely affecting employers. Examining paid family and medical leave policies, Boushey concludes that both are successful for employers as well as employees.

Boushey calls on policy makers to update labor standards and social insurance to reflect the country's changing demographics. In particular, she notes that paid family and medical leave is a missing piece of the nation's social insurance infrastructure and that states are developing viable programs that can serve as a model for federal policy makers.

What Other Countries Do

A final theme that recurs throughout the volume is the extent to which the United States might learn from what other countries do. In virtually every area of work-family policy, provisions in the United States tend to be less well developed and less equitably distributed than those in most peer countries.

In addition, many skeptics in the United States wonder whether more generous work-family policies would impose undue costs on businesses and impede American competitiveness. Although international comparisons cannot answer those questions definitively, they are useful in clarifying the policies of competitive nations abroad. As Alison Earle, of Northeastern University, Zitha Mokomane, of the Human Sciences Research Council of South Africa, and Jody Heymann, of the Institute for Health and Social Policy at McGill University, document, the world's most competitive nations offer quite generous work-family supports, in most cases much more extensive than those in the United States, suggesting that it is possible for such supports to coexist with a robust economy.

Using indicators of competitiveness gathered by the World Economic Forum, the authors identify fifteen countries, including the United States, that have been among the top twenty countries in competitiveness rankings for at least eight years. To this group they add China and India, both rising competitors in the global economy. They find that every one of these countries, except the United States, guarantees some form of paid leave for new mothers. And all but Switzerland and the United States guarantee paid leave for new fathers. Most of these countries also provide paid leave to care for children's health care needs, breast-feeding breaks, paid vacation leave, and a weekly day of rest. Of these, the United States has only breast-feeding breaks (part of the recently passed health care legislation). Comparisons of the same work-family policies in a second group of countries with low unemployment produce similar results.

Policy Implications

Our review of the evidence points to three clear policy implications:

The first is the key role for more workplace flexibility. Although flexibility is not a panacea, it clearly would do more than any other single policy approach to meet the diverse needs of employees with caregiving responsibilities. But to be effective, flexibility must be truly flexible. Traditional flextime policies, whereby employees change their hours to one of a specific set of alternative schedules on a permanent basis with no day-to-day flexibility, may meet the needs of some employees but are likely to be insufficiently flexible for others. Two approaches are more promising. One is to give employees the right to request a change to part-time or flexible hours with the assurance that their requests will be seriously considered and that they will not suffer adverse repercussions for such requests. The other is compensatory time, whereby employees can work extra hours, bank them, and then take off those hours as needed, on a flexible basis.

The second implication is the need for more equitable policies, particularly with regard to paid time off for family responsibilities. The status quo, whereby the lowest-paid workers are least likely to have paid sick leave or other leave that enables them to take care of family responsibilities, forces working parents to choose between not taking care of their family or losing their wages (or losing their job altogether). Such a choice cannot be good for children and families, or for employers who must be paying a price in diminished employee productivity, engagement, and retention. Yet providing additional paid leave would be difficult for many U.S. small businesses, particularly as the nation continues to struggle with the aftereffects of the recession. We concur with Schuster, Chung, and Vestal that it would be reasonable to ask all employers to provide a minimal amount of paid sick leave and other leave time to all employees. But longer leaves, where required

Although flexibility is not a panacea, it clearly would do more than any other single policy approach to meet the diverse needs of employees with caregiving responsibilities.

for parents of newborns or for caregivers of those with serious longer-term health conditions, would probably be better provided through some other mechanism, such as a social insurance fund, like the one that undergirds Social Security retirement and disability programs.

The third policy implication is the need to increase the involvement of sectors other than families and employers in addressing work-family issues. For too long, these issues have been seen as the responsibility solely of families and employers, with government stepping in as a last resort. But as several articles in this volume have pointed out, other service delivery systems could also help reduce demands on family caregivers. Particularly important in this regard are the schools, the health care system, and community-based and other providers serving the elderly, each of which can contribute by updating its assumptions about the availability of family members to acknowledge the reality that most caregivers today are also working in the labor market.

Conclusions

A strong work ethic is a core feature of American culture. Even in this recessionary time, the majority of parents and other caregivers are working, typically long hours. But Americans are also deeply committed to their children and other loved ones. Both mothers and fathers are spending more time with their children today than they did a few decades ago, and time spent caring for or helping the elderly is also on the rise. Parents continue to be the hub of service delivery for their children, providing direct care and coordinating other care, and the same is often true for adults providing care for their parents or other elderly relatives.

It is no wonder, then, that employees are increasingly voicing concerns about having too little time for family life and that both employees and employers are actively exploring ways to create more workplace flexibility. Local, state, and federal governments are also experimenting with new policies to provide benefits such as paid sick leave, paid parental leave, and more extensive support for preschool and school-aged child care. These employer and public policy initiatives reflect a growing recognition that, with more parents working and elder care demands on the rise, policies must adapt.

Although there are no easy solutions to the work-family challenge, the evidence presented in this volume provides useful insights into the types of work-family conflicts American employees are experiencing, as well as the types of employer, governmental, and community policies that might most effectively address them. Particularly promising are employer and governmental initiatives that promote workplace flexibility, provide at least a minimal amount of paid sick leave and other needed leave to all employees, and cover the costs of longer-term leaves to care for newborns or family members with serious illness. Also promising are community initiatives whereby schools, health care, and other service delivery systems acknowledge the realities of American family life and adjust their services to meet the needs of the nation's families and workplaces.

Changing Families, Changing Workplaces

Suzanne M. Bianchi

Summary

American families and workplaces have both changed dramatically over the past half-century. Paid work by women has increased sharply, as has family instability. Education-related inequality in work hours and income has grown. These changes, says Suzanne Bianchi, pose differing work-life issues for parents at different points along the income distribution.

Between 1975 and 2009, the labor force rate of mothers with children under age eighteen increased from 47.4 percent to 71.6 percent. Mothers today also return to work much sooner after the birth of a child than did mothers half a century ago. High divorce rates and a sharp rise in the share of births to unmarried mothers mean that more children are being raised by a single parent, usually their mother.

Workplaces too have changed, observes Bianchi. Today's employees increasingly work nonstandard hours. The well-being of highly skilled workers and less-skilled workers has been diverging. For the former, work hours may be long, but income has soared. For lower-skill workers, the lack of "good jobs" disconnects fathers from family obligations. Men who cannot find work or have low earnings potential are much less likely to marry. For low-income women, many of whom are single parents, the work-family dilemma is how to care adequately for children and work enough hours to support them financially.

Jobs for working-class and lower middle-class workers are relatively stable, except in economic downturns, but pay is low, and both parents must work full time to make ends meet. Family income is too high to qualify for government subsidized child care, but too low to afford high-quality care in the private market. These families struggle to have a reasonable family life and provide for their family's economic well-being.

Bianchi concludes that the "work and family" problem has no one solution because it is not one problem. Some workers need more work and more money. Some need to take time off around the birth of a child without permanently derailing a fulfilling career. Others need short-term support to attend to a family health crisis. How best to meet this multiplicity of needs is the challenge of the coming decade.

www.futureofchildren.org

Suzanne M. Bianchi is the Dorothy Meier Chair and Distinguished Professor in the Department of Sociology at the University of California–Los Angeles.

Suzanne M. Bianchi

A ll workers face times during their lives when the demands of family caregiving grow so intense that balancing work and family life becomes a struggle. A web of obligations—to a child who needs care, a spouse who is ill, an older parent who needs support, a sibling undergoing a divorce—connects workers with their families. Workers are also obligated to their employers, on whom they depend for the income and other satisfactions that paid work provides. The many responsibilities that workers have to their family members and to their jobs are both important—and often in conflict.

Major changes in American families and workplaces over the past half-century form the backdrop for the work and family challenges that face workers today. The biggest changes in the family itself have been increases in paid work by women and in family instability, both of which have altered family-related activities such as housework and child care. Population aging has also increased demand for care of parents and older relatives. Workplace changes include an increase in nonstandard work schedules and greater education-related inequality in work hours and income. Although these family and workplace changes affect all American families, they result in quite different work-life issues for parents at the top, middle, and bottom of the income distribution.

Changing Families

Over the second half of the twentieth century, U.S. family life changed dramatically in two ways. The employment of women, especially mothers of young children, outside the home surged. Family instability too increased sharply, as did the likelihood that children would be raised, at least for part of childhood, in a household with only a single parent,

usually the mother. As a result of these changes, adults in households with children became much more likely to juggle paid work and unpaid family caregiving responsibilities—making the tension between the two spheres much more apparent than it had been during the 1950s and 1960s, when women tended to stay out of the labor force to rear children while men brought home a "family wage" large enough to support everyone.[1]

Increased Maternal Employment

Between 1975 and 2009, the labor force rate of mothers with children under age eighteen increased from 47.4 percent to 71.6 percent (figure 1). For mothers of children under age six, the share in the labor force rose from 39.0 percent to 63.6 percent. Mothers' employment rates rose steadily until about 2000 and then flattened out, leading some observers to believe that a retrenchment in the trend toward gender equality might be under way in the United States.[2] The ensuing debate about whether mothers were increasingly "opting out" of the paid workforce, however, has subsided during the recent recession and its aftermath.[3]

In 2009, 74 percent of all employed mothers worked full time (defined by the Bureau of Labor Statistics as at least thirty-five hours a week at all jobs), and the full-time rate was almost as high—71 percent—for mothers with children under age six. Fathers' rates of participation in the labor force remained higher than those of mothers: 94 percent of fathers who were living with their children were in the labor force, and 94 percent of employed fathers worked full time.[4]

Mothers today work during pregnancy more often and return to work much sooner after the birth of a child than did mothers half a century ago. During 1961–65, the

Figure 1. Labor Force Participation of Mothers

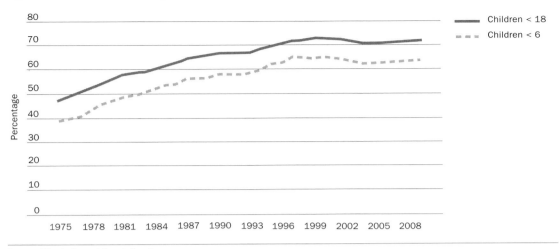

Source: March Current Population Survey.

Figure 2. Return to Work among First-Time Mothers

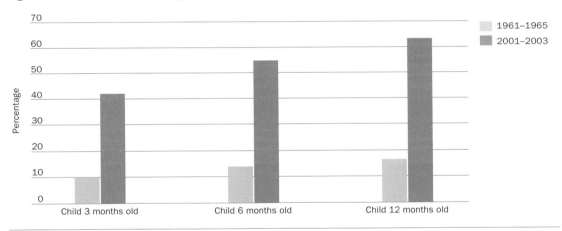

Source: Tallese Johnson, "Maternity Leave and Employment Patterns of First-Time Mothers, 1961–2003," *Current Population Reports,* P70–113 (Washington: U.S. Census Bureau, 2008).

share of women working during their first pregnancy was 44 percent; by 2001–03 it had climbed to two-thirds (based on data collected in the Survey of Income and Program Participation).[5] More dramatic was the change in the speed at which women returned to work after the birth of their child, as shown in figure 2. Among all women having their first child during the early 1960s,

only 10 percent were back at work three months after the baby's birth. By 2001–03, that share was 42 percent; the share back at work six months after the birth was 55 percent; and the share back at work by the child's first birthday was 64 percent.

Some observers might argue that comparisons with the 1960s exaggerate the change

An unmarried mother in the United States today faces a high probability of becoming both the main caregiver and the main breadwinner for her family during at least part of her child's life.

because family roles were highly specialized along gender lines during that decade, with women providing the bulk of unpaid care in the home and men providing the wage labor that economically supported the family. Earlier in the twentieth century—during the 1920s and 1930s—women often combined rearing children with paid work, or unpaid family work, either on farms or in urban ghettos where they took in boarders, laundry, or piecework. Until the mid-twentieth century, however, married women most often did their paid work later in life, after they had raised their children, or in the household, where they could keep an eye on those children. During the second half of the twentieth century, women of childbearing age moved into the workplace. To engage in paid work, they had to leave their children and arrange for other people to care for them.

Susan Short, Frances Goldscheider, and Berna Torr show that as women's paid work was increasingly moving outside the home, the household itself was being transformed. At the very time that parents could have used the help of others in the household to care for children, households were "emptying out" of adult kin.[6] Families that included three generations of kin during the Great Depression and

World War II uncoupled as housing expanded and postwar affluence allowed for more privacy in living arrangements. The large baby boom families with older daughters who could help care for younger children began to disappear as families reduced fertility to replacement levels (two children per family) by the 1970s. Increasingly, parents were "on their own" to juggle the work and family demands of modern life.

Greater Family Instability and More Single Parenting

As mothers' labor force rates were climbing, families were facing other big changes. Divorce rates rose sharply during the 1970s, causing more children to be raised by a single parent, usually their mother. The divorce rate plateaued (at high levels) around 1980, but a second trend—the increase in the proportion of births to unmarried mothers—continued to rise. Today, 40 percent of U.S. births are to a woman who is not married.[7] Sara McLanahan and Audrey Beck document that almost half of unmarried mothers are cohabiting with the father when the child is born and another 30 percent are romantically involved with the baby's father. But these relationships are extremely unstable. Forty percent of cohabiting relationships and 80 percent of those where the couple is romantically involved but not living together dissolve by the child's fifth birthday.[8] An unmarried mother in the United States today faces a high probability of becoming both the main caregiver and the main breadwinner for her family during at least part of her child's life.

High rates of nonmarital births are also common today throughout Europe, but the United States tends to be exceptional in the high rates of dissolution of these nonmarital relationships, their short duration, and the lack of sustained father involvement in rearing children.

Andrew Cherlin, in his book *The Marriage-Go-Round*, documents that 10 percent of all U.S. women have been in at least three different marriages or cohabiting relationships, or both, by the time they turn thirty-five, more than twice the share for women in the European countries with the highest rates of union dissolution.[9] The family system is more turbulent in the United States than elsewhere, and women spend more time as lone mothers, rearing children without a father present, than do their European counterparts.

Single parents now head about one-quarter of U.S. households with children under the age of eighteen. Even though fathers now head about 15 percent of all single-parent households, the overwhelming majority (85 percent) of single parents are mothers.[10] Single parents may have as many child-related demands on their time as married parents do, but their households have only half as many adults to meet those demands.[11] In 2009, single mothers had an overall labor force participation rate of 75.8 percent, and an unemployment rate of 13.6 percent. Married mothers had a lower rate of participation in the labor force, at 69.6 percent, but their unemployment rate, at 5.8 percent, was less than half that for single mothers. Thus, the ratio of "employment to population" was similar for the two groups of mothers. Single mothers' high unemployment rates in part reflect their relatively low educational attainment: 16.4 percent have no high school degree and 30.3 percent have only a high school degree. Not all single mothers are poorly educated: 17.2 percent have college degrees (or higher) and 36.1 percent have spent some time in college. Fully 38.5 percent of two-parent households with children, however, have a parent with a college degree or higher, and an additional 27.3 percent have a parent with some college education.[12]

Changes in Nonmarket Activities in the Home

Labor force surveys, such as the Current Population Survey, track trends in the number and share of parents who work in the paid labor force but not in what parents do in their nonwork hours. Researchers interested in trends in unpaid work in the home have turned to evidence from time diaries in which representative samples of respondents record their activities over a twenty-four-hour period. Time diary data, which are relatively easy to collect, force respondents to respect the constraint of the twenty-four-hour day when reporting activities. Numerous methodological studies confirm that time diary estimates are both reliable and valid.[13] Aggregating diary days across respondents and across days of the week and weeks of the year yields a representative picture of time use for groups such as fathers or single mothers. Beginning in 2003 in the United States, the American Time Use Survey (ATUS) has provided evidence for large representative samples. Combining the ATUS data with data from earlier U.S. time diary studies makes it possible to track trends over longer periods.

Time diary data show that housework hours for U.S. mothers fell from an average of thirty-two hours a week (reported in 1965 time diaries) to just under eighteen hours (reported in the 2003–08 ATUS), a decline of fourteen hours, on average. The change turns out to be close to an equal work-housework trade: mothers averaged thirteen more hours of market work during 2003–08 than in 1965 as they shed housework hours. Most of the change was in "core housework" tasks: The time spent preparing and cleaning up after meals and doing laundry was almost halved, and housecleaning time fell more than one-third.[14]

Mothers' time devoted to child care followed a different pattern. In the United States it declined from ten hours to eight and one-half hours a week between 1965 and 1975 (as large baby boom households gave way to households with fewer children). After 1985, however, mothers' primary child-care time began rising—and reached almost fourteen hours a week during 2003–08 (according to estimates from the ATUS).[15] Time use data from European countries show similar patterns. Maternal time invested in child-care activities increased during the same period, despite rapid increases in women's labor force participation in virtually all European economies.[16] Employed U.S. mothers today spend less time doing child care than non-employed mothers, but the allocation of time to children has ratcheted upward for both groups. A comparison of mothers' diaries shows that employed mothers were recording as much time doing primary child care in 2000 as nonemployed mothers did in 1975.[17]

As mothers increased their market work, fathers' time use patterns at home changed too. Fathers living with their children spent more time on both housework and child care. They more than doubled hours spent on housework between 1965 and 1985, from four to ten hours a week on average. And after 1985, they nearly tripled time devoted to primary child-care activities, averaging seven hours a week during 2003–08 compared with two and a half hours a week during 1965–85.[18] Extra time spent on child care came on top of long work hours—an average of forty hours a week (based on time diary reports)—that varied little by the age of their children.[19]

Numerous qualitative studies suggest why time allocated by mothers to child care may remain the same or even increase despite their greater paid work effort. Sharon Hays describes what she calls the cultural contradiction of modern motherhood: Mothers assume the co-provider role but still feel compelled to be "all giving" and "ever available" to their children.[20] Mary Blair-Loy analyzes a schema of "devotion to family" that competes with "devotion to work" even among high-income professional mothers who are most heavily invested in their jobs.[21] Being a good mother, devoted to one's children, is a core identity that does not change when women take on more hours of paid work.

As adults, especially highly educated adults, postpone parenthood and have smaller families, they may be planning their childbearing for a point in life when they want to devote time to parenting. Middle-class children participate in numerous extracurricular activities, many of which require active parental involvement, such as providing transportation.[22] Parents may increasingly believe that involving their children in a wide range of activities ensures their ultimate educational success.[23] Annette Lareau, in her book *Unequal Childhoods*, labels such parenting "concerted cultivation," and her follow-up interviews with children thus cultivated suggest they perform well in young adulthood, especially compared with peers from families with less education and less involved parenting.[24]

Raising children in the United States today also requires substantial financial investment, because the lengthening transition to adulthood often requires parents to "backstop" children unable to secure a foothold in the job market. The vast majority of children in their early twenties—regardless of whether they are enrolled in school—receive economic assistance from their parents.[25] Frank Furstenberg Jr. argues that as the transition to adulthood grows longer, the burden of supporting adult children grows heavier for U.S. parents than for their counterparts in Europe, where governmental programs invest more heavily in education, health care, and job prospects for young people. Young adults in the United States also experience more inequality in outcomes, reflecting inequality in the economic resources available to parents to assist their children.[26]

Population Aging and Care of Older Adults

One final family change that looms large, as the baby boom begins to retire, is the increased likelihood that working adults will have elderly parents who need care. Getting a reliable sense of either the number of older adults who need care or the number of working-age adults who have an older parent, spouse, or other relative who requires care is difficult, and estimates vary widely. For example, the National Alliance for Caregiving, in collaboration with AARP, estimated in 2009 that 65.7 million Americans, or 29 percent of the adult population, provided care for an adult or a child with special needs in the previous year.[27] The Family Caregiver Alliance has compiled a wide range of estimates of informal caregivers from different data sources. The highest estimate, from the 1987 National Survey of Families and Households, is that 52 million people care for someone aged twenty or older who is ill or disabled. The lowest estimate, from the 1994 wave of the National Long-Term Care Survey, is that between 6 million and 7 million people care for family, friends, or neighbors aged sixty-five and older who need help with everyday tasks.[28]

Another approach to assessing the "risk" of becoming a caregiver is to estimate the number of potential caregivers per elderly adult in need of care. Based on the National Long-Term Care Survey in 1994, when the average number of adult children was at its peak, 5.5 million chronically disabled elderly adults had a total of 14.5 million potential spousal or child caregivers—about 3.1 potential caregivers per care recipient.[29] The baby boom generation, now reaching retirement age, had much smaller families in adulthood than the ones into which they were born—an average of two, rather than three or four, children per family.[30] Smaller family sizes translate to fewer siblings with whom to share care when a health crisis emerges for one's parents. The older baby boom cohorts have also experienced considerable lifetime marital instability, as have their children. Because of the increase in births outside marriage, cohabitation before and after marriage, divorce and repartnering, older parents now have numerous stepchildren, but norms of obligation to assist family members may be less strong among stepfamily than among biological kin.[31]

Improved health and declining disability rates among older people also complicate the task of estimating the future need for elder care. In part because they are healthier, older adults today are working longer than did their peers five decades ago. Over the past fifteen years, in particular, the labor force rates for those in their sixties and seventies have risen.[32] The working lives of older adults are also being extended by the broad societal shift away from traditional defined-benefit retirement plans, the security of which tends to encourage earlier retirement, and by older Americans' increased educational attainment, which enables them to stay in the labor force longer than their less well-educated counterparts.[33]

The lengthening of *healthy* life expectancy means that most workers do not face serious caregiving demands from their parents until their own children are older and less in need of day-to-day care. Here again, though, estimates vary widely. Depending on the definition of caregiving responsibilities, between 1 and 33 percent of women in their late forties and early fifties are providing care and support to children and parents simultaneously. The best estimate is that about 9 percent of women in this age group are "sandwiched" caregivers who are providing substantial care and support both to children and to parents.[34] Although sandwiched caregivers are a little less likely to be in the labor force than those who are not supporting two generations, labor force rates are high for both groups (72 percent compared with 76 percent). The likelihood that middle-aged workers will need to provide care both up and down the generations may increase in coming years, because of delayed childbearing, especially among highly educated women. And because of the increase in women's employment, more and more of the potential caregivers of unmarried elderly parents, the group who most often require assistance from their adult children, will be in the workforce.

Changing Workplaces

As families have changed, so too have workplaces—as well as the economic outlook for working families. Harriet Presser has chronicled the growth in the "24/7" economy—work at nonstandard hours, part-time work, work without fixed hours, and rotating schedules.[35] And because inequality in the workplace has increased, workers at different points in the income distribution face quite different work-family dilemmas.

Nonstandard Work Hours

The standard full-time workweek is typically considered to be thirty-five to forty hours,

Monday through Friday, mostly during the day. About one-fifth of employed Americans, however, work more than half of their hours outside the 8:00 a.m. to 4:00 p.m. standard daytime hours, or work a rotating schedule, or work varying hours. The incidence of nonstandard work schedules in the United States is roughly in line with that in Europe, where between 15 and 25 percent of the workforce works nonstandard hours. One in three employed Americans works at least one day on the weekend, though less than 1 percent work only on the weekend. Weekend work is more variable in Europe, ranging in one study of twelve countries from a low of 10 percent (in Sweden) to a high of 35 percent (in Italy).[36]

Because inequality in the workplace has increased, workers at different points in the income distribution face quite different work-family dilemmas.

Some analysts are concerned that nonstandard work schedules, and the workplaces that require them, may be "family unfriendly"—affecting adversely the health of workers and curtailing the time that parents spend with each other and their children. Virtually all studies of the "effects" of nonstandard work schedules on families find correlations, but not causal links, between the two, because the studies are based on observational rather than experimental designs. One study, which finds that preschool-age children of mothers with nonstandard work hours have lower cognitive scores than do children whose mothers work during the daytime, posits that the lower scores may be attributable to lower-quality child care.[37] Other studies explore whether parental work in the evenings or on weekends may be costly to older children, in terms of lack of supervision, more behavioral problems, less parental availability to help with homework, and poor child mental health.[38] The studies do not establish causal connections, however, because parents who work nonstandard schedules are not a random subset of all workers: Their children may have experienced the same outcomes regardless of their parents' work schedules.

Descriptive evidence from the ATUS suggests that married parents record spending less time with each other and with their children when they work non-standard hours on their diary day. Mothers who work evening hours spend less time in routine child-care activities, such as bathing children, and less time reading to children than do mothers who work during the day. Evening work schedules reduce the likelihood of parents being present at the family dinner table, and parents who work in the evening or at night spend less time with their spouses, and less time watching television and sleeping.[39]

Work schedules may also affect the mental health of adult family members.[40] A study of nurses in dual-earner families found that those who worked evening shifts had more conflict and distress than those working day shifts.[41] Among new parents in working-class, dual-earner families, shift work was linked to higher levels of depression. Parents working a rotating shift experienced lowered marital relationship quality.[42] Particularly stressful were mismatches between children's school schedules and parents' work schedules.[43]

Because all of these studies are observational, however, these links may not be causal.

Not all associations between nonstandard work schedules and the quality of family life are negative. Nonstandard hours may enhance children's welfare when parents coordinate their work schedules (at least in two-parent homes) to reduce the use of nonparental care and make one parent available to their children during both the day and evening hours. Care of children in two-parent families may also be more equitably distributed between mothers and fathers when one or both parents work nonstandard schedules. When mothers work evenings rather than daytime hours, fathers are more involved in child care, spend more time with and take more sole responsibility for children, and are generally more knowledgeable about their children's lives and activities.[44] Parents working at night often spend more hours supervising children than do those working other schedules.[45]

Part-Time Work

In 2007, the Bureau of Labor Statistics (BLS) reported that 17 percent of all workers aged sixteen and over worked part time—defined as usually working less than 35 hours a week. Part-time workers tend to be younger than full-time workers, although many older workers are employed part time. Women much more often work part time than men. The BLS categorizes part-time work as being involuntary (primarily because of economic reasons such as slack work) or voluntary. Working part time because of family caregiving responsibilities is considered voluntary, even though choosing part-time work to meet caregiving obligations may not in fact be completely voluntary. Part-time workers in the United States are much less likely than full-time workers to have benefits such as health care or pension coverage, in part because part-time work evolved to attract married women into the labor market during the 1940s and 1950s, with the presumption that these "secondary" workers would have husbands whose jobs had fringe benefits.[46] Today, however, a little more than one-third of part-time workers are the family's major breadwinner, and that share has been rising. Part-time workers who are a family's primary earner are much less well-off, given their low incomes and lack of fringe benefits, than part-time workers who are secondary earners and enjoy benefits from another household earner.[47]

Inequality in Employment and Work-Family Dilemmas

Workplaces have been characterized by growing inequality in the income of highly skilled and less-skilled workers during the past few decades.[48] For workers at the top of the income-skill distribution, the work-family dilemma often involves well-remunerated, interesting jobs that have long work hours and offer few alternatives to full-time "devotion" to the workplace. For the low-skill worker, a major work-family dilemma often involves work that offers too few hours with too little pay to support a family adequately, or that offers too little flexibility in work shifts to enable workers to care adequately for their children. For families in the middle of the income distribution, the dilemma is that wages are too high to qualify for public assistance, but that work offers little flexibility, requires mandatory overtime on short notice, or offers wages that can support a family only if both parents in two-parent families work full time or if single parents hold multiple jobs. These middle-income families have, in addition, been more deeply affected by the recent recession than higher-income families.[49]

High-Income Families, High-Skill Workers

At the high end of the skill distribution, work hours may be long, but remuneration is high and income has soared. Dual-earner couples increasingly fill these ranks. Growing marital homogamy by educational status means that workers in long-work-hour "good jobs" are increasingly married to each other.[50] Although men have increased their time in the home, this solution to the work-family dilemma has its limits. Hence, upper- and middle-class couples seem to make one of two adjustments in this context of "too much work." Either they forgo having children—childlessness has risen recently among women in the United States (and in Europe and Japan). Or mothers (but not fathers) scale back labor market hours and move in and out of the labor force when children are young.

Childlessness

A sizable proportion of highly educated women in recent cohorts has remained childless. Among American women today aged forty to forty-four, 20 percent have never had a child, double the share thirty years ago. The share rises to 27 percent for those with graduate or professional degrees.[51] Highly educated women, as a group, tend to have fewer children than they say they wanted earlier in their lives. The 1979 BLS National Longitudinal Survey of Youth, which interviewed a large, nationally representative group beginning when they were teenagers or young adults and then regularly conducted follow-up interviews over many years, asked young women how many children they wanted to have. Over time the total fertility rate for college-educated women was lower (by about one-half a child, averaged over the group) than their stated intentions at the beginning of their childrearing years, suggesting either that these women had difficulty realizing their preferences for motherhood or that their preferences changed as they grew older.[52]

Some observers have suggested that sharp fertility declines over the past decade or two in Southern and Eastern Europe and in some countries in Asia, most notably Japan, are attributable to rigid family role expectations for women in these countries.[53] In countries where women's labor market opportunities expand but women are still expected to do most of the housework and child care with little assistance from men, women may remain childless when work and family roles are too difficult to reconcile. The United States has not experienced these sharp declines in fertility: the U.S. average continues to be about two births per woman. But even in the United States, among some groups such as highly educated women, motherhood may also be forgone as women increasingly hold jobs that are both fulfilling and highly remunerative but also demanding of time and energy.

Reduced Employment and Pay Penalties for Women

Many occupations, especially those that are the most highly paid, require almost total absorption in the job, which is problematic for workers who want to spend time with children and other family members. The tension between work and family life may be especially pronounced in the United States, where parents work longer hours and vacation less than do parents in Europe and where a higher share of dual-earner couples work long weeks.[54] Observational studies suggest that a father's long work hours are negatively associated with the breadth of activities he shares with his children, involvement with adolescent children, time with a spouse, and marital quality when he feels

high role overload.[55] Mothers often respond to long work hours—either their own or those of their husband—by cutting back their paid work hours.

Using the 2003–09 ATUS samples, Betsy Thorn has recently calculated how women reallocate time after the birth of a first child. Comparing the diary days of mothers of one child under the age of one year with those of a comparable group of childless young women (aged twenty-three to thirty-four), she shows that mothers spend almost three and a half more hours on family care and housework a day. Mothers average half an hour less in personal care, an hour less in leisure activities, and almost two hours less a day in paid work.[56]

Mothers who can afford to do so exit the labor force or reduce work hours despite the economic disadvantage of interrupted labor market participation and part-time employment. When mothers return to (full-time) employment, they may choose jobs whose hours allow as much overlap as possible with children's school schedules.[57] Mothers may also face subtle discrimination in the labor market—known as the "motherhood wage penalty" or "the family gap"—because they are assumed to be less committed workers than men or women without children.[58]

Mothers' adjustments in their work hours coincide with their subjective reports of time pressure. One-quarter to one-third of workers report feeling that they do not have enough time for themselves or their family because of their jobs.[59] The share of mothers who say that they would prefer to work fewer hours a week is increasing. According to a 2007 report by the Pew Research Center, about 21 percent of mothers reported that full-time work was the ideal situation for them (down from 32 percent in 1997), whereas 60 percent of mothers preferred part-time work (up from 48 percent in 1997).[60] The desire to reduce work hours stems from both job demands and personal and family life considerations.

The noneconomic costs of "too much work" may spill over into subjective assessments of parenting and the quality of family life. In attitudinal surveys, parents express feelings of regret about not spending enough time with children, though expressions of "parental guilt" are higher for fathers who spend more hours away from home in the paid workforce than for mothers.[61] Parents also evidence a yearning for elusive high-quality family time, with some research suggesting that the lack of time for shared family activities may have negative consequences for children, such as more risky behaviors for adolescents.[62]

Low-Income Families, Low-Skill Workers

Although work and family research has been dominated by the assumption that "too much" work is the major problem in balancing the demands of family life, analysts are increasingly noting that "too little" work is also a major work-family issue. The lack of "good jobs" for lower-skill workers tends to disconnect fathers from family obligations and from involved parenting. Low-skill mothers must often balance work and children as a single parent and may rely on older children to help care for younger siblings.

Men's Family Involvement

Breadwinning remains core to men's identity, and when men struggle to find work or have low earnings potential, they are much less likely to marry.[63] Avner Ahituv and Robert Lerman describe a feedback loop in which stable employment enhances the likelihood

of marriage. Once married, men work more hours, leading to higher earnings and, in turn, to greater marital stability.[64] Parenting too is tied to men's ability to provide financially for their children. Fathers with higher earnings more often reside with their children throughout childhood than do fathers with lower earnings, leading to increased inequality in children's life chances.[65] Among low-income families, in which couples are often not married when a child is born, a father's financial contribution is correlated with active parenting—visiting, caring for, and taking responsibility for children.[66]

Family involvement and commitment to children also seem to strengthen ties to the workforce for men, particularly low-income fathers. Observational studies offer some support for several hypotheses about why this might be the case. One hypothesis is that becoming a parent may make men adjust their priorities and commitments, thus strengthening their attachment to extended kin and to paid work. A second is that parents, coworkers, and (prospective) spouses may expect more maturity from a man who marries or becomes a father, or both, and that men may internalize these expectations. Another is that extended kin may provide more support when they think a father is acting responsibly. Finally, it may be that men do not randomly take on responsible adult roles: more mature men may "select" themselves into the father role—marrying, holding onto a job, working hard—and thus fulfill it better than less mature men.[67]

Other studies link the economic hardships and financial insecurities caused by too little or too poorly remunerated work with family health. For parents who experience unemployment, downward mobility, forced early retirement, or economic deprivation, worries about job security or the adequacy of their income may be associated with negative health outcomes, strained marital relationships, and lower parenting quality for both adolescents and young children.[68]

Maternal Employment and Child Outcomes in Low-Income Families

For low-income women, many of whom are single parents, the work-family dilemma is how to care adequately for children and work enough hours to support them financially. Mounting evidence from random-assignment, experimental research with welfare-eligible families shows that young children often benefit from programs that increase a mother's stable employment or income. Maternal employment tends to improve the home environment and encourage stable routines, especially when mothers have a good social support network and good mental health.[69]

Other experimental studies, however, show negative effects for low-income adolescents when their mothers transition from welfare to work. In a meta-analysis of eight random-assignment experimental studies, Lisa Gennetian and her colleagues reported small declines in adolescents' school performance and in their likelihood of performing in the top half of the class, as well as an increased likelihood of grade repetition. One explanation for the negative effects on adolescents is that mothers moving from welfare to work rely on their older children to care for younger siblings and that the new responsibility of child care interferes with adolescents' school attendance and performance.[70]

The finding that maternal work negatively affects older adolescent children is consistent with research that suggests that child

For low-income women, many of whom are single parents, the work-family dilemma is how to care adequately for children and work enough hours to support them financially.

care costs are a barrier to employment and often curtail work hours, particularly for low-income mothers.[71] Using older children as caregivers can be one way to find stable, affordable child care. Single mothers commonly have multiple child care arrangements. Patchwork child care arrangements are particularly prevalent among low-income mothers trying to move from welfare to work. Low-income mothers who use small, home-based nonrelative care are especially likely to stop working. Although mothers using centers and large family day-care settings are more likely to miss work because of sick children than are mothers using small, home-based caregivers, they are less likely to quit their jobs.[72]

Other studies examine whether working parents leave older children unsupervised at too young an age. To date, analysts find that self-care by older children is less common among minority and low-income children than among white, higher-income children, who begin small amounts of self-care between ages eight and ten.[73] Older siblings may substitute for parents in poor, urban settings to ensure that young children are not left alone, perhaps to the detriment of those older children.

Families in the Middle

A large segment of the workforce is neither in highly remunerated professional occupations nor in highly unstable and low-skill jobs. These working-class and lower middle-class workers are in jobs that, in most periods, are relatively stable, but that pay too little to permit one parent in two-parent families to support the family. Both parents must work full time to make ends meet. Finding high-quality child care is difficult and expensive because family income is too high to qualify for government subsidized programs, such as Head Start, but too low to make it easy to afford high-quality care in the private market.

[Some] working-class and lower middle-class workers are in jobs that, in most periods, are relatively stable, but that pay too little to permit one parent in two-parent families to support the family.

These families may often engage in "tag-team parenting" and work different schedules to reduce child-care costs. They also may be in jobs that are unionized but whose rigid work schedules make it difficult to mesh work and family life. Workers may have to work mandatory overtime on short notice and face a high likelihood of losing their jobs if they do not comply with employers' scheduling. Joan Williams and Heather Boushey's review of research on job litigation illuminates the work-family challenges for this large segment of working families.[74] These families feel that they have done everything right—completed high school or some college, married before having children, worked hard at their jobs—and yet they still struggle to carve out a reasonable family life and hold onto jobs that are critical to their family's economic well-being. The authors describe parents who are exhausted by the multitude of work and family demands, worried about debt and bills, and fearful that they are one crisis away from job loss.[75] These are the families who have increasingly lost jobs and faced housing foreclosure in the recent economic downturn.

Conclusion

Men and women seeking to balance work and family life today face intensifying challenges. Since the middle of the twentieth century, women, the nation's unpaid caregivers, have entered the paid workforce in great numbers. They return to work after their children are born far more rapidly than did their peers five decades ago. Their families are more diverse, with more single parenting and greater inequality in employment and income. As the U.S. population ages, issues of elder care loom large on the work-family horizon.

Too little work, most often a problem for low-income workers, is likely implicated in the erosion of less-educated men's connections to families. Although the overhaul of the nation's welfare system in 1996 evoked some concern about the negative impact on children of forcing welfare mothers to work, research has found that increased maternal employment is often neutral or even beneficial for young children in low-income families, though new concerns have arisen about possible negative effects on adolescents.

Too much work may be related to increased childlessness in the United States and elsewhere, particularly among more highly educated workers. The issue is especially intense in Europe, where the need to support an aging population is even more pressing than it is in the United States. Too much work may also slow progress toward greater gender equality in the labor market, because women continue to curtail paid work more often than do men in the face of the need to care for children and close kin.

Families in the middle of the income distribution may be least likely to be able to manage financially if mothers cut back their paid work. These families may thus be especially "time stretched," having much less ability than higher-income workers either to pay substitutes to do their work at home or to negotiate flexible work hours that might ease work-family strains.

The "work and family" problem has no one solution because it is not one problem. Some families need more work and more money. Others need assurances and safeguards that taking some time off from the job around the birth of a child will not permanently derail fulfilling careers. Yet other workers will likely need short-term support later in life to attend to the health (or other) crises of spouses, adult children, and aging parents. Understanding how best to meet this multiplicity of needs—what makes up the best mix of support from employers, the unpaid care of the (extended) family, and incentives from the public sector—is the challenge of the coming decade. Solutions must focus not only on the workplace and home life but also on the institutions that support healthy working families—schools, child care centers, afterschool programs, the medical care system, and support systems for elder care.

Endnotes

1. In 2009, in two-parent families with children under age eighteen, 96 percent had at least one parent employed and 59 percent had both parents employed. In families headed by women, 68 percent had the mother employed. In families headed by a man, 77 percent had the father employed. See the Bureau of Labor Statistics, "Economic News Release—Table 4: Families with Own Children: Employment Status of Parents by Age of Youngest Child and Family Type, 2008–09 Annual Averages" (www.bls.gov/news.release/famee.t04.htm).

2. David A. Cotter, Joan A. Hermsen, and Reeve Vanneman, "Gender Inequality at Work," in *The American People Census 2000 Series* (New York: Russell Sage Foundation and Population Reference Bureau, 2004); Liana C. Sayer, Philip N. Cohen, and Lynne M. Casper, "Women, Men, and Work," in *The American People Census 2000 Series* (New York: Russell Sage Foundation and Population Reference Bureau, 2004).

3. Lisa Belkin, "The Opt-Out Revolution," *New York Times Magazine,* October 26, 2003, pp. 42, 46, 85, 86; Heather Boushey, "Are Women Opting Out? Debunking the Myth," Briefing Paper (Washington: Center for Economic Policy Research, November 2005); Saul Hoffman, "The Changing Impact of Marriage and Children on Women's Labor Force Participation," *Monthly Labor Review* 132, no. 2 (2009): 3–14; Pamela Stone, *Opting Out* (University of California Press, 2007).

4. Bureau of Labor Statistics, "Economic News Release—Table 5: Employment Status of the Population by Sex, Marital Status and Presence and Age of Own Children under 18, 2008–09 Annual Averages" (www.bls.gov/news.release/famee.t05.htm).

5. Tallese Johnson, "Maternity Leave and Employment Patterns of First Time Mothers, 1961–2003," *Current Population Reports,* P70–113 (Washington: U.S. Census Bureau, 2008).

6. Susan E. Short, Frances K. Goldscheider, and Berna M. Torr, "Less Help for Mother: The Decline in Coresidential Female Support for the Mothers of Young Children, 1880–2000," *Demography* 43, no. 4 (2006): 617– 29.

7. B. E. Hamilton, J. A. Martin, and S. J. Ventura, "Births: Preliminary Data for 2007," *National Vital Statistics Reports* 57 (12) (Hyattsville, Md.: National Center for Health Statistics, 2009).

8. Sara McLanahan and Audrey N. Beck, "Parental Relationships in Fragile Families," *Future of Children* 20, no. 2 (2010): 18, 21.

9. Andrew Cherlin, *The Marriage-Go-Round* (New York: Vintage Books, 2009), p. 19.

10. Rose M. Kreider and Diana R. Elliott, "America's Families and Living Arrangements 2007," *Current Population Reports,* P20–561 (Washington: U.S. Census Bureau, 2009).

11. More than three decades ago, Claire Vickery pointed out this problem and coined the term "time poor." See Claire Vickery, "The Time-Poor: A New Look at Poverty," *Journal of Human Resources* 12, no. 1 (1977): 27–48.

12. Data come from the March Current Population Survey, detailed tables, "America's Families and Living Arrangements" on the Census Bureau website. "Table F2: Family Households by Type, Age of Own Children, and Educational Attainment of Householder: 2010" (www.census.gov/population/www/socdemo/hh-fam.html).

13. For a discussion of the time diary methodology and a review of its advantages for estimating time in unpaid activities like family work and leisure, see chapter 2 in Suzanne M. Bianchi, John P. Robinson, and Melissa A. Milkie, *Changing Rhythms of American Family Life* (New York: Russell Sage Foundation, 2006). See also John P. Robinson and Geoffrey Godbey, *Time for Life* (Pennsylvania State University Press, 1999), and Thomas F. Juster and Frank P. Stafford, *Time, Goods, and Well-Being* (Ann Arbor, Mich.: Survey Research Center, Institute for Social Research, University of Michigan, 1985). For an analysis of nonresponse in the ATUS, see Katharine G. Abraham, Aaron Maitland, and Suzanne M. Bianchi, "Non-Response in the American Time Use Survey: Who Is Missing from the Data and How Much Does It Matter?" *Public Opinion Quarterly* 70, no. 5 (2006): 676–703.

14. Author's calculations from the 2003–08 ATUS and earlier time diary data collections; Suzanne M. Bianchi, "Maternal Employment and Time with Children: Dramatic Change or Surprising Continuity?" *Demography* 37, no. 4 (2000): 139–54; Bianchi, Robinson, and Milkie, *Changing Rhythms of American Family Life* (see note 13).

15. Estimates are of the time mothers are doing direct child-care activities, not the overall time mothers spend with their children, which is much higher. Suzanne Bianchi, "Family Change and Time Allocation in American Families," paper prepared for the Focus on Workplace Flexibility Conference, Washington, D.C., November 29–30, 2010, table 1.

16. Anne H. Gauthier, Timothey M. Smeeding, Frank F. Furstenberg Jr., "Are Parents Investing Less Time in Children? Trends in Selected Industrialized Countries," *Population and Development Review* 30, no. 4 (2004): 647–71; Heather Joshi, "The Opportunity Costs of Childbearing: More than Mothers' Business," *Journal of Population Economics* 11, no. 2 (1998): 161–83.

17. Bianchi, Robinson, and Milkie, *Changing Rhythms of American Family Life* (see note 13).

18. Time spent in direct child care. The total time fathers spend with children is much greater. Bianchi, "Family Change and Time Allocation in American Families" (see note 15).

19. Suzanne M. Bianchi and Sara Raley, "Time Allocation in Working Families," in *Work, Family, Health, and Well-Being,* edited by Suzanne M. Bianchi, Lynne M. Casper, and Rosalind B. King (Mahwah, N.J.: Lawrence Erlbaum and Associates, 2005).

20. Sharon Hays, *The Cultural Contradictions of Motherhood* (Yale University Press, 1996).

21. Mary Blair-Loy, *Competing Devotions: Career and Family among Women Executives* (Harvard University Press, 2003).

22. Annette Lareau and Elliot Wieninger, "Time, Work and Family Life: Reconceptualizing Gendered Time Patterns through the Case of Children's Organized Activities," *Sociological Forum* 23, no. 3 (2008): 419–54.

23. Valerie A. Ramey and Garey Ramey, "The Rug Rat Race," *Brookings Papers on Economic Activity,* Spring (2010): 129–76.

24. Annette Lareau, *Unequal Childhoods* (University of California Press, 2003); Annette Lareau, "Class and the Transition to Adulthood: Differences in Parents' Interactions with Institutions," in *Social Class and Changing Families in an Unequal America,* edited by Marcia Carlson and Paula England (Stanford University Press, 2011).

25. Robert Schoeni and Katherine Ross, "Material Assistance Received from Families during the Transition to Adulthood," in *On the Frontier of Adulthood: Theory, Research, and Public Policy,* edited by Richard A. Settersten Jr., Frank F. Furstenberg Jr., and Rubén G. Rumbaut (University of Chicago Press, 2004).

26. Frank F. Furstenberg Jr., "On a New Schedule: Transitions to Adulthood and Family Change," *Future of Children* 20, no. 1 (2010): 67–87.

27. *Caregiving in the U.S. in 2009* (www.caregiving.org/data/Caregiving_in_the_US_2009_full_report.pdf).

28. www.caregiver.org/caregiver/jsp/content_node.jsp?nodeid=439.

29. B. Spillman and L. Pezzin, "Potential and Active Family Caregivers: Changing Networks and the 'Sandwich Generation,'" *Milbank Quarterly* 78, no. 3 (2002), 347–74.

30. Peter Uhlenberg, "Historical Forces Shaping Grandparent-Grandchild Relationships: Demography and Beyond," in Merril Silverstein, ed., *Intergenerational Relations across Time and Place, Annual Review of Gerontology and Geriatrics* 24 (2005): 77–97.

31. Marilyn Coleman and Lawrence H. Ganong, "Normative Beliefs about Sharing Housing with Adult Children after Mid-Life," *International Journal of Aging and Human Development* 66, no. 1 (2008): 49–72.

32. Maury Gendell, "Older Workers: Increasing Their Labor Force Participation and Hours of Work," *Monthly Labor Review* 131, no. 1 (2008): 41–54.

33. Mitra Toosi, "Labor Force Projections to 2018: Older Workers Staying More Active," *Monthly Labor Review* 132, no. 11 (2009): 30–51.

34. Charles R. Pierret, "The 'Sandwich Generation': Women Caring for Parents and Children," *Monthly Labor Review* 129, no. 9 (2006): 3–9.

35. Harriet B. Presser, *Working in a 24/7 Economy: Challenges for American Families* (New York: Russell Sage Foundation, 2003).

36. Harriet B. Presser, Janet C. Gornick, and Sangeeta Parashar, "Gender and Nonstandard Work Hours in 12 European Countries," *Monthly Labor Review* 131, no. 2 (2008): 83–103.

37. Wen-Jui Han, "Maternal Nonstandard Work Schedules and Child Cognitive Outcomes," *Child Development* 76, no. 1 (2005): 137–54.

38. Wen-Jui Han and Jane Waldfogel, "Parental Work Schedules, Family Process, and Early Adolescents' Risky Behavior," *Children and Youth Services Review* 29 (2007): 1249–66; Jody Heymann, *The Widening Gap: Why America's Working Families Are in Jeopardy and What Can Be Done about It* (New York: Basic Books, 2001); Jody Heymann, "What Happens during and after School: Conditions Faced by Working Parents Living in Poverty and Their School-Aged Children," *Journal of Children and Poverty* 6, no. 1 (2000): 5–20; Jody Heymann and Alison Earle, "The Impact of Parental Working Conditions on School-Age Children: The Case of Evening Work," *Community, Work, and Family* 4, no. 3 (2001): 305–25; L. Strazdins and others, "Unsociable Work?: Nonstandard Work Schedules, Family Relationships, and Children's Well-Being," *Journal of Marriage and Family* 68, no. 2 (2006): 394–410.

39. Vanessa Wight, Sara Raley, and Suzanne M. Bianchi, "Time for Children, Spouse and Self among Parents Who Work Nonstandard Hours," *Social Forces* 87, no. 1 (2008): 243–74.

40. K. D. Davis and others, "Nonstandard Work Schedules, Perceived Family Well-Being, and Daily Stressors," *Journal of Marriage and Family* 70, no. 4 (2008): 991–1003; Karen C. Gareis and Rosalind C. Barnett, "Under What Conditions Do Long Work Hours Affect Psychological Distress? A Study of Full-Time and Reduced-Hours Female Doctors," *Work and Occupations* 29, no. 4 (2002): 483–97.

41. Rosalind C. Barnett, Karen C. Gareis, and Robert T. Brennan, "Wives' Shift Work Schedules and Husbands' and Wives' Well-Being in Dual-Earner Couples with Children: A Within-Couple Analysis," *Journal of Family Issues* 29, no. 3 (2008): 396–422.

42. Maureen Perry-Jenkins and others, "Shift Work, Role Overload, and the Transition to Parenthood," *Journal of Marriage and Family* 69, no. 1 (2007): 123–38.

43. Rosalind C. Barnett and Karen C. Gareis, "Parental After-School Stress and Psychological Well-Being," *Journal of Marriage and Family* 68, no. 1 (2006): 101–08.

44. Lynne Casper and Martin O'Connell, "Work, Income, the Economy, and Married Fathers as Child Care Providers," *Demography* 35, no. 2 (1998): 243–50; Harriet B. Presser, "Shift Work and Child Care among Young Dual-Earner American Parents," *Journal of Marriage and the Family* 50, no. 1 (1988): 133–48; Rosalind C. Barnett and K. C. Gareis, "Shift Work, Parenting Behaviors, and Children's Socioemotional Well-Being: A Within-Family Study," *Journal of Family Issues* 28, no. 6 (2007): 727–48.

45. Wight, Raley, and Bianchi, "Time for Children, Spouse and Self among Parents Who Work Nonstandard Hours" (see note 39).

46. H. Luck Schaefer, "Part-Time Workers: Some Key Differences between Primary and Secondary Earners," *Monthly Labor Review* 132, no. 10 (2009): 3–15.

47. Ibid., table 2.

48. David H. Autor, Lawrence F. Katz, and Melissa S. Kearney, "Trends in U.S. Wage Inequality: Revising the Revisionists," *Review of Economics and Statistics* 90, no. 2 (2008): 300–23; Jerry A. Jacobs and Kathleen Gerson, "Who Are the Overworked Americans?" *Review of Social Economy* LVI, no. 4 (1998): 42–53; Jerry A. Jacobs and Kathleen Gerson, "Overworked Individuals or Overworked Families? Explaining Trends in Work, Leisure, and Family Life," *Work and Occupations* 28, no. 1 (2001): 40–63.

49. Joan C. Williams and Heather Boushey, *The Three Faces of Work-Family Conflict: The Poor, the Professionals, and the Missing Middle,* report from the Center for American Progress and the UC Hastings Work Life Law Project, 2010.

50. Christine R. Schwartz and Robert D. Mare, "Trends in Educational Assortative Marriage from 1940 to 2003," *Demography* 42 (2005): 621–46.

51. Jane L. Dye, "Fertility of American Women 2006," *Current Population Reports*, P20-558 (Washington: U.S. Census Bureau, 2008).

52. S. Philip Morgan, "Thinking about Demographic Family Differences," in *Social Class and Changing Families in an Unequal America,* edited by Marcia Carlson and Paula England (Stanford University Press, 2011).

53. Peter McDonald, "Gender Equity in Theories of Fertility Transition," *Population and Development Review* 26, no. 3 (2000): 427–39.

54. Janet C. Gornick and Marcia K. Meyers, *Families That Work: Policies for Reconciling Parenthood and Employment* (New York: Russell Sage Foundation, 2003).

55. R. E. Bulanda, "Paternal Involvement with Children: The Influence of Gender Ideologies," *Journal of Marriage and Family* 66, no. 1 (2004): 40–45; Ann C. Crouter and others, "Implications of Overwork and Overload for the Quality of Men's Family Relationships," *Journal of Marriage and Family* 63 (2001): 404–16; Jean W. Yeung and others, "Children's Time with Fathers in Intact Families," *Journal of Marriage and Family* 63, no. 1 (2001): 136–54.

56. Betsy Thorn, "Work-Family Conflict and the Competition for Mothers' Time Across the Life Course," unpublished manuscript (College Park, Md.: University of Maryland, 2010).

57. Bianchi and Raley, "Time Allocation in Working Families" (see note 19); Jacob A. Klerman and Arleen Leibowitz, "Job Continuity among New Mothers," *Demography* 36, no. 2 (1999): 145–55; Ann C. Crouter and Susan M. McHale, "Work, Family, and Children's Time: Implications for Youth," in *Work, Family, Health, and Well-Being,* edited by Bianchi, Casper, and King, pp. 21–42.

58. Michelle J. Budig and Paula England, "The Wage Penalty for Motherhood," *American Sociological Review* 66, no. 2 (2001): 204–25; Shelly J. Correll, S. Benard, and I. Paik, "Getting a Job: Is There a Motherhood Penalty?"*American Journal of Sociology* 112 (2007): 1297–1338; Ann Crittenden, *The Price of Motherhood* (New York: Metropolitan Books, 2001); Heather Joshi, "Production, Reproduction, and Education: Women, Children, and Work in British Perspective," *Population and Development Review* 28, no. 3 (2002): 445–74; Jane Waldfogel, "The Effect of Children on Women's Wages," *American Sociological Review* 62, no. 2 (1997): 209–17.

59. Jerry A. Jacobs and Kathleen Gerson, *The Time Divide: Work, Family and Gender Inequality* (Harvard University Press, 2004).

60. Kathleen Christensen, "Achieving Work-Life Balance: Strategies for Dual-Earner Families," in *Being Together, Working Apart,* edited by Barbara Schneider and Linda Waite (Cambridge University Press, 2005), pp. 449–57; Jeremy Reynolds, "In the Face of Conflict: Work-Life Conflict and Desired Work Hour Adjustments," *Journal of Marriage and Family* 67, no. 5 (2005): 1313–31; Paul Taylor, Carolyn Funk, and Alison Clark, *From 1997 to 2007: Fewer Mothers Prefer Full-Time Work* (Washington: Pew Research Center, 2007).

61. Melissa A. Milkie and others, "The Time Squeeze: Parental Statuses and Feelings about Time with Children," *Journal of Marriage and Family* 66 (2004): 739–61.

62. Ann C. Crouter and others, "Implications of Overwork and Overload for the Quality of Men's Family Relationships," *Journal of Marriage and Family* 63 (2001): 404–16.

63. S. L. Christiansen and R. Palkovitz, "Why the 'Good Provider' Role Still Matters: Providing as a Form of Paternal Involvement," *Journal of Family Issues* 22 (2001): 84–106; Nicholas Townsend, *The Package Deal: Marriage, Work and Fatherhood in Men's Lives* (Temple University Press, 2002).

64. Avner Ahituv and Robert I. Lerman, "How Do Marital Status, Work Effort, and Wage Rates Interact?" *Demography* 44, no. 3 (2007): 623–47.

65. Sanjiv Gupta, Pamela J. Smock, and Wendy D. Manning, "Moving Out: Transition to Nonresidence among Resident Fathers in the United States, 1968–1997," *Journal of Marriage and Family* 66 (2004): 627–38.

66. Rebecca L. Coley and J. E. Morris, "Comparing Father and Mother Reports of Father Involvement among Low-Income Minority Families," *Journal of Marriage and Family* 64 (2002): 982–97; Nancy S. Landale and R. Salvatore Oropesa, "Father Involvement in the Lives of Mainland Puerto Rican Children: Contributions of Nonresident, Cohabiting, and Married Fathers, *Social Forces* 79 (2001): 945–68.

67. Gail Kaufman and Peter Uhlenberg, "The Influence of Parenthood on the Work Effort of Married Men and Women," *Social Forces* 78 (2000): 931–49; Christopher Knoester and David J. Eggebeen, "The Effects of the Transition to Parenthood and Subsequent Children on Men's Well-Being and Social Participation," *Journal of Family Issues* 27 (2006): 1532–60; Christopher Knoester, R. J. Petts, and David J. Eggebeen, "Commitments to Fathering and the Well-Being and Social Participation of New, Disadvantaged Fathers," *Journal of Marriage and Family* 69 (2007): 991–1004.

68. Rand D. Conger and Glen H. Elder Jr., *Families in Troubled Times* (New York: DeGruyter, 1994); Rand D. Conger and others, "Economic Pressure in African American Families: A Replication and Extension of the Family Stress Model," *Developmental Psychology* 38 (2002): 179–93; T. M. Probst, "Economic Stressors," in *Handbook of Work Stress,* edited by J. Barling, E. K. Kelloway, and M. R. Frone (Thousand Oaks, Calif.: Sage, 2002), pp. 267–97.

69. P. Lindsay Chase-Lansdale and others, "Mothers' Transition from Welfare to Work and the Well-Being of Preschoolers and Adolescents," *Science* 299 (2003): 1548–52; Theresa Ciabattari, "Single Mothers, Social Capital, and Work-Family Conflict," *Journal of Family Issues* 28 (2007): 34–60; Lisa Gennetian and others, "Can Child Care Assistance in Welfare and Employment Programs Support the Employment of Low-Income Families?" *Journal of Policy Analysis and Management* 23 (2004): 723–43; P. A. Morris and others, *How Welfare and Work Policies Affect Children* (New York: Manpower Demonstration Research Corporation, 2001); C. C. Raver, "Does Work Pay Psychologically as Well as Economically? The Role of Employment in Predicting Depressive Symptoms and Parenting Among Low-Income Families," *Child Development* 74 (2003): 1720–36. Interestingly, when negative effects of maternal employment are found, it is more often in higher-income families. See Christopher J. Ruhm, "Maternal Employment and Child Development," in *Handbook of Families and Work*, edited by D. R. Crane and E. J. Hill (University Press of America, 2009), pp. 331–54.

70. Lisa A. Gennetian and others, "How Welfare Policies Affect Adolescents' School Outcomes: A Synthesis of Evidence from Experimental Studies," *Journal of Research on Adolescence* 14 (2004): 399–423.

71. C. L. Baum, "A Dynamic Analysis of the Effect of Child Care Costs on the Work Decisions of Low-Income Mothers with Infants," *Demography* 39 (2002): 139–64; Marcia K. Meyers, T. Heintze, and Douglas A. Wolf, "Child Care Subsidies and the Employment of Welfare Recipients," *Demography* 39 (2002): 165–79.

72. Rachel A. Gordon, Robert Kaestner, and Sanders Korenman, "Child Care and Work Absences: Tradeoffs by Type of Care," *Journal of Marriage and Family* 70 (2008): 239–56; T. W. Morrissey, "Familial Factors Associated with the Use of Multiple Child-Care Arrangements," *Journal of Marriage and Family* 70 (2008): 549–63; E. K. Scott, A. S. London, and A. Hurst, "Instability in Patchworks of Child Care When Moving from Welfare to Work," *Journal of Marriage and Family* 67 (2005): 370–86.

73. Lynne M. Casper and Kristin E. Smith, "Dispelling the Myths: Self-Care, Class, and Race," *Journal of Family Issues* 23 (2002): 716–27.

74. Williams and Boushey, *The Three Faces of Work-Family Conflict* (see note 49); Perry-Jenkins and others, "Shift Work, Role Overload, and the Transition to Parenthood" (see note 42).

75. Joan C. Williams, *Reshaping the Work-Family Debate: Why Men and Class Matter* (Harvard University Press, 2010).

Policies to Assist Parents with Young Children

Christopher J. Ruhm

Summary

The struggle to balance work responsibilities with family obligations may be most difficult for working parents of the youngest children, those five and under. Any policy changes designed to ease the difficulties for these families are likely to be controversial, requiring a careful effort to weigh both the costs and benefits of possible interventions while respecting diverse and at times conflicting American values. In this article, Christopher Ruhm looks at two potential interventions—parental leave and early childhood education and care (ECEC)—comparing differences in policies in the United States, Canada, and several European nations and assessing their consequences for important parent and child outcomes.

By and large, Canadian and European policies are more generous than those in the United States, with most women eligible for paid maternity leave, which in a few countries can last for three years or more. Many of these countries also provide for paid leave that can be used by either the mother or the father. And in many European countries ECEC programs are nearly universal after the child reaches a certain age. In the United States, parental leave, if it is available, is usually short and unpaid, and ECEC is generally regarded as a private responsibility of parents, although some federal programs help defray costs of care and preschool education.

Ruhm notes that research on the effects of differences in policies is not completely conclusive, in part because of the difficulty of isolating consequences of leave and ECEC policies from other influences on employment and children's outcomes. But, he says, the comparative evidence does suggest desirable directions for future policy in the United States. Policies establishing rights to short parental leaves increase time at home with infants and slightly improve the job continuity of mothers, with small, but positive, long-run consequences for mothers and children. Therefore, Ruhm indicates that moderate extensions of existing U.S. leave entitlements (up to several months in duration) make sense. He also suggests that some form of paid leave would facilitate its use, particularly among less advantaged parents, and that efforts to improve the quality of ECEC, while maintaining or enhancing affordability, are desirable.

www.futureofchildren.org

Christopher J. Ruhm is a professor of public policy and economics at the University of Virginia and a research associate at the National Bureau of Economic Research.

Balancing the competing needs of work and family life is a challenge for most households, but the difficulties may be greatest for households with young children, defined here as newborns through age five. Parents in many of these families struggle to find sufficient time both to fulfill work responsibilities and provide the intensive care that young children require.

Two trends exacerbate this struggle in the United States. First, mothers with infants and small children engage in market employment at much higher rates than they once did. Sixty percent of mothers with children under the age of six worked in 2008 compared with 33 percent in 1975.[1] This near-doubling reflects a general increase in the share of all working women as well as particularly fast growth in employment among mothers. Second, more children are now raised by single parents, mostly females: the proportion of children under age eighteen in sole-parent households rose from 23 percent in 1980 to 30 percent in 2008.[2] Clearly, single-parent households do not have the option of one parent working while the other cares for the children, nor do these households have the same flexibility as two-parent families to coordinate work schedules with family obligations. The growing number of single-parent households also suggests that fewer adults are available to share family responsibilities. In combination, these trends imply that a smaller fraction of young children reside in families with an adult who does not work or works only part time: the share of children with a nonworking parent declined from 64 to 34 percent between 1967 and 2009; the fraction with all parents in the household employed full time and full year rose from 14 to 33 percent.[3]

Public policies designed to ease work-family conflicts have been implemented at both the federal and state level. The most significant is the 1993 Family and Medical Leave Act (FMLA), which provides some parents the right to twelve weeks of unpaid leave following the birth of a child or for other reasons. Entitlements to job-protected or paid leave nevertheless remain extremely limited in the United States, particularly in comparison with other countries. In 2006 the United States was 1 of only 4 nations, of a total of 173, that did not guarantee some measure of paid maternity leave.[4] Even more significant, all other developed countries provide new parents rights to paid time off from work, and these entitlements often last well into early childhood.[5] Also important are policies related to the provision and financing of early childhood education and care (ECEC). Indeed, in many countries the distinction between parental leave and ECEC is no longer clear-cut. Parents often have rights to extensive leaves that cover a substantial portion of the early childhood period, and policies related to time off work and care of infants and toddlers are often fairly tightly integrated.[6]

By and large, U.S. parental policies differ dramatically from those in other industrialized countries. Foreigners frequently express surprise at the limited nature of U.S. policies, and changes that would be considered radical by many Americans are modest by their standards. Given these substantial differences in attitudes, traditions, and the institutional environment surrounding families and work, parental leave and ECEC policies in place elsewhere may not produce the same results in the United States. Still, the experiences of other nations may offer useful lessons that could help shape workable policy in the United States.[7]

This article summarizes key characteristics of parental leave and ECEC policies in the United States, Canada, and countries of Western Europe and assesses their consequences for important parent and child outcomes. Isolating the effects of these policies from other influences on the family-work balance is challenging. Recently, however, researchers have begun to use a variety of sophisticated estimation procedures (such as difference-in-difference, instrumental variables, and regression discontinuity methods) in an effort to do so. Although considerable uncertainty often remains, as reflected in the somewhat ambiguous results reported in several places in this article, these findings from the United States and other advanced countries nonetheless point in some interesting policy directions.[8]

Availability of Parental Leave

As noted, the primary parental leave policy in the the United States is the FMLA, which was enacted in 1993 after years of debate. This law entitles eligible workers to twelve weeks of job-protected leave during a twelve-month period to care for newborns or newly adopted children; leave may also be taken for serious medical problems experienced by the employee or relatives. Although historic by U.S. standards, the FMLA contains significant limitations. First, the leaves are unpaid, although employers must continue health insurance coverage, and workers can be required to use accrued sick leave or vacation before taking FMLA leave. Second, small companies (employing fewer than fifty persons within seventy-five miles of the work site) are not covered by the law, and individuals in covered companies must have worked at least 1,250 hours during the previous twelve months to be eligible. Finally, job reinstatement (in the same or an equivalent position) is not guaranteed for certain "key"

employees. Because of these restrictions, only around half of private sector workers are eligible to take FMLA leaves.

Twenty-five states had enacted some type of parental leave before the federal law was put in place.[9] Many of the rights provided in these state laws were less generous than those under the FMLA and so were subsumed by it. However, fifteen states and the District of Columbia currently supply benefits that exceed the federal law in at least some dimension, as detailed in table 1. Most frequently, eligibility is extended by covering smaller firms or relaxing the work history requirements; four states and the District of Columbia also provide for slightly longer unpaid leave periods (between thirteen and seventeen weeks).

Six states provide rights to paid family leave.[10] These entitlements take two forms. First, after passage of the federal Pregnancy Discrimination Act in 1978, the five states providing temporary disability insurance were required to treat pregnancy as a short-term disability. As a result, new mothers in these states receive partial payment (usually one-half to two-thirds of earnings) for around six weeks; job reinstatement at the end of the leave is not guaranteed.[11] Second, three states currently offer or are scheduled to provide explicit paid parental leave. California did so first. Its program, which took effect in 2004, offers six weeks of leave for an employee to bond with a newborn baby or with an adopted or foster child (or to care for a seriously ill parent, child, spouse, or registered domestic partner), with 55 percent of earnings replaced (up to a ceiling).[12] Coverage includes part-time workers and those working in relatively small firms and so is broader than that under the FMLA, but job protection is not guaranteed (unless the employee is

Table 1. Additional State Leave Entitlements beyond FMLA

State	Expanded rights to unpaid leave				Temporary disability insurance	Paid leave
	Smaller firms	Shorter tenure	Fewer work hours	Longer leaves		
California					X	X
Connecticut			X	X		
District of Columbia	X		X	X		
Hawaii		X	X		X	
Maine	X		X			
Massachusetts	X	X	X			
Minnesota	X	X	X			
Montana	X	X	X			
New Jersey			X		X	X
New York					X	
Oregon	X	X	X	X		
Rhode Island				X	X	
Tennessee	X			X		
Vermont	X					
Washington						X
Wisconsin			X			

Sources: Wen-Jui Han and Jane Waldfogel, "Parental Leave: The Impact of Recent Legislation on Parents' Leave Taking," *Demography* 40, no. 1 (2003): 191–200; Sarah Fass, *Paid Leave in the States: Critical Support for Low-Wage Workers and Their Families* (New York: National Center for Children in Poverty, Columbia University, 2009).
Note: The table excludes parental leave laws covering state employees only.

also covered by the FMLA). New Jersey's paid leave law, enacted in 2008, also provides for six weeks away from the job and sets a higher earnings replacement rate than California does (66 versus 55 percent) but a lower maximum weekly benefit ($546 versus $959 in 2009). Job protection is not guaranteed, nor are part-time workers covered. Finally, Washington state enacted a law to provide state payments during five weeks of leave at a flat weekly rate of $250, with prorated pay for part-time workers and job protection for persons meeting a work history requirement and in companies with twenty-five or more employees. This program was scheduled to begin in 2009, but budget issues have delayed its implementation until 2012.

In contrast to the United States, Europe has a long tradition of maternity leave—the first programs were enacted in Germany and Sweden at the end of the nineteenth century. These rights were initially linked to sick leaves, ranged between four and twelve weeks, with limited lump sum or flat rate payment benefits and no job protection.[13] By World War I thirteen countries supplied paid maternity leave (eight more offered unpaid leave), and all major Western European countries did so by the start of World War II. These policies were typically paternalistic in their concern for the health of the child and mother, with mothers required to take at least some of the leave, and often had a pronatalist and nationalistic orientation.

Table 2. Parental Leave Entitlements in Europe and Canada, 2008

Country	Number of months			
	Total leave	Leave exclusive to fathers	Paid leave	Paid 2/3 earnings or more
Austria	24.0	0	24.0	4.0
Belgium	9.5	3.0	9.5	4.0
Canada	12.0	0	11.5	0
Denmark	12.0	0.5	11.5	12.0
Finland	38.0	1.0	38.0	11.0
France	37.5	0.5	10.0	4.0
Germany	39.5	2.0	17.5	15.0
Greece	16.0	6.5	10.0	8.0
Iceland	15.0	6.0	9.0	9.0
Ireland	16.0	3.5	6.0	6.0
Italy	14.5	4.0	10.5	4.5
Netherlands	16.0	6.0	4.0	4.0
Norway	34.5	14.0	12.5	12.5
Portugal	36.0	5.0	12.0	6.5
Spain	72.0	36.0	4.0	4.0
Sweden	36.5	18.0	16.5	13.0
Switzerland	3.5	0	3.5	3.5
United Kingdom	18.5	3.75	9.5	1.5

Sources: Peter Moss, ed., *International Review of Leave Policies and Related Research, 2009* (London: Employment Relations Research Series 102, University of London, 2009); Rebecca A. Ray, *A Detailed Look at Parental Leave Policies in 21 OECD Countries* (Washington: Center for Economic Policy Research, 2008).

After World War II many European countries began to broaden eligibility for maternity leave, expand its durations, and provide or enhance cash payments.[14] Since the 1960s these policies have evolved from prohibitions on employing women before and after birth to job-protected time away from work to care for young children. Many nations that previously mandated compulsory leaves added job protection and, starting in the mid-1990s, extended leave durations through the implementation of parental leave provisions available to mothers or fathers.[15] This latter provision reflects a desire in many European countries for greater gender neutrality in leave policies.[16] Such concerns are particularly salient; extended leave formerly was taken almost exclusively by mothers, raising the possibility that the policies might have reduced rather than increased gender equity.[17]

Current European parental leave policies exhibit substantial cross-country variation, but most share some common elements.[18] Table 2 summarizes key characteristics of these systems, showing total duration of parental leave entitlements in 2008, leave exclusively provided to fathers, and the number of months of paid and highly paid leave (highly paid leave is defined as time off work with at least two-thirds of earnings replaced).[19]

All European nations offer paid maternity leave, typically fourteen to twenty weeks (sometimes subsumed into the broader parental leave system), with 70–100 percent of wages replaced. The variation in leave entitlements is much wider following the end of maternity leave. Three years or more of job-protected leave are provided in Finland, France, Germany, and Spain; the duration ranges between eighteen months and two years in Austria, Norway, and Sweden. These long durations can be misleading, however, because some countries (Austria, France, and Spain, for example) offer high wage replacement rates for only a portion of the period, whereas others (such as Denmark and Italy) provide shorter leaves but at higher rates of pay.

Paternity leave is less common and of shorter duration. All but two of the seventeen European nations listed in table 2 provide fathers at least some time off work, but only five countries (Finland, Germany, Iceland, Norway, and Portugal) replace at least two-thirds of wages for three weeks or more; others offer new fathers only a few days of high-wage replacement (Greece and the Netherlands) or none at all (Austria, Ireland, and Italy).[20] Where fathers take significant time off work, it is usually because countries provide nontransferable leaves or offer "bonus" arrangements extending the total leave period if some is used by fathers.

Leave payments are generally financed through payroll taxes or general government revenues, rather than directly by employers, consistent with standards set by the International Labour Union and the European Union. The government payments are motivated by a desire to spread the costs widely to avoid burdening specific employers and to reduce the likelihood that companies discriminate against those workers most likely to take leave. Employment history

requirements are short—usually six months or less with the firm—although some countries require slightly longer periods of work or social insurance contributions before a worker qualifies for full benefits.[21]

Using the total number of months of highly paid parental leave as a summary indicator of leave rights, Germany and the five Nordic countries (Denmark, Finland, Iceland, Norway, and Sweden) are the most generous, providing nine to fifteen months at high wage replacement. Less generous are Great Britain, which offers less than two months, at high replacement rates, and eight nations (Austria, Belgium, France, Greece, Italy, the Netherlands, Spain, and Switzerland) that provide about four months.[22]

The use of parental (but typically not maternity) leave can be quite flexible. Depending on the country, employees may be able to use the leave at any point until the child reaches a specified age, take longer leaves at lower wage replacement rates or shorter leaves at higher replacement pay, combine part-time work with partial leave payments, reduce work hours, take specified breast-feeding breaks, and refuse overtime or scheduling changes that conflict with family responsibilities.[23]

Canadian leave policies are of interest given the similarities of many Canadian and U.S. institutions and traditions (for example, both countries are federal systems in which some laws and policies differ from state to state). Although only three Canadian provinces offered job-protected maternity leave in 1970, by 1981 all mandated rights to at least fifteen weeks of leave; in 2008 the durations ranged from fifty-two to fifty-four weeks, except in Quebec, where the duration was seventy weeks.[24] Leave is currently paid at

55 percent of average earnings, up to a ceiling (the rate is higher in Quebec). The first fifteen to eighteen weeks are maternity leave, reserved for mothers, while either parent can use the remainder. Leave is administered at the provincial (rather than the national) level, and benefits are provided through the employment insurance system and financed by employee premiums. To qualify for leave, individuals must have worked at least 600 hours and paid employment insurance premiums for the past year.

Canada provides lower wage replacement rates (particularly during maternity leave) and has stricter eligibility criteria than is the case in much of Europe; however, the leave durations exceed those in Austria, Belgium, Ireland, Switzerland, and the United Kingdom. Thus, in the European context, Canada falls in the middle in generosity, while being unusual in administering family leave benefits through the employment insurance rather than social insurance system.

The costs of parental leave are fairly modest. Expenses in the Nordic countries averaged 0.5 to 0.7 percent of gross domestic product (GDP) in 1998; those in other European nations ranged from less than 0.1 to 0.4 percent. These figures had changed only slightly by 2002, despite increased generosity of the programs in some countries, to between 0.5 and 0.8 percent of GDP in the Nordic countries and 0.1 to 0.2 percent of GDP in seven other Western European nations (Austria, Germany, Ireland, the Netherlands, Portugal, Switzerland, and the United Kingdom).[25] These estimates suggest that substantial expansion of leave rights (including paid entitlements) in the United States would not be prohibitively expensive. As further evidence, the California paid-leave program is financed completely by employee

payroll tax contributions that were capped at $64 a worker in 2005.[26] Such costs are also small relative to other related social expenditures. For example, in 2007, the latest year for which common data are available, the United States spent 7.6 percent of its GDP on education, while the OECD average was 5.7 percent.[27]

Consequences of Parental Leave Policies

Governments enact parental leave entitlements to help parents balance the competing demands of work and family, to improve the labor market status of women (including reducing the "family gap" in earnings), and to enhance child and maternal health and development. Some European nations also use these policies in an effort to increase gender equity and raise fertility.

Parental leave permits employees to take time off work, rather than having to quit, to care for a newborn or newly adopted child. Leave policies may therefore increase job continuity—the ability of parents to stay in their prebirth job—and so help them retain use of skills or knowledge specific to their employer, potentially enhancing productivity and resulting in better long-term earnings and career advancement. Leave may also lower stress by decreasing uncertainty about future employment. These benefits are by no means guaranteed, however. For example, long leaves may cause human capital to depreciate, reducing productivity and wages. Extensive leave rights may make employers less likely to employ types of workers with high propensities to use leave or to reduce the costs of these absences by cutting training.

Proponents of leave entitlements believe that these policies also enhance the health and long-term development of children by giving parents more time to invest in their children during the critical first years of life. Although the theoretical rationale for such benefits seems clear (notwithstanding the possibility that the gains could be offset if leave rights lower earnings), these issues are challenging to study, because potential benefits are difficult to measure in most large-scale data sets and may not strongly manifest until many years after birth. The following describes the current state of knowledge on the consequences of parental leave policies, again with attention paid to evidence from Western Europe and Canada, as well as from the United States.

Leave-Taking, Job Continuity, and Employment

An explicit aim of leave policies is to allow parents to spend more time at home with young children. Such efforts appear successful. Availability of highly paid leave delays the return to work by mothers after giving birth. Data from several countries, including Great Britain, Canada, Germany, and the Scandinavian nations, show that many women return to jobs precisely when their paid leave ends.[28] Results for the brief unpaid leaves offered in the United States are more equivocal. Studies examining periods ending shortly after enactment of the FMLA or earlier state mandates find either small but statistically insignificant positive effects or no change in leave-taking.[29] However, recent research that better controls for potential confounding factors and includes more current periods indicates that leave entitlements increase the time mothers take off from work during the birth month and the next two months and are associated with a growth in *paternal* leave-taking during the birth month that is small in absolute size but large in percentage terms.[30] These increases

in leave are concentrated among college-educated and married parents, with no apparent changes for less-educated persons or single mothers, who less often qualify for or can afford to take unpaid leave.

Leave entitlements that are highly paid and of short or intermediate duration also appear to increase long-run employment. In a study using data from 1969 to 1993 for nine European countries, paid leave rights were associated with a 3–4 percent rise in female employment.[31] The estimated impact was similar whether the leave was brief or more extended, indicating that even relatively short leaves may yield benefits by increasing job continuity (the ability of mothers to return to their prebirth employers). Direct evidence from Canada and Great Britain shows that the enactment of fairly brief (seventeen to eighteen weeks) paid entitlements enhances job continuity, compared with having no leave rights, with some effect found in the United States for even shorter (twelve to sixteen weeks) unpaid leaves.[32]

The effects of rights to extended parental leaves are less obvious, because the benefits of improved job continuity may be offset by depreciation of human capital during lengthy periods away from the job. Data from the European study discussed in the previous paragraph ended in 1993, when leave rights were often much shorter than those currently mandated, so the results may not generalize to the consequences of more recent leave extensions.[33] An analysis of Austrian reforms in 1990 (which increased paid leave from twelve to twenty-four months) and 1996 (which reduced paid leave to eighteen months) did not uncover evidence of any long-term changes in employment, nor did a study of multiple changes in German leave policies.[34] Such findings may be less relevant

Leave policies may increase job continuity and so help [parents] retain use of skills or knowledge specific to their employer, potentially enhancing productivity and resulting in better long-term earnings and career advancement.

in the United States, where lengthy leave entitlements such as those granted in much of Europe seem unlikely to be adopted. U.S. research examining shorter (largely unpaid) leaves arrives at mixed conclusions. Two studies suggest that these leaves are associated with small (sometimes statistically insignificant) increases in female employment, while a third argues that enactment of the FMLA led to reductions in the labor force participation of mothers with young children.[35]

Earnings

An important motivation for parental leave policies is to reduce the "family gap" in wages (the low earnings of mothers relative to childless females or males). One early investigation suggests that the family gap was largely eliminated in the United States and Great Britain for mothers of infants who used parental leave and then returned to their pre-birth employer.[36] However, this study focused on leaves voluntarily provided by firms and so suffers from potential selection bias.[37]

Few U.S. studies examine how changes in leave entitlements affect earnings. Those

that do look at these changes obtain mixed and generally inconclusive results, perhaps because the short, mostly unpaid leave rights in the United States are too modest to have much impact.[38] European investigations usually find either no effect or wage gains following short or moderate durations of paid leave. The nine-nation study mentioned earlier found that earnings were unaffected by rights to brief leaves but that employees receiving lengthy leave entitlements (more than five or six months) suffered a small wage penalty.[39] In contrast, Denmark's expansion of leave in 1984 to twenty weeks, from fourteen, appears to have slightly raised mothers' earnings for several years after birth.[40]

Ambiguous evidence is also obtained from single-country studies of rights to lengthy leaves. Research examining policy changes in Austria, Germany, and Sweden finds that women's wages are largely unaffected by the length of the leave.[41] Conversely, evidence from one study in Denmark and another in Germany suggests that human capital losses during the period away from work have lasting (but not necessarily permanent) negative effects on earnings and that employers may reduce the training provided to women of childbearing age, with potential long-term deleterious consequences.[42] A related concern is that parental leave policies might increase occupational segregation and limit the advancement of women. Research on Sweden suggests that such concerns may be justified in the case of lengthy leave entitlements.[43]

Health and Development

Until recently, there have been few high-quality analyses of whether parental leave yields health benefits, for either mothers or children, or positively affects the longer-term developmental outcomes of children.[44] One of the first studies using more sophisticated methods examined data for sixteen European nations from 1969 to 1994 and found that paid parental leave entitlements were associated with decreased mortality for infants and young children. The largest drops in deaths were for babies aged two through twelve months, where parental involvement might be anticipated to have the strongest effect.[45] The estimates suggest that paid leave of about forty weeks has the greatest effect in reducing mortality; longer paid entitlements result in smaller gains, while unpaid leave results in little benefit. A follow-up study that expanded the sample to eighteen nations and the time period through 2000 obtained similar results, plus evidence of reductions in low-weight births.[46]

A reasonable reading of the existing research is that U.S. policies establishing rights to short unpaid leaves have modestly raised time at home with infants and slightly increased the job continuity of mothers.

Maternal leave might benefit child health because it increases breast feeding. Such an effect was found from a doubling of Canadian leave rights in 2000 from around six months to one year.[47] A related investigation showed that this leave expansion increased the time parents spent at home and reduced nonparental child care, but the study found little consistent evidence of changes in

developmental outcomes at seven through twenty-four months of age.[48] One U.S. analysis found that return to work by mothers within twelve weeks of giving birth is associated with decreases in well-baby visits, breast feeding, and child immunizations, and with lower cognitive scores and more behaviorial problems at age four.[49] A second showed that state leave mandates adopted before enactment of the FMLA raised maternity leave use by about one week and that this increase was associated with a drop in the mother's postpartum depressive symptoms and physician visits to address health problems.[50]

The availability of comprehensive national databases for individuals starting at birth and sometimes continuing through adulthood has permitted particularly innovative research on how leave entitlements in Denmark, Germany, Norway, and Sweden are related to child educational and subsequent labor market outcomes.[51] The lengthy time periods such studies require imply that they do not generally evaluate the extremely long leaves currently provided in those countries. However, findings about the extensions of the somewhat shorter (albeit generally paid) time off they do examine may be particularly relevant in the U.S. context. This research typically shows that parental leave has either no or modest benefits for long-run school performance, educational attainment, and subsequent labor market outcomes.

Fertility
Parental leave entitlements sometimes have been expanded in hopes of raising fertility or slowing its decline. Evidence from the Scandinavian countries and Austria suggests that these efforts meet with some success.[52] Increased fertility is probably less desirable in the United States, given its higher birth rates and relatively rapid population growth. In

any event, the relatively modest leave entitlements that might be realistically considered for this country would be unlikely to have much effect on fertility.[53]

Overall Assessment

A reasonable reading of the existing research is that U.S. policies establishing rights to short unpaid leaves have modestly raised time at home with infants and slightly increased the job continuity of mothers, probably with small but positive long-run consequences. Parental leave expansions that do not exceed six months or a year in length are generally associated with either no effect or slight increases in the relative earnings of mothers, as well as with gains in maternal and child health and longer-term outcomes for children. The size of these benefits is difficult to ascertain, however, because of formidable challenges in estimating causal effects, potential differences across specific policies, and the likelihood that leave rights are only one among many types of work-family policies potentially affecting earnings, health, and children's well-being. It seems likely that moderate extensions of existing U.S. leave entitlements (up to several months in duration), with or without pay, would yield further benefits for both mothers and children. Lengthy paid leaves are much less likely to be implemented in the United States, and the benefits of doing so would be less certain in any event. In particular, the right to take a year or more off work may well be associated with reductions in maternal earnings and possibly with increased occupational segregation, as employers try to limit the adjustment difficulties associated with supplying lengthy leaves.

Early Childhood Education and Care

The supply and financing of ECEC services in the United States are primarily private

responsibilities and present formidable challenges to many families. In 2005, 63 percent of U.S. children under age five received care from someone other than the "designated parent" (usually the mother), most commonly in day-care centers or preschools (35 percent), from grandparents (23 percent), or in informal settings such as in the care provider's or child's home (13 percent). About 17 percent of children used more than one of these arrangements, a situation that itself suggests the balancing act engaged in by many parents.[54] Use of nonparental care is closely linked to maternal employment. Almost 90 percent of children with employed mothers received care from someone else (fathers were the primary caregivers about one-sixth of the time), with multiple arrangements used for 25 percent of these children. Preschool-aged children averaged about nineteen hours a week in care if their mother did not work compared with thirty-five hours if she did.

In 1999 families with children under age six spent an average of 4.9 percent of their after-tax (and transfer) income paying for their young children's care.[55] One reason this amount was not larger is that 63 percent of these households incurred no child care expenses because they did not use nonparental care, used only free care (like relatives) or, less commonly, received subsidies for formal care. On the other hand, 10 percent of such families devoted at least one-sixth of their income to child care, and 5 percent of families spent one-quarter or more of their income caring for young children. Sole-parent households spent twice as much of their income on care as two-parent households did (7.9 versus 3.9 percent). The share of income spent on care fell as income rose, but not by as much as might be expected (from 6.2 for the bottom income decile to 4.4

percent for the top) for three reasons. First, families with a nonemployed parent have lower incomes on average but also use less paid care. (However, high child-care costs may be one reason why the parent does not work.) Second, poorer families more often use free or inexpensive modes of nonparental care and pay lower rates within modes. Finally, low-income parents are more likely to receive subsidized care.

The federal government has played a limited but gradually increasing role in supporting ECEC. Probably the best-known federal ECEC program is Head Start, which has operated since 1965 to provide compensatory education and other services to children from low-income families (primarily those below the poverty line or receiving welfare assistance) and to disabled preschool children.[56] In fiscal year 2009, $7.1 billion was appropriated to the program, which served 904,000 children. Most of those served (87 percent) were three- and four-year-olds, but 10 percent were younger than three and were enrolled in Early Head Start, which began in 1994. Four-fifths of program costs are paid directly to local public and private service providers, with the remainder taking the form of local match or in-kind contributions. Head Start services are offered on a part-time basis (approximately three and a half hours a day) in some localities and full time (at least six hours daily) in others. The program serves only a small fraction of those economically eligible, however, suggesting that its reach is limited, even among the low-income population.[57]

The Child Care Development Fund (CCDF) is the largest federal source of child-care subsidies. Formally implemented in 1996, the CCDF consolidated several previously existing child-care programs. It grew rapidly

through 2003 but has had relatively stable nominal funding since then, meaning that funding is declining in real terms. In fiscal year 2006 program expenditures totaled about $9.1 billion, of which $5 billion came from direct federal appropriations, around $2.2 billion from required state matching funds, and $1.9 billion from state transfers from the Temporary Assistance for Needy Families (TANF) block grant.[58] CCDF funds can be used for children up to age thirteen, but about two-thirds goes to those aged six or under. Subsidies cannot be provided to children in families whose income exceeds 85 percent of the state median income; in practice the actual thresholds are usually considerably lower (for example, in half the states, the ceiling for receiving subsidies is 55 percent or less of median income). The program serves 1.7 million children a month, or about 20 percent of income-eligible children. Parents have substantial choice regarding the setting in which subsidized care occurs: 57 percent used center-based care in fiscal 2006, while 29 percent used family day care; most of the rest of the subsidized children were cared for in their own home or that of another family. Eighty-nine percent of subsidies take the form of vouchers or cash. States are allowed to establish payment rates (within federal guidelines), and most families pay for a portion of the care on a sliding basis.

A second much smaller source of federal subsidies is the Social Services Block Grant (SSBG). Forty-one states provided child-care subsidies in 2006 under this program, primarily to low-income families; but appropriations have been falling, with only about $180 million allocated to day care in that year.[59]

A substantial share of children aged five and under in low-income families have access to subsidized child care through one of these programs: 51 percent of young poor children and 28 percent of young nonpoor children eligible for CCDF subsidies received care through the CCDF, TANF, or SSBG programs in 2005.[60] These estimates do not include enrollments in Head Start or state prekindergarten (pre-K) programs. However, eligibility for and enrollment in the subsidized programs fall rapidly for families with incomes above the poverty level, and the required co-payments imply that even subsidized families often devote a substantial portion of their incomes to child care.[61] Also, with the exception of Head Start, the care need not have an explicit educational orientation, even for children approaching the age of formal school entry.

States have attempted to fill some of these gaps through pre-K programs. Thirty-eight states provided such services, in the 2008–09 school year, to 150,000 three-year-olds and more than 1 million four-year-olds (3.7 and 25.4 percent of these age groups).[62] The programs mostly serve low- and moderate-income children. Average spending levels are modest ($4,100 a student annually in 2009 compared with $8,400 for Head Start) and have declined somewhat, adjusting for inflation, during the past decade. The percentage of three- and four-year-olds served has trended upward (from 3.0 and 14.0 percent of these age groups, respectively in 2002), but this growth has recently slowed or reversed in many states. Services can be received in a variety of venues, with about one-third of children in state-funded private programs. Pre-K is typically provided five days a week during the academic year but with substantial local variation—facilities operate fewer than five days a week in about one-third of states. Most children attend pre-K for two to four hours a day, although "full-day" programs (six to seven hours) are an option in some states and

standard in others. Even in these cases, however, most employed parents need to make additional care arrangements to fill any gap between the school day and the workday.[63]

Tax policies assist some families in paying for child care. Employed parents could use the Child and Dependent Care Tax Credit to receive a tax credit for between 20 and 35 percent of their expenses, up to $6,000 in 2010, to care for two or more children age twelve and under ($3,000 for one child).[64] The tax credit is nonrefundable, however, limiting its benefit for low-income families whose tax bills are low, and the percentage of expenses credited begins to phase out at incomes of $15,000; the minimum (20 percent) credit rate applies to families with adjusted gross incomes of $43,000 or more.

Alternatively, up to $5,000 can be tax-sheltered for persons in companies with flexible spending accounts (where employees are allowed to set aside a portion of pay to cover specified expenses on a pre-tax basis). These provisions tend to offer the greatest benefits to high-income families, who have the largest marginal tax rates and highest probabilities of being offered flexible spending plans. Families must generally choose between the child care tax credit or flexible spending plans, because income sheltered through the latter must be excluded when the tax credit is calculated.

The average quality of child care in the United States is not high. An evaluation of the "process" quality of care (based on direct observation of the interactions between caregivers and children) in nine states revealed that just 9 percent of children aged fifteen months to three years (observed between 1996 and 1999) generally received positive caregiving, while 61 percent rarely or

Table 3. Early Care and Education Arrangements

| Country | 0- to-2-year-olds | | | In formal care by age (%) | | |
	In formal care (%)	Average hours (no.)	No nonparental care (%)	3	4	5
Austria	11	23	72	48	83	93
Belgium	42	30	42	100	100	100
Canada	24	32	—	16	42	100
Denmark	63	34	27	94	93	85
Finland	26	35	75	66	70	74
France	43	30	50	99	100	100
Germany	14	22	63	82	93	93
Greece	18	31	37	—	56	86
Iceland	56	36	39	94	95	97
Ireland	25	25	59	—	47	100
Italy	29	30	51	97	100	100
Netherlands	23	17	25	—	74	98
Norway	42	31	51	87	92	93
Portugal	44	40	34	63	81	93
Spain	34	28	49	96	97	100
Sweden	45	29	48	82	87	88
Switzerland	<10	—	—	9	38	97
United Kingdom	40	18	46	79	91	100
United States	31	31	51	39	58	78

Sources: OECD Family Database (www.oecd.org/els/social/family/database); OECD, *Starting Strong II: Early Childhood Education and Care* (Paris: Organization for Economic Cooperation and Development, 2006).
Notes: "Formal care" refers to care in licensed centers and accredited family day care; it is measured in 2006 (2005 in the Netherlands and United States). "Average hours" indicate the weekly time in formal care and is conditional on some use. No nonparental child care is measured in 2008 (except 2007 in France and 2005 in the United States) and refers to families without a usual child-care arrangement during a typical week.
— Not available.

never did.[65] A 1993–94 study of 749 classrooms in 401 child-care centers indicated that the quality of care was so low in 12 percent of the centers that basic health and safety needs were unmet. Quality was rated mediocre in nearly three-fourths of the centers, with only 14 percent supplying high-quality care; just 8 percent of infants and toddlers were in classrooms where the care was rated as high quality.[66] This low process quality is accompanied by, and almost certainly related to, the deficiencies found when "structural" indicators of care such as group size, child-staff ratios, and caregiver training and pay are examined.[67]

A Cross-National Perspective

ECEC arrangements in the comparison nations, while heterogeneous, can often be usefully separated into the periods before and after the third birthday.[68] In the earliest years, emphasis is typically on care, health, and safety. Depending on the country, this early care might occur in formal modes (child-care centers or crèches) or informal settings (family day care, relative care, or play groups). Starting at age three, educational skills receive more emphasis, often in preschools, and institutional responsibility for care usually shifts from the social insurance to educational system. Public provision and

Table 4. Early Care and Education Financing and Costs

Country	Public ECEC spending as a % of GDP	Public spending per child ($)		Net child-care costs as a % of family income	
		0- to 2-year-olds	3- to 5-year-olds	Dual earners	Sole parents
Austria	—	—	—	15	17
Belgium	0.79	2,333	4,698	4	4
Canada	—	—	4,052	22	30
Denmark	1.17	6,376	3,743	8	9
Finland	0.94	7,118	2,420	7	7
France	1.00	2,858	4,679	11	10
Germany	0.38	860	3,538	8	8
Greece	—	—	—	5	5
Iceland	1.18	5,733	4,589	15	11
Ireland	—	—	—	29	45
Italy	0.61	1,558	4,626	—	—
Netherlands	0.47	1,092	5,881	12	9
Norway	0.77	6,425	4,127	8	–2
Portugal	0.40	—	3,293	4	4
Sweden	0.98	5,928	3,627	6	6
Switzerland	0.23	1,129	2,515	30	18
United Kingdom	0.58	3,563	4,255	33	23
United States	0.35	794	4,660	19	37

Sources: OECD Family Database (www.oecd.org/els/social/family/database); *Benefits and Wages 2007: OECD Indicators* (Paris: Organization for Economic Cooperation and Development, 2007).
Notes: The first column shows public ECEC spending on children aged five and younger. Public spending per child is in U.S. dollars for 2005, adjusted for purchasing power parity. Net child-care costs are for 2004 for full-time formal care of children aged two or three, and are defined as total fees minus cash benefits, rebates, and tax concessions measured as a percentage of family income. Net child-care costs are calculated for dual-earner families whose incomes are equal to 167 percent of the national average wage and for sole-parent families with incomes equal to 100 percent of the average wage.
— Not available.

payment generally become nearly universal at some point during this later period, although families are still often required to make a financial contribution.

At one end of the continuum, the Nordic countries use an integrated and nearly universal ECEC system, where care starts when parental leave ends (generally around age one or two) and continues with an increasingly education-oriented component until the child enters primary school at the relatively late age of seven. ECEC spending is high in these countries—around 1 percent of GDP for children five and under in Denmark, Iceland, and Sweden—and the

expenditures are especially large during the first three years of life. One reason is that care facilities are open about eleven hours a day year-round. Another is that the child-care workers in these nations typically have a university degree and are highly trained in early child care. In other countries training levels are typically lower for infant and toddler caregivers than for those caring for older children in preschool settings. Belgium, France, and Italy provide fewer services during the first three years of life, but formal care becomes nearly universal and extensive by age three. Tables 3 and 4 provide descriptive information on care arrangements, costs, and financing.

Gender roles in Austria, Germany, and the Netherlands are fairly traditional in that mothers provide most of the care to young children. As a result, relatively few infants or toddlers are regularly placed in nonparental settings, particularly in formal modes, and then for relatively few hours. Public ECEC spending is therefore limited during the first three years but becomes more generous thereafter. Universal entitlements to preschool begin at age three or four but the programs often run for only part of a day or involve long (two-hour) lunch breaks or closures on some weekday afternoons, making it difficult for parents to work full time without alternative sources of care.

Care arrangements during the first three years of life are often integrated with parental leave rights, with lengthier leaves implying less extensive use of nonparental care. For example, Finland combines long durations of highly paid parental leave with minimal support for publicly financed early child care, whereas Denmark provides shorter leave but higher rates of child-care coverage. Figure 1 illustrates how lengthy paid leaves are typically associated with reductions in the use of formal care and increased (exclusive) reliance on parents for regular child care.[69]

The U.S. system is most similar to other Anglo-Saxon nations (Canada, Great Britain, and Ireland) and Switzerland, which all rely on private, market-driven decentralized child care for much of the preschool period. Universal rights to early education begin at relatively late ages, with one result being that three- and four-year-olds are placed in early education programs or other types of formal care comparatively infrequently. Public ECEC spending is limited in these countries, particularly during the first three years, and most of it comes as (narrowly focused) tax

deductions or credits.[70] One consequence is that the net cost to parents of placing two- and three-year-olds in formal care is high (see the last two columns of table 4). However, Great Britain is moving toward the more typical European system, where education-oriented preschool is common and inexpensive beginning around age three.

ECEC in the United States remains distinctive in at least two ways. First, public investment in care during the first three years of life is smaller, both in absolute terms and as a percentage of GDP, than in any of the comparison countries (the most similar are Germany and the Netherlands). Second, the United States has the lowest enrollment in formal care (which includes preschool) by five-year-olds and among the smallest for four-year-olds, suggesting continuing challenges for many working families during these years, as well as possible negative consequences for children not receiving education-oriented care at these ages.

Employment Consequences

A large body of U.S. research has examined how child-care prices influence the employment rates of mothers (less often these studies also look at work hours). Virtually all analyses indicate that higher prices reduce labor supply, although the predicted magnitudes differ substantially. Two reviews of research conducted before 2000 suggest that child-care cost elasticities of maternal employment range from 0 to slightly over -1.0, with the most credible estimates varying between -0.1 and -0.5 (an elasticity of -0.5 indicates that a 10 percent increase in child-care prices reduces maternal employment by around 5 percent).[71] This uncomfortably wide range of predicted effects reflects the difficulties researchers face in adequately accounting for the choice of preferred child-care modes

Figure 1. Use of Care during First Three Years of Life As a Function of Paid Parental Leave

a. Share using formal child care

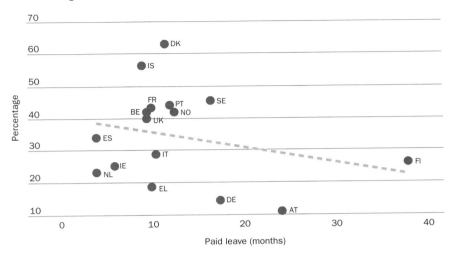

b. Share using only parental care

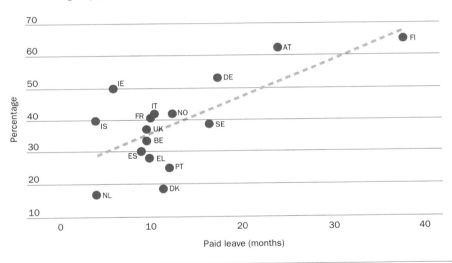

Source: See tables 2 and 3.
Note: The dashed line indicates the linear regression estimate of the predicted relationship. Country abbreviations: Austria (AT), Belgium (BE), Denmark (DK), Finland (FI), France (FR), Germany (DE), Greece (EL), Iceland (IS), Ireland (IE), Italy (IT), the Netherlands (NL), Norway (NO), Portugal (PT), Spain (ES), Sweden (SE), United Kingdom (UK).

(which may include inexpensive or free sources of informal care) and for nonrandom selection into child-care use and employment.

Research that examines the period since the 1996 reform of the welfare system continues to provide disparate estimates of child-care cost elasticities, within the range of those obtained using data from before the mid-1990s. Nevertheless, almost all studies indicate that lower child-care costs promote maternal work, particularly full-time employment, especially for single mothers and those with young children or relatively high child-care expenses.[72] Research for other countries also typically finds a negative relationship between child-care prices and maternal employment, although with small effects where nonparental day care at young ages is common.[73]

These investigations may not fully indicate the effects of direct government subsidies, because families may treat these subsidies differently from other sources of child-care cost reductions.[74] Analyses of child-care subsidies focused on low-income families during the era before welfare reform indicate positive but, again, often widely varying and small employment effects.[75] Subsidies provided after welfare reform appear to have large effects, however, especially for the low-income (usually single-parent) families they target. In particular, the probability that single mothers work and use formal, center-based care increases while rates of nonemployment or employment combined with the use of informal child care falls.[76] Public ECEC funding also increases maternal employment in other countries. An analysis of nineteen OECD countries predicts that raising public child-care expenditures from the sample average to the level spent in Denmark—the highest of the nations analyzed—would increase the labor force participation rates of women aged twenty-five to fifty-four by 4.4 percentage points, from a base of 76.4 percent.[77]

Universal ECEC entitlements also appear to raise the number of women in the workforce. Two innovative U.S. studies find that the availability of public kindergarten strongly increased the employment of single mothers whose youngest child was five years old (and so eligible for kindergarten) but had a weaker or nonexistent influence on married women or unmarried females who also had younger children.[78] A program in Quebec that charged just $5 a day for child care for one- to four-year-olds, between 1997 and 2000, led to a 13–14 percent rise in the employment of mothers with children of this age.[79]

ECEC service expansions, particularly those aimed at younger children, did not always increase maternal employment, however. The provision of free prekindergarten services to four-year-olds in Georgia and Oklahoma had little impact on maternal employment, nor did a Norwegian reform, during the mid-1970s, that dramatically increased the availability of heavily subsidized child-care slots for three- to six-year-olds.[80] In both cases, public subsidies may have "crowded out" the use of informal care. Whether that is a desirable outcome depends on relative costs and benefits of different modes of ECEC.

Child Health and Development

The consequences of ECEC policies for child health and cognitive or social development cannot be completely separated from those of parental leave policies or of parental employment during the child's first years of life. This discussion thus largely abstracts from studies of work and infancy, most of which suggest that maternal job-holding or long work hours have negative consequences for their infants.[81] Although the related literature is too vast to be fully described, an overall conclusion is that the quality of care matters. Put simply, high-quality care mitigates any negative consequences of ECEC and enhances its benefits.[82] At one extreme, favorable short- and long-term benefits (such as gains in cognitive development and eduational attainment) have been obtained from expensive, high-quality, and comprehensive "model" interventions aimed at disadvantaged children, such as the Carolina Abecedarian Project or Perry Preschool Project. But these projects are unlikely to be replicated in broad nationwide or state-level interventions, so I do not elaborate upon them.

Formal (center- or school-based) ECEC received immediately before kindergarten appears to promote school readiness. Children, particularly those who are disadvantaged, who attend prekindergarten in the year before formal schooling begin that formal schooling with better math and reading skills, although some of these gains may be transitory or offset by later compensatory education that targets less-prepared children.[83] Early center-based care also predicts somewhat higher rates of behavior problems in the late toddler years and at school entry, however.[84] More generally, formal day care earlier in life may have fewer beneficial effects, particularly for children who receive long hours of such care at very young ages.[85]

ECEC has mixed and generally modest effects on child health and safety. Use of nonparental care in the first two years of life increases the risk of infectious diseases, particularly respiratory ailments, but this exposure may confer some subsequent protection from allergies and asthma (because exposure to microorganisms stimulates immune system responses).[86] On average, children are safer in child-care settings than at home. Head Start participation is also associated with better dental care and overall health as well as with reductions in obesity.[87]

Research on other countries indicates diverse consequences of establishing or expanding formal child-care programs. The provision of almost free universal care to preschool-age children in Quebec was associated with increased behaviorial problems among two- and three-year-olds.[88] No similar behavioral

effects were found for most Danish three-year-olds enrolled in preschools (although the study found some deleterious consequences for those in family day care).[89] Finally, expansion of highly subsidized formal child care in Norway during the 1970s may have increased completed education and earnings at thirty to thirty-three years of age.[90] The very different findings in these studies might reflect heterogeneous quality and age effects. Expensive and presumably high-quality care was provided in the two Scandinavian countries, whereas the Quebec expansion consisted largely of (generally lower-quality) home-based care, often supplied to very young children.

Overall Assessment

Taken together, the studies are more ambiguous about the overall consequences of ECEC policies than of parental and maternity leave policies. One reason for this uncertainty is the diverse nature of the policies themselves, which vary substantially in the types of services provided or subsidized, the ages of the children covered, and the modes in which the care occurs. A second reason is the difficulty of determining which outcomes are of key interest (for example, cognitive test scores at school entry versus long-term educational and developmental outcomes) and how to accurately measure them. That said, it seems clear that new U.S. efforts to cut the cost or increase the availability of ECEC services would make it easier for mothers to work, although the size of the employment response is uncertain and probably dependent on the specific changes implemented. From the perspective of children, the arguments for expanding ECEC policies are strongest for those focused on disadvantaged toddlers or children approaching school entry. Many other countries have implemented or moved toward providing public prekindergarten to all children. The case for doing so in the United States would be considerably strengthened if such efforts were combined with improvements in the quality of the (often poor) care currently provided.

Where Do We Go from Here?

The United States provides relatively limited public support for the efforts of households with preschool-age children to balance the competing responsibilities of work and family life. Rights to parental leave are short and unpaid in all but a few states, in contrast to the paid and often lengthy work absences available in many other industrialized countries. The contrasts between the United States and the comparison nations are not quite as stark for the provision of ECEC. Nonetheless, in the United States ECEC is primarily a private responsibility, whereas most of the comparison nations have moved toward universal entitlements to public prekindergarten, beginning at age three or four, and many have much greater public involvement in child care at younger ages.

A first issue, therefore, is to determine the extent of any desire among Americans to raise the support for families with young children. The answer is not entirely obvious. The United States has long followed a path of "exceptionalism," where citizens have viewed differences between U.S. policies and practices and those of other countries with pride. This perspective complements a long tradition of limited government involvement, reliance on the free market, and suspicion of public efforts to solve social problems. There is nevertheless reason to believe that most Americans would like to see more comprehensive efforts to address issues of work-family balance. For instance, a poll conducted in 2009 by the Rockefeller Foundation and *TIME* revealed that 77 percent of adults

think that "businesses should be required to provide paid family and medical leave for every family that needs it," with 73 percent stating that "business should provide their employers with more child care benefits," and 59 percent agreeing that "the government should provide more funding for child care to support parents who work."[91] The remaining discussion therefore assumes that increased assistance is desirable and considers how such help could be provided.

Probably the first question to address is whether parental leave and ECEC policies should be universal or targeted. Observed practices vary across both countries and policies. All of the comparison nations provide universal entitlements to paid parental leave, although often with more extended rights for selected groups (such as those with birth complications or larger families). ECEC policies exhibit more variation. Expansions of prekindergarten programs and the integration of early day care into broader education systems suggest a movement toward universality. Yet several countries remain closer to the U.S. model of fragmented and mostly privately financed care, providing public support only to specific groups such as low-income or sole-parent families. Nor does the empirical evidence unambiguously indicate the desired direction for policy. Most studies suggest that children gain from high-quality ECEC immediately before school entry, but the results are less clear for care at younger ages (particularly if its quality is questionable). ECEC generally has the most positive consequences for disadvantaged children, a finding that suggests potential support for targeted interventions. However, universality may offer additional benefits, including increasing the political support for high-quality (usually more expensive) programs.

Any policy change designed to ease the difficulties in balancing the needs of work and family will be controversial, requiring a careful effort to weigh both the costs and benefits of possible interventions while respecting diverse and at times conflicting American values.

If greater assistance is to be provided to families with young children, it must be paid for. International evidence suggests that the costs are not overwhelming, particularly when compared with those of other programs targeting children (such as formal education) or seniors (such as public pensions and medical care). But these financing issues are nontrivial in the current era of large budget deficits and rising costs of other public programs. Once again there are two main alternatives: public versus private funding. In nations with strong traditions of social insurance, parental leave policies and ECEC programs are viewed as a national responsibility, and the costs are largely borne by the general public. At the other extreme, the expenses can be directly covered by individuals or their employers or through taxes whose incidence falls largely upon the affected groups.

"Employer mandates" have often been implemented in the United States and are attractive because they do not impose costs directly on the government. However, they are likely to result in wage decreases for groups most likely to use the benefits (such as women of childbearing age) as employers attempt to pass the costs through to their employees.[92] Moreover, if institutional barriers are enacted to prevent reductions in earnings for these workers, companies may become reluctant to hire persons likely to use the benefits, leading to an overall decline in their employment.

From an economic perspective, broad payment systems have the substantial advantage of reducing the incentives employers might otherwise have to avoid employing (or investing in) groups with high levels of expected program use. Such systems also provide insurance, in the most fundamental sense, for the costs of expensive and not fully predictable outcomes. Moreover, to the extent that children represent a "public good," it is appropriate to spread these costs throughout the economy.

Public financing can be provided through either broadly distributed payroll taxes or general revenues. Payroll taxes reduce incentives to work because they decrease the net (after-tax) wage, although when program expenses are spread across all workers, the effect on incentives may be fairly small. In addition, payroll taxes can be quite regressive (that is, the tax rate is greater for low earners than for high earners) if the taxes are paid only up to an earnings threshold, as currently occurs for Social Security but not Medicare.[93]

The use of general tax revenues has several advantages. First, it is the broadest-based source of funding and so provides the fewest incentives to discriminate against high-use groups. Second, financing comes from unearned as well as earned sources of income, implying that work disincentives are minimized. Finally, such financing is consistent with the perspective that parental leave and ECEC represent social investments in children and families. Conversely, the use of general revenues may engender particularly strong political opposition, particularly in an era of tight budgets and limited political support for federally funded social programs. It may also encourage some individuals to "game the system" (by working just long enough to qualify for public benefits, for example), and may sometimes crowd out efficiently operating private arrangements.

The United States faces many challenges in supporting the efforts of households with young children to balance the competing needs of work and family life. Any policy change designed to ease the difficulties in balancing these needs will be controversial, requiring a careful effort to weigh both the costs and benefits of possible interventions while respecting diverse and at times conflicting American values. That said, previous research suggests that policies establishing rights to short parental leaves increase time at home with infants and slightly improve the job continuity of mothers, with small, but positive long-run consequences for mothers and children. Therefore, it probably makes sense to provide moderate extensions of existing U.S. leave entitlements (up to several months in duration), with some form of payment during the leave period being necessary to facilitate its use among less-advantaged parents. The consequences of lengthy paid leaves are much less certain, but there is little realistic possibility that these will be considered in the United States in the foreseeable future.

Reaching consensus on desired changes in policies related to early care and education may be still more complicated, given the often ambiguous results of previous research. However, efforts to improve the quality of care provided, while maintaining or enhancing affordability, are almost certainly desirable. The most obvious method of achieving these twin objectives is to provide increased government support through subsidy arrangements or the direct provision of services. In an ideal world, such efforts would probably be most efficiently targeted toward low-income and disadvantaged parents, for whom the need and benefits are probably the greatest. However, the history of social programs in the United States and Europe suggests that there may be greater benefits from universal programs that build a stronger base of political support both for financing and the maintenance of quality.

Endnotes

1. U.S. Bureau of Labor Statistics, *Women in the Labor Force: A Databook,* Report 1018 (September 2009). The employment rate of mothers with children aged five and under has remained fairly stable, ranging between 58 and 60 percent since 1996.

2. U.S. Census Bureau, *Statistical Abstract of the United States: 1999,* 119th ed. (Government Printing Office, 1999); U.S. Census Bureau, *Statistical Abstract of the United States: 2010,* 129th ed. (Government Printing Office, 2009).

3. Liana Fox and others, "Time for Children: Trends in the Employment Patterns of Parents, 1967–2009" (Columbia University, March 2011).

4. Jody Heymann, Alison Earle, and Jeffrey Hayes, "The Work, Family Equity Index: How Does the United States Measure Up?" (Montreal: McGill University Project on Working Families and the Institute for Health and Social Policy, 2007). The three other countries that do not provide paid leave are Liberia, Papua New Guinea, and Swaziland. In many developing countries these rights are likely to be limited to formal sector employment and may not always be provided in practice.

5. Australia supplies a lump-sum payment to new parents but no additional payment during the leave period. However, a newly introduced paid leave scheme is scheduled to make eighteen weeks of paid leave available starting in 2011; see Peter Moss, ed., *International Review of Leave Policies and Related Research, 2009,* Employment Relations Research Series 102 (University of London, 2009).

6. Many other government policies with relevance for work-family balance do not receive much attention here. For example, reforms to the U.S. welfare system have created additional pressures for many families, particularly where exemptions from work requirements for parents with infants or toddlers have been shortened or eliminated. Although potentially important, such effects are by-products of policies enacted for other reasons and a careful treatment of them is beyond the scope of this discussion. Nor is significant attention paid to the Women, Infants, and Children program, which provides federal food subsidies and other support to pregnant women and some families with young children, or to private employer policies that certainly play a significant role for many families. Because the focus here is on families with preschool-age children, policies with more general impacts such as family allowances in Europe or the Earned Income Tax Credit in the United States are not examined. Finally, policies supporting breast feeding (breast-feeding breaks in the workplace) or time off work to take care of one's own health problems or to care for sick children, are detailed in other chapters of this volume and so receive little attention here.

7. Households with young children may find it more difficult to achieve work-family balance in the United States than in the other industrialized nations, but that is not entirely because of higher rates of maternal employment. The fraction of mothers in the United States with children under age three who work is greater than the average for all advanced countries (54 versus 45 percent in 2007) but substantially below rates in Sweden, Denmark, the Netherlands, Portugal, and Belgium, and similar to those in France, Canada, Germany, Spain, and the United Kingdom; see Organization for Economic Cooperation and Development, OECD Family Database (www.oecd.org/els/social/family/database). Part-time work is more common in other advanced countries, however, and rights to lengthy maternity and parental leave imply that parents with young children are often formally "employed" but not working, in contrast to the United States, where such leaves are almost always brief; see Wen-Jui Han, Christopher Ruhm, and Jane Waldfogel, "Parental Leave Policies and Parents' Employment and Leave-Taking," *Journal of Policy*

Analysis and Management 28, no. 1 (2009): 29–54. Europeans also generally receive four to five weeks of paid vacation (plus public holidays) annually, whereas vacation is not guaranteed in the United States and rarely exceeds two or three weeks; see U.S. Department of Labor, *National Compensation Survey: Employee Benefits in the United States, March 2009,* Bulletin 2731 (September 2009). Finally, the share of children living in single-family homes is significantly lower in Europe than in the United States; see OECD Family Database.

8. Policy outcomes may also vary with other aspects of the institutional environment. For example, the impact of parental leave may depend on the quality of the nonparental child care.

9. Eileen Trzcinski and William T. Alpert, "Pregnancy and Parental Leave Benefits in the United States and Canada," *Journal of Human Resources* 29, no. 2 (1994): 535–54. A distinction is often made between maternity leave occurring at or near the time of birth and parental leave, which takes place subsequently. The term *parental leave* is used to cover both types of time off work in most of the discussion here.

10. Employers occasionally give some workers paid leave, even when such rights are not mandated, but the practice is uncommon: In 2008 just 8 percent of private industry employees worked for companies providing paid family leave to some of their workforce; U.S. Census Bureau, *Statistical Abstract of the United States: 2010* (see note 2). Paid leave is also sometimes received on an informal basis or through the use of accrued vacation, sick leave, or personal leave.

11. Sarah Fass, *Paid Leave in the States: A Critical Support for Low-Wage Workers and Their Families* (Columbia University, National Center for Children in Poverty, March 2009). Payments are received directly from employers (or their insurers) in some states and from the government in others.

12. This paragraph is based on information in Fass, *Paid Leave in the States* (see note 11), and Alex Stone, *Paid Family Leave: U.S. Families Falling (Way) behind the Rest of the World* (Washington: Washington Family Leave Coalition, 2010).

13. This discussion is based on Christopher J. Ruhm and Jackqueline L. Teague, "Parental Leave Policies in Europe and North America," in *Gender and Family Issues in the Workplace,* edited by Francine D. Blau and Ronald G. Ehrenberg (New York: Russell Sage Foundation, 1997), pp. 133–56; Sheila B. Kamerman, "A Global History of Early Childhood Education and Care," background paper prepared for the Education for All Global Monitoring Report 2007: *Strong Foundations: Early Childhood Care and Education* (Paris: UNESCO, 2006); Meryl Frank and Robyn Lipner, "History of Maternity Leave in Europe and the United States," in *The Parental Leave Crisis: Toward a National Policy,* edited by Meryl Frank and Robyn Lipner (Yale University Press, 1988), pp. 3–22; and Anne-Marie Brocas, Anne-Marie Cailloux, and Virginie Oget, *Women and Social Security: Progress towards Equality of Treatment* (Geneva: International Labour Office, 1990).

14. These expansions followed the 1952 International Labour Organization Maternity Protection Convention, which called for widening coverage to include women in nonindustrial and agricultural occupations, extending maternity leave to twelve weeks (with at least six weeks after birth remaining compulsory), and providing cash payments of not less than two-thirds of previous earnings from social insurance or other public funds (rather than from the employer).

15. European Union Council Directive 96/34/EC of June 3, 1996, requires EU members (except Great Britain) to provide at least three months of parental leave as an individual right, to mothers and fathers, with guaranteed return to the same or an equivalent job.

16. Some changes are motivated by other considerations. For instance, the 2007 German replacement of a means-tested parental leave benefit with a benefit that instead depended on previous wages was designed to increase female labor force participation and fertility rates, particularly for high-income families; see Katharina C. Spiess and Katharina Wrohlich, "The Parental Leave Benefit Reform in Germany: Costs and Labour Market Outcomes of Moving towards the Nordic Model," *Population Research and Review* 27, no. 5 (2008): 575–91.

17. For example, fewer than 1 percent of Austrian fathers and 1–2 percent of German fathers used parental leave during the mid-1990s, compared with 96 percent of corresponding mothers; even in Finland, Norway, and Sweden, where most men take some parental leave, the vast majority of total time off work was taken by women; see Gwennaële Bruning and Janneke Plantenga, "Parental Leave and Equal Opportunities: Experiences in Eight European Countries," *Journal of European Social Policy* 9, no. 3 (1999): 195–209.

18. This chapter focuses on Western European nations because they have the longest traditions of providing parental leaves. Some innovations developed elsewhere, however, such as paid child-rearing leaves in Central and Eastern Europe.

19. The leave durations do not reflect the extra entitlements available to limited groups (such as government workers or those covered under collective agreements) or additional time off given for multiple births or medical complications, or in other situations such as second or later children). Leave restricted to men is separately broken out because benefits available to either parent are almost always taken by women. There is often a maximum benefit, implying that less than two-thirds of wages are replaced for persons earning above the threshold. Some countries offer a limited period of leave at a high replacement rate or longer durations at lower pay. A portion of the leave is also often paid at a (typically low) flat rate.

20. Longer paid work absences are often available to fathers if mothers choose not to take leave or explicitly transfer the entitlement to their husbands; however, mothers rarely take those options.

21. Self-employed persons may have stricter qualification conditions or higher social insurance contribution rates, and fathers sometimes face additional eligibility criteria.

22. Rebecca Ray, Janet C. Gornick, and John Schmitt, *Parental Leave Policies in 21 Countries: Assessing Generosity and Gender Equity* (Washington: Center for Economic Policy Research, 2008), obtain similar results using an alternative calculation of the amount of "full-time equivalent" paid leave.

23. For additional details, see Peter Moss and Fred Deven, "Country Notes: Introduction and Main Findings," in *International Review of Leave Policies and Related Research 2009*, edited by Moss, pp. 77–99; Ray, Gornick, and Schmitt, *Parental Leave Policies in 21 Countries* (see note 22); and Ariane Hegewisch and Janet C. Gornick, *Statutory Routes to Workplace Flexibility in Cross-National Perspective* (Washington: Institute for Women's Policy Research, 2008).

24. For details see Michael Baker and Kevin Milligan, "How Does Job-Protected Maternity Leave Affect Mothers' Employment?" *Journal of Labor Economics* 26, no. 4 (2008) 655–91; Rebecca A. Ray, *A Detailed Look at Parental Leave Policies in 21 OECD Countries* (Washington: Center for Economic Policy Research, 2008).

25. Janet C. Gornick and Marcia K. Meyers, *Families That Work: Policies for Reconciling Parenthood and Employment* (New York: Russell Sage Foundation, 2003); Nabanita Datta Gupta, Nina Smith, and Mette

Verner, "The Impact of Nordic Countries' Family Policies on Employment, Wages, and Children," *Review of the Economics of the Household* 6, no. 1 (2008): 609–29.

26. Fass, *Paid Leave in the States* (see note 11).

27. OECD, "Education at a Glance 2010: OECD Indicators" (www.oecd.org/document/52/0,3746,en_2649_ 39263238_ 45897844_1_1_1_1,00.html).

28. Marit Rønsen and Marianne Sundström, "Family Policy and After-Birth Employment among New Mothers: A Comparison of Finland, Norway and Sweden," *European Journal of Population* 18, no. 2 (2002): 121–52; Christian Dustmann and Uta Schönberg, "The Effects of Expansions in Maternity Leave Coverage on Children's Long-Term Outcomes," IZA Discussion Paper 3605 (Bonn: Institute for the Study of Labor, 2008); Simon Burgess and others, "Maternity Rights and Mothers' Return to Work," *Labour Economics* 15, no. 2 (2008): 168–201; Maria Hanratty and Eileen Trzcinski, "Who Benefits from Paid Leave? Impact of Expansions in Canadian Paid Family Leave on Maternal Employment and Transfer Income," *Journal of Population Economics* 22, no. 3 (2009): 693–711.

29. Charles L. Baum, "The Effects of Maternity Leave Legislation on Mothers' Labor Supply after Childbirth," *Southern Economic Journal*, 69, no. 4 (2003): 772–99; Wen-Jui Han and Jane Waldfogel, "Parental Leave: The Impact of Recent Legislation on Parents' Leave Taking," *Demography* 40, no. 1 (2000): 191–200.

30. Han, Ruhm, and Waldfogel, "Parental Leave Policies and Parents' Employment and Leave-Taking" (see note 7). The control group includes persons having children approximately one year in the future. Leave rights increase predicted maternal leave taking by 5 to 9 percentage points (13 to 20 percent) in the birth month and next two months and paternal leave taking by 3.9 percentage points (54 percent) in the birth month.

31. Christopher J. Ruhm, "The Economic Consequences of Parental Leave Mandates: Lessons from Europe," *Quarterly Journal of Economics* 113, no. 1 (1998): 285–317.

32. Baker and Milligan, "How Does Job-Protected Maternity Leave Affect Mothers' Employment?" (see note 24); Jane Waldfogel, "The Family Gap for Young Women in the United States and Britain: Can Maternity Leave Make a Difference?" *Journal of Labor Economics* 16, no. 3 (1998): 505–45; Baum, "The Effects of Maternity Leave Legislation on Mothers' Labor Supply after Childbirth" (see note 29).

33. For instance, in 1993 mothers were entitled to twenty-eight, sixteen, fourteen, and forty-two weeks of paid leave in Denmark, France, Ireland, and Norway, respectively, versus forty-eight, forty-two, twenty-six, and ninety weeks in 2008.

34. Rafael Lalive and Josef Zweimüller, "How Does Parental Leave Affect Fertility and Return to Work: Evidence from Two Natural Experiments," *Quarterly Journal of Economics* 124, no. 3 (2009): 1363–1402; Uta Schönberg and Johannes Ludstek, "Maternity Leave Legislation, Female Labor Supply, and the Family Wage Gap," IZA Discussion Paper 2699 (Bonn: Institute for the Study of Labor, 2007). The latter study investigated German changes lengthening paid leave from two to six months in 1979, six to ten months in 1986, and eighteen to thirty-six months in 1992.

35. Positive employment effects were found by Charles L. Baum, "The Effect of State Maternity Leave Legislation and the 1993 Family and Medical Leave Act on Employment and Wages," *Labour Economics* 10, no. 5 (2003): 573–96; Han, Ruhm, and Waldfogel,"Parental Leave Policies and Parents' Employment

and Leave-Taking" (see note 7). Negative impacts were found by Natalie K. Goodpaster, "Leaves and Leaving: The Family and Medical Leave Act and the Decline in Maternal Labor Force Participation," *B. E. Journal of Economic Analysis and Policy (Contributions)* 10, no. 1 (2010), Article 6. The employment reductions are hypothesized to occur because some women on leave discover that they prefer being home with their young children to returning to work.

36. Waldfogel, "The Family Gap for Young Women in the United States and Britain" (see note 32).

37. For instance, the family gap in Denmark is overestimated by failing to account for the self-selection of mothers into relatively low-paid public sector jobs; see Helena Skyt Nielsen, Marianne Simonsen, and Mette Verner, "Does the Gap in Family-Friendly Policies Drive the Family Gap?" *Scandinavian Journal of Economics* 106, no. 4 (2004): 721–24.

38. Jane Waldfogel, "The Impact of the Family and Medical Leave Act," *Journal of Policy Analysis and Management* 18, no. 2 (1999): 281–302; Baum, "The Effect of State Maternity Leave Legislation and the 1993 Family and Medical Leave Act on Employment and Wages" (see note 35).

39. Ruhm, "The Economic Consequences of Parental Leave Mandates" (see note 31).

40. Astrid W. Rasmussen, "Increasing the Length of Parents' Birth-Related Leave: The Effect on Children's Long-Term Educational Outcomes," *Labour Economics* 17, no. 1 (2010): 91–100.

41. James W. Albrecht and others, "Career Interruptions and Subsequent Earnings: A Reexamination Using Swedish Data," *Journal of Human Resources* 34, no. 2 (1999): 294–311; Dustmann and Schönberg, "The Effects of Expansions in Maternity Leave Coverage on Children's Long-Term Outcomes" (see note 28); Lalive and Zweimüller, "How Does Parental Leave Affect Fertility and Return to Work" (see note 34).

42. Nabanita Datta Gupta and Nina Smith, "Children and Career Interruptions: The Family Gap in Denmark," *Economica* 69, no. 276 (2002): 609–29; Helena Skyt Nielsen, "Causes and Consequences of a Father's Child Leave: Evidence from a Reform of Leave Schemes," IZA Discussion Paper 4267 (Bonn: Institute for the Study of Labor, 2009); Patrick A. Puhani and Katja Sonderhof, "The Effects of Maternity Leave Extension on Training for Young Women," *Journal of Population Economics* 24, no. 2 (2011): 731–60.

43. James Albrecht, Anders Björklund, and Susan Vroman, "Is There a Glass Ceiling in Sweden?" *Journal of Labor Economics* 21, no. 1 (2003): 145–77. "Glass ceiling" effects are hypothesized to manifest through larger gender differentials higher in the earnings distribution. No such differential existed in 1968, but one emerged by the early 1980s and strengthened in the 1990s, when parental leave rights were expanded. Occupational segregation also increased over time.

44. Such research is reviewed in Katharina Staehelin, Paola Coda Bertea, and Elisabeth Zemp Stutz, "Length of Maternity Leave and Health of Mother and Child: A Review," *International Journal of Public Health* 52, no. 4 (2007): 202–09.

45. Christopher J. Ruhm, "Parental Leave and Child Health," *Journal of Health Economics* 19, no. 6 (2000): 931–60.

46. Sakiko Tanaka, "Parental Leave and Child Health across OECD Countries," *Economic Journal* 15, no. 501 (2005): F7–F28.

47. Michael Baker and Kevin Milligan, "Maternal Employment, Breastfeeding, and Health: Evidence from Maternity Leave Mandates," *Journal of Health Economics* 27, no. 4 (2008): 871–87. They also provide

evidence of reductions in asthma, chronic conditions, allergies, and ear infections at seven to twelve months but raise concern about the robustness of these findings.

48. Michael Baker and Kevin Milligan, "Evidence from Maternity Leave Expansions of the Impact of Maternal Care on Early Child Development," *Journal of Human Resources* 45, no. 1 (2010): 1–32.

49. Lawrence Berger, Jennifer Hill, and Jane Waldfogel, "Maternity Leave, Early Maternal Employment and Child Health and Development in the US," *Economic Journal* 115, no. 501 (2005): F29–F47. These results suggest but do not explicitly test for effects of leave.

50. Pinka Chatterji and Sara Markowitz, "Does the Length of Maternity Leave Affect Maternal Health?" *Southern Economic Journal* 72, no. 1 (2005): 16–41.

51. Pedro Carneiro, Kartine Løken, and Kjell G. Salvanes, "A Flying Start? Maternity Leave and Long-Term Consequences of Time Investments in Infants in Their First Year of Life" (University College London, March 2010); Dustmann and Schönberg, "The Effects of Expansions in Maternity Leave Coverage on Children's Long-Term Outcomes" (see note 28); Qian Liu and Oskar Nordström Skans, "The Duration of Paid Parental Leave and Children's Scholastic Performance," *B. E. Journal of Economic Analysis and Policy (Contributions)* 10, no. 1 (2010): Article 3; Rasmussen, "Increasing the Length of Parents' Birth-Related Leave" (see note 40).

52. Anders Björklund, "Does Family Policy Affect Fertility," *Journal of Population Economics* 19, no. 1 (2006): 3–24; Gupta, Smith, and Verner, "The Impact of Nordic Countries' Family Policies on Employment, Wages, and Children" (see note 25); Lalive and Zweimüller, "How Does Parental Leave Affect Fertility and Return to Work" (see note 34).

53. Higher fertility in Austria and Sweden largely result from a "speed premium," where having an additional child during the original period of leave extends its duration. Leaves in excess of one year are required to allow for such strategic behavior because of the biological difficulty in timing births within a shorter period.

54. Lynda Laughlin, "Who's Minding the Kids? Child Care Arrangements: Spring 2005/Summer 2006," *Current Population Reports*, P70-121 (U.S. Census Bureau, August 2010).

55. Dan T. Rosenbaum and Christopher J. Ruhm, "Family Expenditures on Child Care," *B. E. Journal of Economic Analysis and Policy (Topics)* 7, no. 1 (2007): Article 34.

56. Except where noted, the information on government programs in this section is from *Green Book, 2008: Background Material and Data on Programs within the Jurisdiction of the Committee on Ways and Means* (Washington: House of Representatives, Committee on Ways and Means, 2009) (http://waysandmeans.house.gov/singlepages.aspx?NewsID=10490). Additional information on Head Start was obtained from the Administration for Children and Families, "Head Start Program Fact Sheet Fiscal Year 2010" (http://eclkc.ohs.acf.hhs.gov/hslc/Head%20Start%20Program/Head%20Start%20Program%20Factsheets/fHeadStart-Progr.htm); and Melinda Gish, "Head Start: Background and Issues," CRS Report for Congress RL30952 (Washington: Congressional Research Service, updated January 9, 2006).

57. Using fiscal year 2009 enrollment figures from Administration for Children and Families, "Head Start Program Fact Sheet Fiscal Year 2010" (see note 56) and estimates of the economically eligible population in 2004, from Gish, "Head Start: Background and Issues" (see note 56), I estimate that the program served 47 percent of income-eligible three- and four-year-olds and 3 percent of income-eligible children below age three in fiscal year 2009.

58. States are permitted to transfer up to 30 percent of their TANF block grant to CCDF and can directly spend TANF funds on child care. In 2006 they allocated around $1 billion for the latter.

59. A few states have implemented at-home infant care programs that subsidize low-income parents who provide child care in the home; see National Partnership for Women & Families, "At-Home Infant Care (AHIC): A Side-by-Side Comparison of Federal and State Initiatives" (www.nationalpartnership.org/site/DocServer/AHICchartOct05.pdf?docID=1048).

60. "Child Care Eligibility and Enrollment Estimates for Fiscal Year 2005," *ASPE Issue Brief* (Washington: U.S. Department of Health and Human Services, Office of the Assistant Secretary for Planning and Evaluation, July 2008).

61. The average family receiving CCDF benefits paid 4.7 percent of its income for subsidized child-care services in fiscal year 2006.

62. In addition, 319,000 three- and four-year-olds received special education services. Information in this paragraph is from W. Steven Barnett and others, *The State of Preschool, 2009* (Rutgers University, National Institute for Early Education Research, 2009).

63. Also deserving mention is the U.S. Department of Defense child-care program, the nation's largest employer-sponsored child-care system, which has been transformed from a low-quality program to one viewed as a national model for providing high-quality care; see M.-A. Lucas, "The Military Child Care Connection," *The Future of Children*, 11, no. 1 (2001): 128–33.

64. Internal Revenue Service, *Child and Dependent Care Expenses: For Use in Preparing 2010 Returns*, Publication 503 (2010) (www.irs.gov/pub/irs-pdf/p503.pdf).

65. NICHD (National Institute for Child Health and Human Development) Early Child Care Research Network, "Characteristics and Quality of Child Care for Toddlers and Preschoolers," *Applied Developmental Science* 4, no. 3 (2000): 116–35.

66. Suzanne W. Helburn, ed., *Cost, Quality and Child Outcomes in Child Care Centers: Technical Report* (University of Colorado, Center for Research in Economic and Social Policy, 1995). These results overestimate the overall quality of care if centers eligible for the study but choosing not to participate in it had lower-than-average quality.

67. In addition to the study mentioned in the previous note, see Deborah Lowe Vandell and Barbara Wolfe, "Child Care Quality: Does It Matter and Does It Need to Be Improved?" Institute for Research on Poverty Special Report 78 (University of Wisconsin–Madison, 2000); and David M. Blau, *The Child Care Problem: An Economic Analysis* (New York: Russell Sage Foundation, 2001).

68. This section is based on Gornick and Meyers, *Families That Work* (see note 25); OECD, *Starting Strong II: Early Childhood Education and Care* (Paris: 2006); Jérôme de Henau, Danièle Meulders, and Síle O'Dorchai, "Parents' Care and Career: Comparing Public Childcare Provision," in *Social Policies, Labour Markets and Motherhood*, edited by Daniela Del Boca and Cécile Wetzels (Cambridge University Press, 2007), pp. 28–62; Eurydice, *Tackling Social and Cultural Inequalities through Early Childhood Education and Care in Europe* (Brussels: European Commission, Education, Audiovisual and Culture Executive Agency, 2009). For historical perspective, see Kamerman, "A Global History of Early Childhood Education and Care" (see note 13).

69. An extra week of paid leave decreases the predicted use of informal care by a statistically insignificant 0.5 percentage point and raises parent-only care by a significant 1.2 points.

70. For additional details, see Jérôme de Henau, Daniéle Meulders, and Síle O'Dorchai, "Support for Market Care: Comparing Comparing Child Care and Tax Systems," in *Social Policies, Labour Markets and Motherhood*, edited by Del Boca and Wetzels, pp. 107–51; OECD, *Benefits and Wages 2007: OECD Indicators* (Paris: 2007).

71. Patricia M. Anderson and Phillip B. Levine, "Child Care and Mothers' Employment Decisions," in *Finding Jobs: Work and Welfare Reform*, edited by David Card and Rebecca M. Blank (New York: Russell Sage Foundation, 2000), pp. 420–62; David M. Blau, "Child Care Subsidy Programs," in *Means-Tested Transfer Programs in the United States*, edited by Robert A. Moffitt (University of Chicago Press, 2003), pp. 443–516. Higher child-care costs also decrease work hours, conditional on employment, but probably by a smaller amount.

72. Rachel Connelly and Jean Kimmel, "The Effect of Child Care Costs on the Employment and Welfare Recipiency of Single Mothers," *Southern Economic Journal* 69, no. 3 (2003): 498–519; Erdal Tekin, "Childcare Subsidies, Wages, and the Employment of Single Mothers," *Journal of Human Resources* 42, no. 2 (2007): 453–86; Chris M. Herbst, "The Labor Supply Effects of Child Care Costs and Wages in the Presence of Subsidies and the Earned Income Tax Credit," *Review of Economics of the Household* 8, no. 2 (2010): 199–230.

73. For instance, price reductions for publicly provided care implemented in Sweden in 2002 and 2003 led to small or no increases in employment for mothers of one- to nine-year-olds; see Daniela Lundin, Eva Mörk, and Björn Öckert, "How Far Can Reduced Childcare Prices Push Female Labour Supply," *Labour Economics* 15, no. 4 (2008): 647–59.

74. This variation may occur for several reasons. Costs may be low in areas where wages or labor market conditions are depressed, muting the observed child-care price elasticities. Families may view subsidies as direct encouragement to use child care and so respond more than for other price changes. Public provision of ECEC may provide some guarantee of quality and reduce transaction costs of using it.

75. For reviews of this research, see Anderson and Levine, "Child Care and Mothers' Employment Decisions" (see note 71), and Blau, "Child Care Subsidy Programs" (see note 71).

76. Erdal Tekin, "Child Care Subsidy Receipt, Employment, and Child Care Choices of Single Mothers," *Economics Letters* 89, no. 1 (2005): 1–6; Herbst, "The Labor Supply Effects of Child Care Costs and Wages in the Presence of Subsidies and the Earned Income Tax Credit" (see note 72).

77. Florence Jaumotte, "Labour Force Participation of Women: Empirical Evidence on the Role of Policy and Other Determinants in OECD Countries," *OECD Economic Studies* no. 37 (2003/2) (June 2004): 51–108.

78. Jonah B. Gelbach, "Public Schooling for Young Children and Maternal Labor Supply," *American Economic Review* 92, no. 1 (2002): 307–22, uses quarter-of-birth as an instrument for kindergarten enrollment. Elizabeth Cascio, "Maternal Labor Supply and the Introduction of Kindergartens into American Public Schools," *Journal of Human Resources* 44, no. 1 (2009): 140–69, exploits differences in the timing of the introduction of state funding for kindergarten. Gelbach finds that Head Start availability also increases employment.

79. Pierre Lefebvre and Philip Merrigan, "Child-Care Policy and the Labor Supply of Mothers with Young Children: A Natural Experiment from Canada," *Journal of Labor Economics* 26, no. 3 (2008): 519–48; Michael Baker, Jonathan Gruber, and Kevin Milligan, "Universal Child Care, Maternal Labor Supply and Family Well-Being," *Journal of Political Economy* 116, no. 4 (2008): 709–45. The largest subsidy increases occurred at middle and high incomes, because the poor were eligible for subsidies before implementation. Hours and annual weeks of work also rose.

80. Maria Donovan Fitzpatrick, "Preschoolers Enrolled and Mothers at Work? The Effects of Universal Prekindergarten," *Journal of Labor Economics* 28, no. 1 (2010): 51–84; Tarjei Havnes and Magne Mogstad, "Money for Nothing? Universal Child Care and Maternal Employment," IZA Discussion Paper 4504 (Bonn: Institute for the Study of Labor, 2009).

81. See, for example, Christopher J. Ruhm, "Parental Employment and Child Cognitive Development," *Journal of Human Resources* 39, no. 1 (2004): 155–92; Jennifer Hill and others, "Towards a Better Estimate of Causal Links in Child Policy: The Case of Maternal Employment and Child Outcomes," *Developmental Psychology* 41, no. 6 (2005): 833–50; and Raquel Bernal and Michael P. Keane, "Quasi-Structural Estimation of a Model of Childcare Choices and Child Cognitive Ability Production," *Journal of Econometrics* 156, no. 1 (2010): 164–89. More neutral results were obtained by Jeanne Brooks-Gunn, Wen-Jui Han, and Jane Waldfogel, "First-Year Maternal Employment and Child Development in the First Seven Years," *Monographs of the Society for Research in Child Development* 75, no. 2 (2010).

82. Much of the information in this section comes from David Blau and Janet Currie, "Pre-School, Day Care, and After School Care: Who's Minding the Kids?" in *Handbook of the Economics of Education*, vol. 2, edited by Eric A. Hanushek and Finis Welch (New York: North Holland, 2006), pp. 1163–278; Jane Waldfogel, *What Children Need* (Harvard University Press, 2006), pp. 81–125; Douglas Almond and Janet Currie, "Human Capital Developments before Age 5," Working Paper 15827 (Cambridge, Mass.: National Bureau of Economic Research, March 2010); National Institute of Child Health and Human Development, *The NICHD Study of Early Child Care and Youth Development: Findings for Children up to 4 ½ Years*, NIH Pub. 05-4318 (2006).

83. Katharine Magnuson, Christopher Ruhm, and Jane Waldfogel, "Does Prekindergarten Improve School Preparation and Performance?" *Economics of Education Review* 26, no. 1 (2007): 33–51; Katherine Magnuson, Christopher Ruhm, and Jane Waldfogel, "The Persistence of Preschool Effects: Do Subsequent Classroom Experiences Matter?" *Early Childhood Research Quarterly* 22, no. 1 (2007): 18–38.

84. NICHD Early Child Care Research Network, "Does the Amount of Time Spent in Child Care Predict Socioemotional Adjustment during the Transition to Kindergarten?" *Child Development* 74, no. 4 (2003): 976–1005; NICHD Early Child Care Research Network, "Type of Child Care and Children's Development at 54 Months," *Early Childhood Research Quarterly* 19, no. 2 (2004): 203–20; Magnuson, Ruhm, and Waldfogel, "Does Prekindergarten Improve School Preparation and Performance?" (see note 83); Susanna Loeb and others, "How Much Is Too Much? The Influence of Preschool Centers on Children's Social and Cognitive Development," *Economics of Education Review* 26, no. 1 (2007): 52–66. These results do not apply to the intensive model interventions, for which evidence of benefits has been obtained.

85. Jay Belsky, "Early Child Care and Early Child Development: Major Findings of the NICHD Study of Early Child Care," *European Journal of Developmental Psychology* 3, no. 1 (2006): 95–110, and the references contained therein supply extensive discussion of these issues. However, Duan Peng and Philip Robins,

"Who Should Care for Our Kids? The Effects of Infant Child Care on Early Child Development," *Journal of Children and Poverty* 16, no. 1 (2010): 1–45, uncover beneficial effects of nonparental care for disadvantaged infants.

86. For details, see Marcia Meyers and others, "Inequality in Early Childhood Education and Care: What Do We Know?" in *Social Inequality*, edited by Kathryn M. Neckerman (New York: Russell Sage Foundation, 2004), pp. 223–69.

87. Janet Currie and Matthew Neidell, "Getting Inside the 'Black Box' of Head Start Quality: What Matters and What Doesn't," *Economics of Education Review* 26, no. 1 (2007): 83–99; Janet Currie and V. Joseph Hotz, "Accidents Will Happen? Unintentional Injury, Maternal Employment, and Child Care Policy," *Journal of Health Economics* 23, no. 1 (2004): 25–59; David E. Frisvold and Julie C. Lumeng, "Expanding Exposure: Can Increasing the Daily Duration of Head Start Reduce Childhood Obesity?" *Journal of Human Resources* 46, no. 2 (2011): 373-402.

88. Baker, Gruber, and Milligan, "Universal Child Care, Maternal Labor Supply, and Family Well-Being" (see note 79).

89. Nabanita Datta Gupta and Marianne Simonsen, "Non-Cognitive Child Outcomes and Universal High Quality Child Care," *Journal of Public Economics* 94, no. 1–2 (2010): 30–43.

90. Tarjei Havnes and Magne Mogstad, "No Child Left Behind: Universal Child Care and Children's Long-Run Outcomes," Research Department Discussion Paper 582 (Oslo: Statistics Norway, 2009).

91. John Halpin and Ruy Teixeira with Susan Pinkus and Kelly Daley, "Battle of the Sexes Gives Way to Negotiation," in *The Shriver Report: A Woman's Nation Changes Everything*, edited by Heather Boushey and Ann O'Leary (Washington: Center for American Progress, 2009), pp. 395–417.

92. See Jonathan Gruber, "The Incidence of Mandated Maternity Benefits," *American Economic Review* 84, no. 3 (1994): 622–41, for a comprehensive review of this issue in the context of mandated health insurance coverage for maternity-related expenses; and Christopher J. Ruhm, "The Economic Consequences of Parental Leave Mandates" (see note 31) for a discussion specific to parental leave benefits.

93. Payroll taxes can be levied on both employers and employees (as is done for Social Security and Medicare) or on just one of the parties (California's paid leave program is financed by payroll taxes paid only by employees). The actual tax burden is more complicated because employers often offset their payroll tax payments by reducing wages.

Families with School-Age Children

Kathleen Christensen, Barbara Schneider, and Donnell Butler

Summary

Most working parents face a common dilemma—how to care for their children when they are not in school but the parents are at work. In this article Kathleen Christensen, Barbara Schneider, and Donnell Butler describe the predictable and unpredictable scheduling demands school-age children place on working couples and single working parents.

The authors assess the potential capacity of schools to help meet the needs of working families through changes in school schedules and after-school programs and conclude that the flexibility parents need to balance family-work responsibilities probably cannot be found in the school setting. They argue that workplaces are better able than schools to offer the flexibility that working parents need to attend to basic needs of their children, as well as to engage in activities that enhance their children's academic performance and emotional and social well-being.

Two types of flexible work practices seem especially well suited to parents who work: flextime arrangements that allow parents to coordinate their work schedules with their children's school schedules, and policies that allow workers to take short periods of time off—a few hours or a day or two—to attend a parent-teacher conference, for example, or care for a child who has suddenly fallen ill. Many companies that have instituted such policies have benefited through employees' greater job satisfaction and employee retention.

Yet despite these measured benefits to employers, workplaces often fall short of being family friendly. Many employers do not offer such policies or offer them only to employees at certain levels or in certain types of jobs. Flexible work practices are almost nonexistent for low-income workers, who are least able to afford alternative child care and may need flexibility the most.

Moreover the authors find that even employees in firms with flexible practices such as telecommuting may be reluctant to take advantage of them, because the workplace culture explicitly or implicitly stigmatizes or penalizes employees for choosing these work arrangements. The authors conclude by making a case for creating a workplace culture that supports flexibility. Such a culture, they argue, would enable working parents to better meet the responsibilities of their jobs as they care for and build strong relationships with their children.

www.futureofchildren.org

Kathleen Christensen is the program director of the Alfred P. Sloan Foundation. Barbara Schneider is the John A. Hannah Distinguished Professor at Michigan State University. Donnell Butler is a postdoctoral fellow at Educational Testing Service.

Kathleen Christensen, Barbara Schneider, and Donnell Butler

M ore than half of all children under age eighteen now live in households with two employed parents or an employed single parent.[1] For many of these households, parenting has grown increasingly complicated, with the structure and demands of the workplace often colliding with parents' basic responsibilities for supervision and involvement in their children's lives. The collision is most noticeable where the relatively rigid schedules governing when and where work is to be done conflict not only with equally rigid school schedules but also with children's needs, both predictable and unpredictable. Parents whose work schedules do not coincide with their school-age children's schedules must arrange for the predictable—transporting their children to and from school and finding care for them during the gap between the end of the school day and the end of the workday and during school vacations. Parents must also be prepared for the unpredictable—an emergency such as a child's sudden illness that requires them either to leave work to care for the child or to find someone quickly who can provide that care.

This article examines the scheduling challenges working families with school-age children face and the ways flexibility at school and at parents' workplaces might help parents meet the needs of their children and fulfill their responsibilities to their employer. Seeing little likelihood that changes in school schedules can provide sufficient flexibility to aid parents, we argue not only that the necessary flexibility is best offered in the parents' workplaces but that a supportive workplace culture needs to be developed for flexibility practices to reach their full potential. We conclude by identifying several employers with well-designed flexibility practices that genuinely serve both working parents and their employers.

Parent Roles in Their Children's Lives: Supervision and Involvement

Full-time jobs that require rigid start and end times or that entail early morning and evening meetings or overnight travel can encroach on the time available to parents to supervise and be involved in their children's lives.[2] Parents must either provide child care for the times when they cannot be present or alter their work schedules so they can be at home at the same time their school-age children are. For those in low-paying jobs, the added constraint of limited resources makes child-care arrangements even more complicated and problematic.[3]

Supervision, a primary responsibility of parenting, includes those activities parents undertake to ensure that their children's basic physical and safety needs are met. Being late to pick up a child at school, for example, can have grave safety consequences, especially if the school closes and no adults are on the premises. The degree of supervision to keep school-age children safe varies depending on the chronological age of the child and the location of the school and home. At a minimum, parents have to ensure that someone is available to take care of children's meals and transportation needs before and after the school day. Some older children can manage these responsibilities on their own, but someone should still check on their whereabouts before and after school, on how they spend their weekends and with whom, and on how they are handling their nutritional needs.

The structure of the workplace constrains the ability of working parents to attend to these basic supervisory responsibilities.[4] For those in autonomous jobs, communicating with children during the day is not a problem; however, in many kinds of jobs, employees are prohibited from making personal calls or their communications are monitored. Moreover, the nature of some jobs severely curtails opportunities to attend to the basic needs of children, such as leaving work early to take a child to a pediatric appointment.[5]

Involvement represents those parental activities that directly relate to children's academic, social, and emotional well-being. Parents provide the most direct and salient role models for their children's academic and social development. One of the most important factors in children's school success is how actively involved their parents are in their education.[6] Overwhelming evidence from decades of research shows that the actions parents take with their children—from reading to them to attending school meetings to helping them with homework—can enhance their motivation to learn, raise their educational expectations, and improve their performance.[7] This confidence in the value of parental engagement has prompted federal legislators to include specific guidance in the latest reauthorization of the Elementary and Secondary Education Act on the activities parents may undertake to assist their children's education.[8] States have also responded by developing websites showing how parents can become involved in their children's learning.[9]

The press for more parental involvement in education activities is related in part to the evolving societal view of what now constitutes "good parenting." The term "helicopter parents" captures this theme of paying close attention to one's child even through young adulthood.[10] Concerned that their children might lose out in the schooling game, parents (primarily those in the middle and upper

The structure of the workplace constrains the ability of working parents to attend to basic supervisory responsibilities.

classes) are heavily engaged, perhaps overly so, in "cultivating" their children for successful adult lives.[11] But even parents who do not "hover" over their school-age children face a scheduler's dilemma of organizing and shuffling transportation for play dates, team practices, arts and music lessons, and tutoring sessions.[12]

Much like supervision, parents' involvement with their children can be determined in part by work schedules. How parents cope with the demands of supervision and involvement depends on the predictability of the situation. But even in the most predictable situations, the structure of the workplace can take a toll on parents' abilities to provide adequate supervision and involvement.

Predictable Supervision

One of the most predictable responsibilities of parents is to ensure that their children attend school. (Although the number of students being home schooled is growing, their parents' supervisory responsibilities are considerably different from the ones described here.) Most states require that children start school by age five and remain in school until age eighteen. In 2010 approximately 55.9 million children were enrolled in public and private schools in the United States.[13] The number of days in the school year and the number of instructional hours per day that children are expected to attend are mandated by each state (or local school districts in the seven states with no formal policy). Most states require a minimum of 180 days; however, several states require fewer than 175 days.[14] These laws apply to both public and private schools.

A 180-day school year leaves at least 185 days in the year when parents have to manage their children's full day care. Weekends can be especially troublesome for parents who have to work on those days. But even parents who do not work on weekends still have to make arrangements for their children's care on at least 81 weekdays during the year when their children are not scheduled to be in school—holidays, school vacations, and summer breaks. Among industrialized countries, the United States has one of the shortest school years, with two and a half months for summer vacation.[15]

Although school holidays and vacations are predictable, they are not always convenient for working parents, who may not be able to take a day off when schools close on a Monday for Washington's Birthday, Columbus Day, or Veteran's Day or for ten days around Christmas. Moreover, teacher professional days, mandated by states or union contracts, can add up to another five to ten full or half-days a year when school is closed and working parents must arrange care for their children.[16]

More recently, schools facing budgetary constraints and pressure to increase or maintain the number of instructional hours have altered their school calendar, which typically starts in September and ends in June. Some schools have moved to year-round schedules with more breaks during the year.[17] Several

news stories have suggested that more breaks make it even more difficult for parents to juggle their schedules and supervise their children.[18] Some schools have moved to a four-day school week, which presents problems for parents working standard shifts who now have to find child care for one full day during the workweek.[19]

A typical school day rarely coincides with a typical workday. A U.S. Department of Labor report estimates that only "64 percent of a fulltime worker's standard work schedule is covered by the hours children are typically in school."[20] The commute to and from work can lengthen that coverage gap. Typically, students are dismissed from school between 2:00 p.m. and 3:00 p.m., while most full-time employed parents leave work sometime between 5:00 p.m. and 7:00 p.m., leaving a gap between school and work of roughly fifteen to twenty-five hours a week.[21] These numbers can be even more daunting for a parent who works long hours or mandatory overtime.

The proportion of time that working parents spend directly with their school-age children on their care and educational activities seems somewhat limited. Parents with standard thirty-five-hour workweeks spend on average slightly under six hours a week, including weekends, providing direct care for their children aged six through seventeen.[22] Women are more likely to spend more time (a little more than seven hours) compared with men, who spend about four hours a week. Most direct care is related to physical needs, such as feeding (one-and-a-half hours a week), followed by education-related activities, such as helping with homework (fifty minutes a week).

What is important to underscore about these hours is that they are averaged across a wide spectrum of age groups, and certainly older children are on their own for much more time than younger children. Nevertheless, the total amount of time working parents spend with their children on school days, either in direct care or just being together, seems relatively small.

School-age children, on average, are alone without adult supervision before and after school for nearly fourteen hours a week, or nearly three hours a day.[23] The number of children in kindergarten through eighth grade left alone after school rose from 14.3 million (25 percent) in 2004 to 15.1 million (26 percent) in 2009.[24] Children with regularly scheduled non-self-care arrangements spend an average of nearly five hours a week before school and nine hours a week after school in such care. Generally younger children are more likely to be in the care of a nonrelative or center before and after school, whereas older children are more likely to care for themselves. Black children are more likely than any other racial or ethnic group to receive nonparental care before school and to care for themselves. Regularly scheduled nonrelative before- and after-school care appears related to household income, with families earning more than $25,000 more likely to use center or school-based care.

A nationally representative parent study, conducted by the National Center for Education Statistics, examined the before- and after-school care of kindergarteners through eighth graders and found that about one-fifth of these children were in regularly scheduled nonparental arrangements before school at least once a month, and about half were in such arrangements after school.[25] Children not in nonparental care arrangements were in their parents' care. A later NCES study looked just at after-school arrangements and found that 40 percent of children in eighth grade or under were in formal nonparental care arrangements at least once a week. The three most commonly used after-school arrangements were center- or school-based care (20 percent of all kindergarteners through eighth graders), care by a relative (15 percent), and self-care (12 percent); some children were in more than one arrangement.[26]

Single-parent households and households where mothers work full time are likely to have nonparental care arrangements for their children before and after school. Children of mothers who work full time are more likely to have before-school arrangements (31 percent of all mothers working full time) than children of mothers who work part time (12 percent) or who are not employed (9 percent). The patterns for after-school care are similar. Although most children of working mothers participate in one after-school care arrangement on a regular basis, almost a third of working mothers (32 percent) piece together different arrangements to cover the hours when they cannot provide supervision.[27]

Children who care for themselves or who receive care from a relative are more likely to be cared for in their own home than somewhere else. Most relatives who provide care are grandmothers of the children (52 percent) or siblings (21 percent). Public schools provide the majority of center- or school-based care (55 percent); the remainder is provided by private schools and care centers outside the school. Surprisingly, parents report no statistically significant differences among the types of activities children engage in before and after school regardless of the kind of care arrangement. Homework is the most frequent activity in all types of care, followed by television watching (with the exception of center- or school-based care), and then outdoor and indoor play.[28]

As children mature, the activities they engage in change. Eighth graders are more likely to participate in sports, academic pursuits, and community service activities than children in kindergarten through fifth grade. Most of these activities are sponsored by the children's schools. Parents often count on organized after-school programs to bridge the gap in supervision and enrichment for their children between the end of the school day and the time parents return home from work.

After-School Programs
In the past two decades, private foundation and government funding has resulted in a significant increase in the number of after-school programs, defined as programs that provide enriching activities for children in a safe space after the school day ends. Afterschool Alliance, a coalition of public, private, and nonprofit groups dedicated to raising awareness and expanding resources for after-school programs, estimates that the number of school-age children participating in these programs rose from 6.5 million (11 percent) in 2004 to 8.4 million (15 percent) in 2009.[29] In addition to helping fill the gap between the end of the school day and the end of the workday, these programs are often credited with reducing crime and drug use and otherwise keeping kids out of trouble, and with increasing student academic achievement.[30] The strength of these claims is limited, however, because most after-school program evaluations have serious methodological limitations related to selection bias, accurate counts of the actual number of after-school participation hours per student, the types of activities engaged in, and program attrition.[31]

Barriers to children's participation in after-school programs include access, program costs, and age-appropriateness of offerings.[32] Many children lack transportation to programs that are located away from their school. According to one survey, 38 percent of parents of kindergarten children through eighth graders who are not in an after-school program would enroll them if a program were available in their community.[33] On average, after-school programs cost $67 a week per child, and 52 percent of parents report cost as being a barrier to enrollment.[34] Additionally, after-school programs often fit the developmental trajectory of a specific age range. This issue is particularly challenging for preteens who have lost interest in after-school programs aimed at younger elementary school students but are not yet developmentally ready for activities targeted to older adolescents.

Other extracurricular activities that can take place on weekends and in summers and that can be sponsored by organizations other than schools include sports, clubs, and lessons. Nationally, nearly 60 percent of children aged six through seventeen participated in at least one extracurricular activity in 2000, with older children participating more frequently (37 percent for those aged twelve through seventeen; 31 percent for those aged six through eleven).[35] Younger children were more likely to participate in lessons after school or on the weekends, whereas older children were more likely to participate in sports.

Out-of-school activities have been shown to positively influence adolescents' social, educational, civic, and physical development.[36] Selection of these activities appears to be affected not only by the interests of adolescents and their peers but also by parents' work schedules, family resources, and the

Out-of-school activities have been shown to positively influence adolescents' social, educational, civic, and physical development.

offerings in surrounding communities.[37] Transportation is always a concern especially if the child needs to be driven to the program when the parents are at work.[38] Less is known about how parents cope, both at work and emotionally, with arranging for such activities.[39] One notable study of 936 full-time employed dual-earner couples with a school-age child found that working parents' concerns about their children's after-school arrangements were associated with job disruptions such as being distracted or drained of energy at work, making on-the-job errors, turning down requests for overtime or travel, and missing deadlines or meetings. Although we are unaware of any definitive studies on the issue, parental stress related to after-school arrangements appears to have an impact not only on parents and their children but also on employers in the form of untold losses in productivity.

Reorganizing School Schedules to Accommodate Working Parents

Because schools are places where children are likely to receive adequate supervisory care and because some school-based after-school programs have been instrumental in improving children's performance, one frequent suggestion is to reorganize the formal school day to more closely match parents' work schedules either by extending the school day or lengthening the school year.

Seemingly reasonable solutions on their face, these proposals may not garner much support among parents or their children. A recent poll conducted by Heather Boushey and funded by the Rockefeller Foundation and *Time* surveyed 3,500 adults, who were asked what changes were necessary for working parents to balance their job or business, their marriage, and their children. Fifty-one percent of respondents said that their own workplaces should be more flexible, while only 11 percent suggested lengthening school hours or the school year.[40]

Why so little apparent interest in changing the length of the school day? One reason may be the roughly 3.5 million teachers working in schools in the United States. The majority of them are women, more than 70 percent of them are married, and some of them are likely to have children in school.[41] Historically, women chose this occupation in part because the workday corresponded to their own children's school schedule.[42] A recent study found that most teachers chose the profession because of the flexibility it gave them with their families.[43] It seems reasonable to assume that the current school schedule is compatible with family needs for a considerable number of teachers. Parents who are self-employed or who work shifts also may find the current school day compatible with their work schedules.

Lengthening the school year is typically proposed as a way to raise academic achievement, not as a solution to problems of family-work balance. Whether a longer school year would in fact raise achievement is questionable. The quality of the research evidence is uneven, and even the most rigorous studies show that four-day school weeks and year-round schooling have little effect on student performance.[44] Empirical evidence of the consequences of changing the school schedule on the family-work balance is limited, and the issue clearly suggests a direction for future research.

Another proposal for addressing the needs of working parents and children is to increase access to after-school programs. This option may be desirable for primary school children, but whether it has much appeal for families with middle or high school children is unknown. Little research examines whether parents and their children aged twelve to eighteen, regardless of their discretionary resources, would actively support and participate in after-school programs if they were more widely available. In the current climate of intense parenting, many families may have neither the time nor the interest in having their children participate in after-school or community-based programs that extend the formal school day because their children are already overscheduled in fee-for-service tutoring or academic engagement programs.[45] Lack of interest is also likely among families with limited economic resources, because they rely on their teenagers to help with after-school care of younger children or to work after school to contribute to household expenses. In addition, adolescence is marked by independence and separation, so the appeal of after-school programs may be limited for many of today's teenagers, especially if friends or other sources of entertainment are beckoning.

Regardless of the extent of parental demand for after-school programs, the suppliers—which often include U.S. public elementary and secondary schools—are experiencing severe economic cutbacks, with teachers being dismissed and programs being discontinued out of concern for costs. Current resources barely cover formal school programs

for most children. In public schools across the country, parents are making donations to keep art and music classes and libraries operational. In many schools students have to pay a fee to participate in after-school sports. Given the current economic climate and the public cries to cut public spending, even for education, it seems unrealistic to expect changes in the school schedule or significant additions to after-school programs that would help parents balance their work-family responsibilities.

Unpredictable Supervision

From time to time all parents must cope with unpredictable situations involving their children. By their very definition, unpredictable situations can occur on any given day and fall outside prearranged care; it is in these situations where workplace flexibility is most salient.[46] The most common example is a child who falls ill and needs direct personal care. On average, a child is likely to miss three to five days a school year because of illness or injury.[47] The Centers for Disease Control and Prevention estimate that 20–25 percent of all children under age eighteen will sustain a severe injury that entails medical attention, missed school, or bed rest.[48] The financial and emotional costs of children's illnesses on working parents have not been well researched; however, a recent study found that at least 25 percent of surveyed households in Pennsylvania reported lost vacation or sick time during an unexpected week-long school closing resulting from an influenza outbreak.[49] Unforeseeable weather-related events such as storms may require parents either to keep their child at home or pick their child up early at school. Threats of severe weather-related events such as hurricanes and tornadoes can evoke fear and worry on the part of parents, leading them to take unexpected time off from work to ensure their children are safe.

Living in high-risk neighborhoods troubled by social disorganization, limited social networks, and insufficient community-based resources, such as public recreational programs, can create additional challenges for working parents who themselves are likely to have limited household resources.[50] For example, the local tax revenue base for low-income neighborhoods often impedes the establishment and sustainability of adequate out-of-school programs for youth.[51] Parents with limited resources are more likely to rely on in-home management to protect their child from the dangers of their surroundings.[52] The stress on parents in these situations is also exacerbated because of heightened concern that something life threatening could unexpectedly happen to their child in the neighborhood or in their home. Both at work and while commuting, these working parents spend countless hours worrying that their child is safe and has not been caught up in a violent assault, home invasion, or random shooting.[53]

For families in more advantaged neighborhoods, the events, predictable and unpredictable, of everyday life requiring parent supervision are often more manageable, in part because parents may be able to afford more care for their children. These parents are also more likely to have social networks they can rely on to look after their children.[54] The concept of reciprocity in strong social networks can be especially helpful for working parents as they juggle arrangements for car pools, sports events, and unexpected early dismissals from school. Working parents, even those with economic resources, do not necessarily form neighborhood social networks on their own but rely on their children to do so for them.[55] Furthermore, social networks that parents form at work do not necessarily transfer to their neighborhood

lives, especially when most workplaces are on average fifteen miles away from their homes.[56] Most working parents travel an extra five to six miles a day dropping off and picking up their children.[57] Depending on family and friends for unpredictable, and in some cases even for predictable, events is often problematic for working parents; thus making even small improvements to workplace flexibility will be substantially beneficial to these parents and their children.

Discretionary Action: Involvement and Enrichment

While parental supervision entails meeting the physical and safety needs of the child, parental involvement covers those activities that parents undertake to enhance their child's academic performance and emotional and social well-being. Involvement is voluntary on the part of the parent and can be predictable; examples are setting aside time for the parent to help with homework, arranging summer school or camps, visiting prospective colleges, and being accessible through text messages or calls. Being involved with the school can help parents learn how best to help their children with homework, what school-related topics to discuss at home, and the importance of high educational expectations. But involvement requires time and resources that are generally related to household income and family priorities. Most middle- and upper-income parents realize the importance of navigating the U.S. educational system by selecting the best schools possible and the right teachers and by emphasizing to their children the consequences of mediocre test score performance. Given the complexity of the educational system, securing advantages for one's children requires parents not only to engage with the school but also to know teachers and school policies.[58] Low-wage workers, even those who place a priority on being involved with their children's education, are unlikely to have the financial resources or flexible work schedules needed to help ensure their children's success in school.

Parental involvement can have an element of unpredictability about it, when, for example, a child is diagnosed with a special learning need and requires tutoring, or when a child needs extra help with a homework assignment. Such instances can create additional pressure and stress on both the child and the working parent. Being able to help with homework, be engaged with the school, and troubleshoot academic problems requires time, which is in short supply for many working parents, who have little to no flexibility to alter their schedules so they can be home when their children are home or at school to advocate for their children's best interests.

Low-wage workers face multiple problems when interfacing with the school. First, many of these parents believe that they can trust the school to take care of their children, and that their own personal involvement is less important in their children's education than that of the teacher.[59] Second, because of their work situations parents may be unable to visit the school for teacher conferences or other activities that would support their children's educational success.[60] The school staff may view parents who are not at school as uncaring or uninterested.[61] Lack of flexible work situations can make it difficult for parents to build social relationships and acquire informational material that parents who frequently visit the school and interact with teachers can more easily obtain.

A synthesis of empirical experimental studies of welfare-to-work programs by Lisa Gennetian and her colleagues suggests that,

when mothers become employed full time, adolescents show poorer school performance, including a higher rate of grade repetition and greater use of special education services.[62] Adolescents with younger siblings had the most negative effects. Not only were these children more likely to have poor school performance, they also were more likely to be suspended or expelled from or drop out of school.

With millions of children needing care at predictable times before and after school, flexibility in start and end times for work could greatly reduce the parental stress of finding alternative care arrangements.

One of the possible explanations for these results is that low-income parents, especially those who are single, are likely to have little control over scheduling their work hours and are less likely to have access to flexible work arrangements than do professional employees.[63] These types of work conditions are likely to interfere with parents' abilities to be involved with their children's education, as well as to supervise their children.

Workplace Flexibility as an Intervention

According to Labor Department statistics, more than one-fifth of all working women have school-age children.[64] As that proportion has increased in the past few decades, working parents have begun to look to the workplace for the flexibility they need to meet their parental responsibilities.

Although workplace flexibility is generally perceived as valuable for both the employer and employee,[65] designing and implementing flexibility that can meet working parents' needs present considerable challenges. In general, two types of flexibility are particularly relevant for working parents: flexible work arrangements that allow employees more control over when and where they work on a daily basis; and formal and informal time-off policies that allow for short-term time off (STO). Flexible work arrangements include flextime (allowing variability in the start and end times for the workday); compressed workweeks; and various forms of reduced hours, including part-time, job sharing, and part-year work. Some flextime programs also allow employees to bank hours, that is, to work longer hours, which they may later "draw out" for a variety of purposes, including providing care for their children during school breaks (predictable) or when they fall ill (unpredictable). Parents report that banking hours is one of the most preferred options for allowing greater workplace flexibility with respect to scheduling.[66]

With millions of children needing care at predictable times before and after school, flexibility in start and end times for work could greatly reduce the parental stress of finding alternative care arrangements. Making flexible the start and end times of the workday could involve a formal policy or an accepted informal practice that also benefits employers in the form of increased employee job satisfaction, engagement, and retention.[67] Daily flextime practices that enable employees to vary when they start and end their workdays, as well as the ability to take time

off during the day if needed, can relieve the stress of unexpected events involving their children.

Many companies find that flexibility benefits the company as well as the parents. Kraft Foods, for example, experienced increased worker satisfaction and retention after it set up a program that allowed its hourly plant workers to swap shifts, take single-day vacations, and request job-sharing arrangements. Similarly, Texas Instruments implemented a workplace flexibility policy that allows most, but not all, employees to meet their personal needs by adjusting their work schedule or telecommuting. The company specifically highlighted the policy as a way for employees to cope with doctor's appointments, sick children, or late-night conference calls. As a result, Texas Instruments saw improvements in employee retention rates, stress levels, and job effectiveness. Moreover, the company found that team members temporarily assumed some of the work tasks of those taking time off, which broadened and diversified employee skills.[68]

KPMG LLP, an audit, tax, and advisory firm, adopted an Alternative Work Arrangement program, which provides flextime and flexplace options that employees who are parents of school-age children now use regularly. These options include reduced hours, starting the workday early and ending it at the end of the school day, and "logging off" after school and then logging back on from home in the evening. During the current recession, KPMG has leveraged its need to cut costs with employees' desire for greater work flexibility and more time off, particularly during the summer months. The company now offers a sabbatical program that provides partially paid leave of four to twelve weeks. Employees receive 20 percent of their regular salary during their time away and may use accrued personal time off to offset the pay differential. More than 450 people had signed up for the program between April 2010, when the program launched, and the end of 2010. Recognizing that employees may run short of their own accrued personal time off during a family crisis, KPMG has also established a "shared leave bank" that lets employees donate hours to help out colleagues in need of additional personal time off when faced with a medical crisis in their family.[69]

Where employers do not provide formal flexibility, there is evidence that some employees arrange for it informally. Recent research at an automotive parts plant found that unionized, hourly workers negotiated informal agreements among themselves to cover for workers who wanted time off to see their children in a ball game or to attend a school event. The workers also share an understanding that reporting such activities to the supervisor is problematic, and an informal sanctioning mechanism has made the workplace uncomfortable for those employees who do not go along with the practice.[70] The researchers concluded that while informal flexibility created a sense of camaraderie among employees, it would not be sustainable if unexpected work conditions occurred.

Telecommuting

One type of flexibility that can be useful to working parents is telecommuting—working from home. Despite the increased use of computers that allow for instant messaging, Internet calls, and video conferencing, however, telecommuting does not seem to be gaining momentum. The U.S. government was an early adopter of telecommuting, but relatively few workers took advantage of the program. Currently, the federal government

lags behind the private sector in this option, with a smaller percentage of federal employees than private employees telecommuting.[71] One reason, found even among high-wage workers in the private sector, is that those who telecommute are often perceived as being less committed to their work than those employees who work in the office. One nationally representative sample of college-educated women and men found that women are the more stigmatized when they telecommute. Four of ten women sampled report having difficulties with co-workers' behavior toward them when taking advantage of this option.[72]

Even though telecommuting has not been as popular as other forms of flexibility, well-designed programs can suit the needs of employers and employees. 1-800 CONTACTS, the world's largest contact lens retailer, attributes its strong business performance in large part to its flexibility. The company's technology allows its call-center staff to handle even the most complex orders at home; those who work in-house may choose their own schedules. As a result, almost half of the call-center employees work from home, and the company has more than 225 different work schedules. Its use of flexible work arrangements has not only benefited its employees but also yielded positive business outcomes; the company's employee turnover rates are below one-third of the national average for the call-center industry.[73] And in 2007 J. D. Power & Associates, a global marketing information services company, awarded 1-800 CONTACTS its highest service rating ever for a call center.

While telecommuting can work well when well designed, what seems most problematic about it is that working parents are already using computers at home and on the weekends for spillover work from their workdays, thereby blurring the boundaries between work and family. Parents have been estimated to work about 160 extra hours a year, counting the hours worked early in the morning, late in the evening, and over the weekend. This is time that parents are often not compensated for; when asked why they are working, the answer is often to keep up with work-related responsibilities.[74] These long work hours take a toll; parents are often emotionally drained, stressed, and resentful of the intrusion of work into family life.[75] For parents, working extra hours on the job at home can hurt their relationships with their children.[76] Although physically present, they may be distracted and pay little close attention to their children or education-related activities.

Workplace flexibility is critical for working parents trying to ensure the safety and health of their children.

Short-Term Time Off

Employers can also provide flexibility in the form of paid time off, which allows employees to take a limited number of days off in a year for personal or family reasons, including caring for a sick child, without losing pay or having to use vacation days. Currently, employers provide STO through a variety of employer-sponsored benefit packages and government regulations. However, access to STO varies between and within organizations depending on the company's size and function, workers' occupations, and employment status.[77] Most firms employing more than five

hundred workers provide paid holiday leave, paid bereavement leave, short-term disability, paid vacation, and paid sick days. These types of short leaves tend to be disproportionately available to full-time but not part-time employees and to those working in large firms.[78] Firms with fewer than five hundred employees rarely provide such benefits. In their studies of employers and employees in large and small firms, Ellen Galinsky and her colleagues found that more than 60 percent of employers permit all or most of their employees to take time off for important family or personal needs.[79] Approximately 31 percent of employees say it is "not hard at all" to take time off during the workday for personal or family reasons without a loss of pay. Conversely, 37 percent of employees report that taking time off for personal reasons is somewhat hard or very hard.[80]

The value of STO is obvious: workers periodically need time away from work to help resolve conflicts that can occur because there are not enough persons and resources to cover the unexpected events and needs that arise in everyday life. On the employer side, STO benefits are commonly perceived as relatively low cost and an incentive for higher productivity, and as a contributing factor to a healthier workforce. However, employers express concerns that employees could overuse the benefit, creating an undesirable work ethic, reducing morale, and becoming a drain on resources.

Culture of Flexibility

Even in firms where different forms of workplace flexibility are available, some employees are reluctant to take advantage of these benefits. In a 2003 nationally representative study of 3,504 workers, only 30 percent of employees at companies with advertised workplace flexibility options felt "strongly" that they could use these options without jeopardizing their chances for job or career advancement.[81] This finding was consistent across levels of income and workplace sizes. In difficult economic times, employees are particularly worried about using flexibility options because they are afraid of being fired or laid off if they do not appear completely dedicated to their jobs.[82]

These flexible work arrangements are relatively economically neutral for the employers: workers typically put in the same number of hours but on different schedules. Nonetheless, workers who are hesitant to use minimal flexibility benefits may be even less likely to avail themselves of other options such as part-time work and job sharing that they perceive as being costly to their employers and therefore more likely to place their jobs at risk.[83] However, these are the very options that are critical when parents require more intensive interaction with their children.

Flexibility practices are likely to become workplace standards only if work cultures develop that support flexibility and minimize the stigma of using it. First Tennessee Bank developed such a culture, educating its managers to "market" the company's flex options to employees placing an emphasis on "family." Within five years more than 60 percent of employees used some sort of flexibility, and the bank reports saving over $3 million in turnover costs.[84]

Conclusion

Workplace flexibility is critical for working parents trying to ensure the safety and health of their children. No one wants a primary school child left unattended in the school yard waiting for a parent. The issues around involvement with one's child are more ephemeral because the degree of

engagement is to some extent a matter of choice. High parental involvement can make a difference in children's achievement and behavior, but parents have to have the time as well as the motivation to become involved with their children. The problem is not work per se but rather how much time working families have to spend together as a family and how that time is spent.

For low-wage workers these problems multiply exponentially. Most of these workers hold jobs that have fluctuating hours or overnight shifts and few benefits, such as paid sick or vacation days. The need to stay home and care for a sick child can translate into a day without pay or even the loss of one's job. Expanded workplace flexibility for these workers could help them to meet the educational needs of their children.

Some of the most valuable workplace options for all parents of school-age children are having time off to care for their children when holidays, weather, illness, or emergencies keep them from school. Other helpful options include allowing workers to change their starting and quitting times periodically (or, even better, daily), allowing employees to work from home or off-site occasionally, and enabling them to job-share or work part time without loss of benefits and with the ability to return to full time when needed.

Some research shows positive results for employees and their employers when workers have more control over their work schedules. A quasi-experimental study of work groups in Best Buy, a large U.S. retail firm, found that workers with a say in their work schedule had lower commuting times, more and higher-quality sleep, more energy, less work-family conflict, and lower absenteeism than those in the control groups.[85] However, in workplaces that employ primarily low-wage workers, opportunities for changing work conditions remain limited.

It is the culture of the workplace that really makes a difference. Creating a workplace flexibility culture is not something that can occur over a short-term basis. Workplace flexibility requires both employers and employees to find a common ground for discourse and to craft consensus-based solutions that benefit all parties. There has to be a common purpose, dialogue, and dedication to change. If flexibility options are not widely viewed as acceptable business practices, they are unlikely to be used—even though workplace flexibility appears to be the solution that most working parents desire to meet the needs of their jobs and their families and to build healthy, strong relationships with their children.[86] As more and more mothers and fathers work, it becomes critical to find more appropriate workplace flexibility practices that are better suited for families with children, especially if society hopes to continue to see engaged workers who have strong family relationships with their children.

Endnotes

1. Bureau of Labor Statistics, "Employment Characteristics of Families Summary May 27, 2010," Economic News Release (www.bls.gov/news.release/famee.nr0.htm). Even in this period of economic slowdown with an increase in unemployment especially among mothers, 69.6 percent of married women with children under age eighteen are employed. The percentage for employed mothers with no spouse present is 67.8 percent.

2. Elaina Marchena, "Adolescents' Assessment of Parental Role Management in Dual-Earner Families," in *Being Together, Working Apart: Dual Career Families and the Work-Life Balance*, edited by Barbara Schneider and Linda Waite (Cambridge University Press, 2005), pp. 333–60. The book reports on the 500 Family Study, which collected data on 500 families from 1999 through 2000. In her chapter, Marchena analyzed results from several multivariate models to examine the relationships between parents' work and family role management from the perspective of parents and their adolescents.

3. Heather Boushey and Joseph Wright, *Working Moms and Childcare*, Data Brief 3 (Washington: Center for Economic and Policy Research, 2004).

4. Ellen Galinsky, *Navigating Work and Family: Hands-On Advice for Working Parents* (New York: Families and Work Institute, 2002).

5. James T. Bond, *The Impact of Job and Workplace Conditions on Low-Wage and Low-Income Employees and Their Employers* (New York: Families and Work Institute, 2003).

6. The literature on parent involvement is extensive. Two new meta-analyses targeted on urban minority children are William H. Jeynes, "A Meta Analysis: The Effects of Parental Involvement on Minority Children's Academic Achievement," *Education and Urban Society* 35, no. 2 (2003): 202–18; and William H. Jeynes, "A Meta-Analysis of the Relation of Parental Involvement to Urban Elementary School Student Academic Achievement," *Urban Education* 40, no. 3 (2005): 237–69. Two other highly cited reviews that address involvement at the elementary and secondary level are by Kathleen V. Hoover-Dempsey and Howard M. Sandler, "Why Do Parents Become Involved in Their Children's Education?" *Review of Educational Research* 67, no. 1 (1997): 3–42; and Xitao Fan and Michael Chen, "Parental Involvement and Student's Academic Achievement: A Meta-Analysis," *Educational Psychology Review* 13, no. 1 (2001): 1–22.

7. On motivation, see Allan Wigfield and Jacquelynne Eccles, *Development of Achievement Motivation* (San Diego: Academic Press, 2002); on educational expectations, see Barbara Schneider and David Stevenson, *The Ambitious Generation: America's Teenagers, Motivated but Directionless* (Yale University Press, 2000); and on relating these factors to achievement, see James P. Connell, Margaret B. Spencer, and J. Lawrence Aber, "Educational Risk and Resilience in African-American Youth: Context, Self, Action, and Outcomes in School," *Child Development* 65, no. 2 (1994): 493–506 (also see note 6).

8. U.S. Department of Education, *A Blueprint for Reform: The Reauthorization of the Elementary and Secondary Education Act* (2010) (www2.ed.gov/policy/elsec/leg/blueprint/blueprint.pdf).

9. North Dakota Department of Public Instruction, "Title I Website for Parents" (www.dpi.state.nd.us/title1/parent/index.shtm); Public Schools of North Carolina, "Parents, Family, and Community Information" (www.ncpublicschools.org/parents/); State of Michigan, "MI Parent Resources" (2009) (www.michigan.gov/miparentresources).

10. Richard A. Settersten Jr. and Barbara E. Ray, *Not Quite Adults: Why 20-Somethings Are Choosing a Slower Path to Adulthood* (New York: Bantam, 2010).

11. Annette Lareau, "Invisible Inequality: Social Class and Childrearing in Black Families and White Families," *American Sociological Review* 67, no. 5 (2002): 747–76; Annette Lareau, *Unequal Childhoods* (University of California Press, 2003). For a more contemporary popular view, see Hilary Levey, "Pageant Princesses and Math Whizzes: Understanding Children's Activities as a Form of Children's Work," *Childhood* 16, no. 2 (2009): 195–212; and Karen Sternheimer, *Childhood in American Society: A Reader* (Boston: Pearson Allyn & Bacon, 2010).

12. Elinor Ochs and others, "Coming Together at Dinner: A Study of Working Families," in *Workplace Flexibility: Realigning 20th-Century Jobs for a 21st-Century Workforce,* edited by Kathleen Christensen and Barbara Schneider (Cornell University Press, 2010), pp. 57–70.

13. National Center for Education Statistics, *The Condition of Education: 2010* (2010) (http://nces.ed.gov/programs/coe/).

14. National Center for Education Statistics, *Digest of Education Statistics* (2008), table 166 (http://nces.ed.gov/programs/digest/d08/tables/dt08_166.asp).

15. UNESCO Institute for Statistics, "Statutory Number of Teaching Hours and Weeks per Year in Public Institutions by Level of Education," Data file (2000) (www.uis.unesco.org/ev.php?ID=5378_201&ID2=DO_TOPIC).

16. Laurie L. Dove, *How Professional Development for Teachers Works* (2010) (http://money.howstuffworks.com/business/professional-development/professional-development-for-teachers.htm/printable); also see how professional development days affect low-income children in Barbara Moldauer, *Union Champions Equity Schools for Neediest Students* (2010) (http://neapriorityschools.org/2010/04/13/union-champions-equity-schools-for-neediest-students).

17. Tracy A. Huebner, "Reimagining School: Year-Round Schooling," *Educational Leadership* 67, no. 7 (2010): 83–84; National Association for Year-Round Education, *Typical Year-Round Calendars* (2009) (www.nayre.org/cal.htm).

18. Zach Miners, *Chicago Tests a Year-Round School Schedule* (2009) (www.usnews.com/blogs/on-education/2009/04/28/chicago-tests-a-year-round-school-schedule.html).

19. National Conference of State Legislatures, *Four Day School Week* (2010) (www.ncsl.org/default.aspx?tabid=12934).

20. U.S. Department of Labor, *Futurework: Trends and Challenges for Work in the 21st Century* (1999).

21. This calculation assumes a thirty-five-hour workweek. U.S. Bureau of Labor Statistics, "American Time Use Survey Summary" (2010) (www.bls.gov/news.release/atus.nr0.htm).

22. Ibid., table 9, "Time Spent Caring for Household Children under 18 by Sex of Adult (1) and Age of Youngest Child by Day of Week, Average for the Combined Years 2005-09."

23. Brian Kleiner, Mary Jo Nolin, and Chris Chapman, *Before- and After-School Care, Programs, and Activities of Children in Kindergarten through Eighth Grade: 2001,* NCES 2004-008 Statistical Analysis Report (U.S. Department of Education, Institute of Education Sciences, 2004).

24. Afterschool Alliance, "Facts and Research" (2009) (www.afterschoolalliance.org/AA3PM.cfm).

25. Kleiner, Nolin, and Chapman, *Before- and After-School Care* (see note 23).

26. Priscilla R. Carver, Iheoma Iruka, and Chris Chapman, *National Household Education Surveys Program of 2005, After-School Programs and Activities: 2005,* NCES 2006-076 (U.S. Department of Education, 2006).

27. Kleiner, Nolin, and Chapman, *Before- and After-School Care* (see note 23).

28. Ibid.

29. Afterschool Alliance, "Facts and Research" (see note 24).

30. Afterschool Alliance, "Afterschool for All" (2010) (www.afterschoolalliance.org/Research%20 Factsheets%202010/Fact_Sheet_Afterschool_Essential_3_22_2010.pdf).

31. Robert Apsler, "After-School Programs for Adolescents: A Review of Evaluation Research," *Adolescence* 44, no. 173 (2009): 1–19.

32. Forum for Youth Investment, "Policy Commentary 2: High School After-School: What Is It? What Might It Be? Why Is It Important?" (2003) (www.forumforyouthinvestment.org/files/OSTPC2.pdf).

33. Afterschool Alliance, "Facts and Research" (see note 24).

34. Afterschool Alliance, "Uncertain Times 2009: Recession Imperiling Afterschool Programs and the Children They Serve" (2009) (www.afterschoolalliance.org/UncertainTimes2009.cfm).

35. Terry A. Lugaila, "A Child's Day: 2000 (Selected Indicators of Child Well-Being," *Current Population Reports* (Washington: U.S. Census Bureau, 2003), 70–89.

36. Joseph Mahoney and others, "Adolescent Out-of-School Activity," in *Handbook of Adolescent Psychology,* edited by Richard Lerner and Laurence Steinberg (Hoboken, N.J.: Wiley and Sons, 2009), pp. 228–67.

37. Joseph L. Mahoney, Angel L. Harris, and Jacquelynne S. Eccles, "Organized Activity Participation, Positive Youth Development, and the Over-Scheduling Hypothesis," *Social Policy Report* 20, no. 4 (Ann Arbor, Mich.: Society for Research in Child Development, 2006) (www.srcd.org/press/mahoney.pdf).

38. Nancy Darling, "Participation in Extracurricular Activities and Adolescent Adjustment: Cross-Sectional and Longitudinal Findings," *Journal of Youth and Adolescence* 34, no. 5 (2005): 493–505; Bonnie L. Barber, Jacquelynne S. Eccles, and Margaret R. Stone, "Whatever Happened to the Jock, the Brain, and the Princess? Young Adult Pathways Linked to Adolescent Activity Involvement and Social Identity," *Journal of Adolescent Research* 16, no. 5 (2001): 429–55; Bonnie L. Barber and others, "Benefits of Activity Participation: The Roles of Identity Affirmation and Peer Group Norm Sharing," in *Organized Activities as Contexts of Development: Extracurricular Activities, After-School and Community Programs,* edited by Joseph L. Mahoney, Reed W. Larson, and Jacquelynne S. Eccles (Mahwah, N.J.: Erlbaum, 2005), pp. 185–210; Jacquelynne S. Eccles and others, "Extracurricular Activities and Adolescent Development," *Journal of Social Issues* 59, no. 4 (2003): 865–89.

39. Rosalind C. Barnett and others, "Parental Concerns about After-School Time: Antecedents and Correlates among Dual-Earner Parents," *Journal of Family* 31, no. 5 (2010): 606–25.

40. Heather Boushey, "It's Time for Policies to Match Modern Family Needs: New Polling Data Shows Widespread Support for an Agenda to Address Work-Family Conflict" (Washington: Center for American

Progress, 2010). Schools received the lowest rating, with respondents wanting more paid time off and better day care.

41. For data on teachers, see Bureau of Labor Statistics, *Occupational Outlook Handbook, 2010-2011* (2009) (www.bls.gov/oco/ocos318.htm); and NCES, *Digest of Education Statistics* (2009) (http://nces.edu.gov/prgrams/digest/d09/tablesdt09 069.asp).

42. Claudia Goldin, *Understanding the Gender Gap: An Economic History of American Women* (Oxford University Press, 1990).

43. Robert Drago, "Time on the Job and Time with Their Kids: Cultures of Teaching and Parenthood in the U.S.," *Feminist Economics* 7, no. 3 (2001), 1–31.

44. Literature reviews of nontraditional school schedules include Julie Aronson, Joy Zimmerman, and Lisa Carlos, "Improving Student Achievement by Extending School: Is It Just a Matter of Time?" (1998) (www.wested.org/online_pubs/po-98-02.pdf); Christine Donis-Keller and David L. Silvernail, "Research Brief: A Review of the Evidence on the Four-Day School Week" (2009) (http://usm.maine.edu/cepare/pdf/CEPARE%20Brief%20on%20the%204-day%20school%20week%202.10.pdf); and Elena Silva, "On the Clock: Rethinking the Way Schools Use Time" (2007) (www.educationsector.org/sites/default/files/publications/OntheClock.pdf).

45. Paul Sullivan, "Wealth Matters: As Private Tutoring Booms, Parents Look at the Returns," *New York Times*, August 20, 2010 (www.nytimes.com/2010/08/21/your-money/21wealth.html).

46. Jerry A. Jacobs and Kathleen Gerson, "Overworked Individuals or Overworked Families? Explaining Trends in Work, Leisure, and Family Time," *Work and Occupations: An International Sociological Journal* 28, no. 1 (2001): 40–63.

47. Centers for Disease Control and Prevention and the National Center for Health Statistics, *Vital Health and Statistics: Current Estimates from the National Health Interview Survey, 1996 series 10* (1999), p. 109, table 69, "Number of Days per Person per Year and Number of Days of Activity Restriction Due to Acute and Chronic Conditions, by Type of Restriction and Sociodemographic Characteristics: United States, 1996."

48. Centers for Disease Control and Prevention, *State of CDC 2004* (2004) (www.cdc.gov/about/stateofcdc/pdf/SOCDC2004.pdf).

49. Thomas L. Gift and others, "Household Effects of School Closure during Pandemic (H1N1), 2009, Pennsylvania, USA," *Emerging Infectious Diseases* 16, no. 8 (2010): 1315–17.

50. Delbert S. Elliott and others, "The Effects of Neighborhood Disadvantages on Adolescent Development," *Journal of Research in Crime and Delinquency* 33, no. 4 (1996): 389–426; J. Lawrence Aber and others, "Development in Context: Implications for Studying Neighborhood Effects," in *Neighborhood Poverty: Context and Consequences for Children,* vol. 1, edited by Jeanne Brooks-Gunn, Greg J. Duncan, and J. Lawrence Aber (New York: Russell Sage Foundation, 1997), p. 4461; Anne R. Pebley and Narayan Sastry, "Neighborhoods, Poverty, and Children's Well-Being," in *Social Inequality,* edited by Kathryn M. Neckerman (New York: Russell Sage Foundation, 2004), pp. 119–45; Catherine E. Ross, John R. Reynolds, and Karlyn J. Geis, "The Contingent Meaning of Neighborhood Stability for Residents' Psychological Well-Being," *American Sociological Review* 65, no. 4 (2000): 581–97.

51. A 2001 report examined strategies at both the state and local levels to generate revenue for child-care programs; see Anne Mitchell, Louise Stoney, and Harriet Dichter, *Financing Child Care in the United States: An Illustrative Catalog of Current Strategies* (Kansas City, Mo.: Ewing Marion Kauffman Foundation, 2001).

52. Jacquelynne S. Eccles and Rena D. Harold, "Parent-School Involvement during the Early Adolescent Years," *Teachers College Record* 94, no. 3 (1993): 568–87.

53. Laurel J. Kiser, "Protecting Children from the Dangers of Urban Poverty," *Clinical Psychology Review* 27, no. 2 (2007): 211–25.

54. This point was made by Coleman in his original conception of social capital; see James S. Coleman, "Social Capital in the Creation of Human Capital," *American Journal of Sociology* 94, Supplement (1988), S95–S120.

55. Shira Offer and Barbara Schneider, "Children's Role in Generating Social Capital," *Social Forces* 85, no. 3 (2007): 1125–42.

56. Research and Innovative Technology Administration, "From Home to Work, the Average Commute Is 26.4 Minutes," *Bureau of Transportation Statistics* 3 (2003) (www.bts.gov/publications/omnistats/volume_03_issue_04/html/entire.html).

57. Kristen Anderson, *Planning for Child Care in California* (Point Arena, Calif.: Solano Press Books, 2006).

58. Elizabeth M. Hassrick and Barbara Schneider, "Parent Surveillance in Schools: A Question of Social Class," *American Journal of Education* 115, no. 2 (2009): 195–225.

59. Ibid.

60. S. Jody Heymann and Alison Earle, "Low-Income Parents: How Do Working Conditions Affect Their Opportunity to Help School-Age Children at Risk?" *American Educational Research Journal* 37, no. 4 (2000): 833–48; Nancy E. Hill and Lorraine C. Taylor, "Parental School Involvement and Children's Academic Achievement: Pragmatics and Issues," *Current Directions in Psychological Science* 13, no. 4 (2004): 161–64.

61. Nancy E. Hill and Stacie A. Craft, "Parent–School Involvement and School Performance: Mediated Pathways among Socioeconomically Comparable African American and Euro-American Families," *Journal of Educational Psychology* 95, no. 1 (2003): 74–83.

62. Lisa A. Gennetian and others, *How Welfare and Work Policies for Parents Affect Adolescents: A Synthesis of Research* (New York: Manpower Demonstration Research Corporation, 2002).

63. Corporate Voices for Working Families, "Workplace Flexibility for Lower Wage Workers" (2006) (www.cvworkingfamilies.org/system/files/lowerwageflexreviewreport.pdf); and Executive Office of the President, Council of Economic Advisers, "Work-Life Balance and the Economics of Workplace Flexibility" (2010) (www.whitehouse.gov/blog/2010/03/31/economics-workplace-flexibility).

64. Data for 2010 from the U.S. Department of Labor and the U.S. Bureau of Labor Statistics shows 54.7 percent of all women are in the workforce. Of these women employees, 36.3 percent have children under age eighteen and 21.9 percent have school-age children. Keith Hall and Hilda L. Solis, *Women in the Labor Force: A Data Book* (U.S. Department of Labor, U.S. Bureau of Labor Statistics, 2010).

65. Workplace Flexibility 2010, "Flexible Work Arrangements: Selected Case Studies" (Washington: Georgetown Law, 2010) (http://workplaceflexibility2010.org/images/uploads/FWA_CaseStudies.pdf).

66. James T. Bond and others, *Highlights of the 2002 National Study of the Changing Workforce* (New York: Families and Work Institute, 2003).

67. James T. Bond and Ellen Galinsky, "Using Survey Research to Address Work-Life Issues," in *The Work and Family Handbook,* edited by Marcie Pitts-Catsouphes, Ellen E. Kossek, and Stephen Sweet (Mahwah, N.J.: Lawrence Erlbaum Associates, 2006), pp. 411–33.

68. Workplace Flexibility 2010, "Flexible Work Arrangements" (see note 65).

69. Families and Work Institute and Society for Human Resources Management (SHRM), *2011 Guide to Bold New Ideas for Making Work Work* (Alexandria, Va.: Society for Human Resources Management, 2011).

70. Lawrence Root and Alford Young Jr., "Workplace Flexibility and Worker Agency," paper presented at Focus on Workplace Flexibility (Georgetown Law, November 29–30, 2010) (http://workplaceflexibility.org/images/uploads/program_papers/root_young_-_workplace_flexibility_and_worker_agency.pdf).

71. Kathleen Christensen, Matthew Weinshenker, and Blake Sisk, "Workplace Flexibility for Federal Civilian Employees," in *Workplace Flexibility: Realigning 20th-Century Jobs for a 21st-Century Workforce,* edited by Christensen and Schneider, pp. 178–95 (see note 12).

72. Sylvia A. Hewlett and others, *The Hidden Brain Drain: Off-Ramps and On-Ramps in Women's Careers* (New York: Center for Work-Life Policy, 2005).

73. Families and Work Institute and SHRM, *2010 Guide to Bold New Ideas for Making Work Work* (see note 69).

74. Holly Sexton, "Spending Time at Work and at Home: What Workers Do, How They Feel about It, and How These Emotions Affect Family Life," in *Being Together, Working Apart: Dual Career Families and the Work-Life Balance,* edited by Schneider and Waite, pp. 49–71 (see note 2); Emma Adam, "Momentary Emotion and Cortisol Levels in the Everyday Lives of Working Parents," in *Being Together, Working Apart: Dual Career Families and the Work-Life Balance,* edited by Schneider and Waite, pp. 105–33 (see note 2).

75. Heather Boushey and Ann O'Leary, eds., *The Shriver Report: A Woman's Nation Changes Everything* (Washington: Center for American Progress, 2009); Jerry A. Jacobs and Kathleen Gerson, *The Time Divide: Work, Family, and Gender Inequality* (Harvard University Press, 2004); Schneider and Waite, eds., *Being Together, Working Apart* (see note 2); Suzanne Bianchi and Melissa Milkie, "Work and Family Research in the First Decade of the 21st Century," *Journal of Marriage and Family* 72, no. 3 (2010): 705–25.

76. Adam, "Momentary Emotion and Cortisol Levels in the Everyday Lives of Working Parents" (see note 74); and Marchena, "Adolescents' Assessment of Parental Role Management in Dual-Earner Families" (see note 2).

77. Schneider and Waite, eds., *Being Together, Working Apart* (see note 2).

78. Workplace Flexibility 2010, "Flexible Work Arrangements" (see note 65).

79. Ellen Galinsky and others, "Employer-Provided Workplace Flexibility," in *Workplace Flexibility: Realigning 20th-Century Jobs for a 21st-Century Workforce,* edited by Christensen and Schneider, pp. 131–56 (see note 12).

80. James T. Bond and others, *National Study of Employers: Highlights of Findings* (New York: Families and Work Institute, 2005); Bond and others, *Highlights of the 2002 National Study of the Changing Workforce* (see note 66).

81. Bond and Galinsky, "Using Survey Research to Address Work-Life Issues" (see note 67).

82. John Blake, *More Workers Are Choosing Fear over Flex Time, Experts Say*, 2010 (www.cnn.com/2010/LIVING/worklife/03/29/flex.time/index.html).

83. Ellen Galinsky, James T. Bond, and E. Jeffrey Hill, *A Status Report on Workplace Flexibility: Who Has It? Who Wants It? What Difference Does It Make?* (New York: Families and Work Institute, 2004); Ellen Galinsky, James T. Bond, and E. Jeffrey Hill, *When Work Works: A Status Report on Workplace Flexibility* (New York: Families and Work Institute, 2004).

84. Workplace Flexibility 2010, "Flexible Work Arrangements" (see note 65).

85. Phyllis Moen, Erin Kelly, and Kelly Chermack, "Learning from a Natural Experiment: Studying a Corporate Work-Time Policy Initiative," in *Work-Life Policies*, edited by Ann C. Crouter and Alan Booth (Washington: Urban Institute Press, 2008), pp. 97–131.

86. Boushey and O'Leary, *The Shriver Report: A Woman's Nation Changes Everything* (see note 75); Heather Boushey and Joan C. Williams, "Resolving Work-Life Conflicts: Progressives Have Answers" (2010) (www.americanprogress.org/issues/2010/03/work_life_conflict.html).

Children with Health Issues

Mark A. Schuster, Paul J. Chung, and Katherine D. Vestal

Summary

All children, even the healthiest, have preventive and acute health care needs. Moreover, a growing number of children are chronically ill, with preventive, acute, and ongoing care needs that may be much more demanding than those for healthy children.

Because children are unable to care for themselves, their parents are expected to provide a range of health care services without which the current health care system for children would not function. Under this "shadow health care system," parents or parent surrogates often need to be with the child, a requirement that can create difficulties for working parents, particularly for those whose children are chronically ill. How federal, state, and employer policies and practices mesh with the child health care needs of families is therefore a central issue in any discussion about work and family balance.

In this article Mark Schuster, Paul Chung, and Katherine Vestal describe the health care needs of children; the essential health care responsibilities of parents; the perspective of employers; and the existing network of federal, state, and local family leave benefits that employed parents can access. They also identify current gaps in policies that leave unmet the needs of both parents and their employers.

The authors suggest the outlines of a national family leave policy that would protect the interests of parents and employers. In essence, such a policy would build on the federal Family and Medical Leave Act, which gives some workers time off with no advance notice required and no loss of job or health insurance. But it would also include elements of California's Paid Family Leave Insurance, which expands coverage to more workers and provides partial pay during leave. Employers could be given some financial protections as well as protections against employee fraud and abuse. Such a policy, the authors conclude, would help to provide security to parents, minimize effects on employers, raise societal expectations for family-friendly work environments, and help maintain the parental shadow system of care on which health care professionals depend.

www.futureofchildren.org

Mark A. Schuster is the William Berenberg Professor of Pediatrics at Harvard Medical School and chief of the Division of General Pediatrics and vice-chair for health policy in the Department of Medicine at Children's Hospital Boston. Paul J. Chung is an associate professor of pediatrics and health services at the David Geffen School of Medicine and School of Public Health at the University of California–Los Angeles. Katherine D. Vestal is with the Division of General Pediatrics at Children's Hospital Boston. The authors thank Gregor Brodsky and Jessica Ratner for research assistance and Katie Alijewicz for assistance with the manuscript.

Mark A. Schuster, Paul J. Chung, and Katherine D. Vestal

For the past two decades, family leave has been viewed in the United States as one of the core tools in helping parents address their children's health care needs. The federal Family and Medical Leave Act (FMLA) of 1993 provides unpaid family leave primarily to long-term employees working more than half time for public agencies or large private employers. Several states and the federal government have implemented or are considering implementing expansions that provide pay during leave, reach more employees, or both. Employers, meanwhile, are increasingly introducing greater scheduling flexibility, access to child care, and paid leave. For these governmental and employer policies to be most effective, they must take into account children's preventive, acute, and chronic health care needs, the associated health care responsibilities of parents, and the costs for employers.

Even the healthiest children have substantial health care needs.[1] All children are expected to receive routine preventive care that addresses not only the screening and prevention of disease but also the promotion of healthy development. Virtually all children also need acute intermittent care (at home, in outpatient settings, or in hospitals), often multiple times a year, for illnesses ranging from minor to serious. Moreover, a large and growing subset of children is chronically ill, with ongoing preventive, acute, and chronic health care needs that may be dramatically greater than those of healthy children.[2]

A distinct feature of health care for children is that parents are expected to perform nearly all of the support roles that make direct services by health care professionals possible. Moreover, parents themselves must provide (free of charge) direct health care services,

many of which were once considered to be the responsibility of health care professionals. In general, the number, frequency, and complexity of these parent-provided services increase with the severity of the illness, and health care system reforms that encourage home care over hospital care typically do so with the full expectation that parent responsibilities will increase. It is not an exaggeration to view parents as the linchpin of a shadow health care system without which the formal child health care system would be unable to function. To provide this shadow care, parents or parent surrogates must be present with the child.

Employed parents currently rely on a patchwork system of employment policies and family leave benefits (as well as the informal accommodations of employers and coworkers) to maintain this shadow system of care. Employers, meanwhile, have interests in ensuring that provision of this shadow care does not unduly affect workplace productivity. How federal, state, and employer policies and practices mesh with the child health care needs of families is therefore a central issue in the ongoing national discussion about work and family balance. In this article, we describe the health care needs of children, the essential health care responsibilities of parents, the perspective of employers, and the existing network of benefits that employed parents can access. We also identify gaps in these benefits that may be particularly salient for the types and patterns of care responsibilities that parents shoulder.

What Are Children's Health Care Needs?

Although children are, on average, healthier than adults, their health care needs, even in the best of circumstances, are considerable.[3] Like adults, children require care in three

Figure 1. Domains of Pediatric Care and Examples of Care in Each Domain

Routine preventive	**Intermittent acute**	**Ongoing chronic***
· Immunizations	· Acute office visits	· Multispecialty physician services
· Developmental screening	· Emergency department visits	· Specialty nursing services
· Disease screening	· Hospitalizations	· Speech, physical, and occupational therapy services
· Anticipatory guidance	· Home care and services	· Home care and services
· Preventive dental care		· Mental, developmental, and behavioral services

Source: Authors.
* Chronically ill children require enhanced routine preventive and intermittent acute care, as well as ongoing chronic care.

basic domains: routine preventive care to promote health, prevent disease, and reduce unhealthy behaviors; intermittent care to diagnose and treat acute illnesses ranging from minor to life-threatening; and ongoing care to manage chronic conditions that persist over months or years. Figure 1 gives examples of the health care services that fall in each of these three categories.

Until a few decades ago, these three types of care were weighted toward preventive and acute care; chronic care needs affected relatively few children. Therefore, parents generally needed only occasional brief absences from their work on behalf of their children. Moreover, traditional gender roles, with mothers typically staying home with the children, ensured that such absences for employed parents (usually fathers) would be few and far between.[4]

In recent decades, however, chronic care needs have substantially expanded with no diminution of preventive and acute care needs. Illnesses that previously killed children (such as severe prematurity, cancer, and genetic diseases) have become, in many instances, nonfatal conditions with long-lasting effects that require extensive,

sometimes lifelong, management. Meanwhile, the number of childhood preventive services now recommended has greatly increased, leading to even higher frequency and intensity of routine care.[5] For the most part, workplaces have not developed effective strategies to adapt to these changing demands, and gender role shifts have guaranteed that the need for absences related to child health and health care, once uncommon, are now a ubiquitous part of workplace life.

Preventive Care
All children are expected to receive a large and ever-growing amount of routine preventive care, including immunizations, developmental surveillance and disease screening, anticipatory guidance (providing education and advice to promote health and prevent disease), and dental care. Currently, the American Academy of Pediatrics and Bright Futures (a national child health promotion and disease prevention initiative that is explicitly referenced in the 2010 Patient Protection and Affordable Health Care Act[6]) jointly specify a minimum of seven visits in a child's first year, six more in the next three years, and a total of twenty-six before the age of eighteen, a frequency far greater than recommended for most adults.[7]

> *The underlying causes of the relationship between socioeconomic status and child health are not yet well understood, but the discrepancy in health status between social classes has persisted over time.*

Immunizations are a public health priority. They protect recipients and the public at large, through "herd immunity," against serious diseases. The number of diseases for which immunizations are recommended continues to grow, and most immunizations require multiple doses at multiple visits.

Developmental and disease screenings are also staples of preventive care. Developmental screening detects delays and problems in physical maturation; speech and language acquisition; gross and fine motor skills; and behavioral, social, and emotional growth. Disease screening consists of a general history, a physical exam, and specific tests. The history and physical exam elicit parent and child concerns and attempt to find incidental signs or patterns of early or hidden illness. Specific tests detect congenital diseases, vision and hearing deficits, anemia, lead exposure, obesity, hypertension, and sexually transmitted infections. Early detection and treatment of delays and diseases in these areas have been associated with short- and long-term health, educational, and economic benefits.[8]

Anticipatory guidance is considered by many pediatric clinicians to be the cornerstone of the childhood preventive care experience. It consists of education given to parents and children (especially adolescents) regarding the prevention of diseases and the promotion of healthy growth and development. Recommended anticipatory guidance topics are far too numerous to detail but include advice on topics such as breast feeding and sleeping position for infants, discipline and injury prevention for toddlers, school performance and nutrition for elementary-school-age children, and substance use and sexual health for adolescents.[9]

Finally, regular dental care has become increasingly recognized as a major determinant of health. Tooth decay and periodontal disease are associated with complications caused by infection and chronic inflammation.[10] Some health care professionals now recommend that children have their first routine dental visit as early as age one, with routine follow-ups recommended as frequently as every six months.[11]

Care of Intermittent Acute and Ongoing Chronic Illnesses

Children may experience a great range of illnesses, from mild to severe, and from common to rare. These conditions may last for a day or two or for a child's whole life.[12] Most are intermittent acute illnesses such as infectious diseases (common colds, pneumonias) and injuries (car accidents, falls), but a substantial and growing percentage are chronic illnesses. The most common chronic childhood illnesses include allergies, asthma, attention-deficit/hyperactivity disorder (ADHD), and emotional problems. Other well-known and relatively common chronic illnesses include cancers, developmental and behavioral disabilities (such as autism), congenital abnormalities, cerebral palsy, complications of prematurity, cystic fibrosis, and diabetes.

The prevalence of many of these conditions (both acute and chronic) has been shown to vary by socioeconomic status.[13] On average, children with poorer parents are less healthy than children whose parents are financially better off. For instance, more than twice as many poor children as nonpoor children are reported by their mothers to be in less than "very good" health, a gap that increases as children age.[14] The underlying causes of the relationship between socioeconomic status and child health are not yet well understood, but the discrepancy in health status between social classes has persisted over time.[15]

Intermittent Acute Care. In addition to receiving routine preventive care, almost all children will have one or more illness episodes serious enough to require an outpatient or emergency ward visit, hospitalization, or care at home. It is difficult to disentangle preventive from acute office visits in administrative data sets. Nevertheless, about three of four children under age eighteen have at least one office visit in a given year, with an average rate of about four visits a year; that rate would suggest an average frequency far in excess of the recommended routine visit schedule. Moreover, about one in eight children in a given year has at least one emergency ward visit, and about one in thirty is hospitalized at least once. For children described by their parents as being in only fair or poor health, the numbers are dramatically higher, with five of six having at least one office visit (at an average rate of nine visits a year), one in four having at least one emergency room visit, and one in seven being hospitalized at least once.[16]

On top of these acute health care encounters are days in which children suffer minor illnesses that may not require care by medical professionals but still prevent them from attending day care or school or that otherwise require parental presence at home. About 70 percent of children in elementary school miss some school each year because of illness, with 15 percent missing more than one week.[17] Thus, it is entirely likely that intermittent acute care necessitates multiple days of health care services (by providers or parents) each year even for otherwise healthy children, and potentially weeks of services for children who are seriously ill.

Ongoing Chronic Care. Finally, about 15 percent of children are considered children with special health care needs—children "who have or are at increased risk for a chronic physical, developmental, behavioral or emotional condition and who also require health and related services of a type or amount beyond that required by children generally."[18] For instance, children with conditions such as ADHD, asthma, autism, cancer, cerebral palsy, cystic fibrosis, depression, diabetes, and sickle cell anemia generally fall into this category. These children require ongoing care, including frequent monitoring, interventions aimed at preventing or managing complications of the illness, and often high-intensity acute care for severe episodes of illness. They account for a vastly disproportionate number of hospital days, health care encounters, and school absences.[19] Although fewer children are chronically ill than adults overall, the number of children with special health care needs appears to be growing. Moreover, these children are at high risk for permanent physical and developmental impairments that may create large societal costs lasting an entire lifetime. Intervening in an appropriate and timely fashion is critical for their health maintenance and long-term prognosis.

Intervening, however, is often an enormously complex undertaking. Chronically ill children typically do not have a single health care provider who delivers all necessary services. Instead, management of childhood chronic illnesses is generally a multisystem, multiprovider effort requiring intensive coordination. Most chronically ill children require specialty physician services, and many require the input of multiple physician specialists, often in separate venues. In addition, about 20 percent of all children in a given year receive health care from nonphysician providers, with much of this care focused on the chronically ill. These services include specialty nursing visits; speech, physical, and occupational therapy; home health services for intensive or complex therapies as a way to avoid long-term or even permanent hospitalizations; and mental, developmental, and behavioral health services. About a quarter of children with special health care needs use speech, physical, or occupational therapy each year, and about one in twenty uses home health services each year.[20] Typically, these services require separate providers who do not routinely communicate with each other, forcing constant and active supervision.

Variations in Patterns of Care Needs

There is an additional factor complicating children's health care needs—the large and unpredictable variations in need that occur not only among different children but also for the same child over time. As noted, a single health care episode can last a day, a week, a month, or a lifetime. A history of shorter durations of illness for an individual child does not eliminate the possibility of a serious or even catastrophic event in the future. Conversely, the fact that a child experiences long-term health care needs does not mean that additional short-term needs are somehow diminished. In fact, chronically ill children exhibit, on average, greater use of preventive and acute care services than other

There is an additional factor complicating children's health care needs—the large and unpredictable variations in need that occur not only among different children but also for the same child over time.

children.[21] Therefore, as the complexity of illness increases, so does the variation in the durations of health care episodes.

The same can be said with respect to frequency. Children with special health care needs typically use health care services more frequently than children without such needs. However, children can become chronically ill at any time, and many may recover or improve substantially over time. Childhood cancers, for instance, can appear at any age (depending on the type of cancer) and, once they present, can immediately increase health care needs for long periods of time. But those health care needs are not static. Instead, they fluctuate dramatically depending on factors that are largely outside the family's control—available treatment options, initial response to treatment, acute or chronic complications resulting from either the cancer or its treatment, and spread or recurrence of the cancer. These fluctuations can occur both rapidly and suddenly—children with special health care needs, for instance, are more than three times as likely as other children to have an acute illness episode requiring admission to an intensive care unit.[22] That does not mean, however, that all children with special health care needs will require such services, or that all other children will not.

What it does mean is that health care needs vary enormously among children, especially among those with special health care needs, and that this variation is often unpredictable. Thus, an examination of children's health care needs suggests that policies designed to help parents care for their children will be most effective if they take into account this most basic fact of life and health.

Parents: The Central Hub of the Child Health Care System

Children occupy a special position with respect to health care. Few other populations are as dependent on others for their health care. Because of this dependence, a societal obligation is attached to the parents (or parent substitutes). Whether the care is preventive, acute, or chronic, parents are simply expected to be there, and many of the processes of care have been arranged based on an assumption of parental presence.

Parent Responsibilities during Outpatient and Emergency Visits

It may be easy to forget the myriad background duties expected of parents during something as seemingly simple as an outpatient visit. Parents are responsible for scheduling the visit. They are responsible for arranging transportation. In most offices and emergency wards, parents are responsible for filling out all the necessary paperwork, displaying proof of insurance, and handling co-pays. Parents are expected to entertain or otherwise supervise their children while waiting, sometimes for hours, first in a waiting room and then in a patient room. They are expected to provide most or all of the relevant historical information to clinicians

and to assist clinicians in the gathering of additional data, including talking with their child, comforting him or her during examinations or procedures, and helping collect urine or other samples. They are expected to work with clinicians to develop appropriate health care plans, to learn how to execute these plans at home, and to ask any and all necessary questions before leaving. They are then expected to arrange follow-up appointments, fill pharmacy prescriptions, follow through on lab requests, and provide or arrange for transportation home.

Typical clinician offices, clinics, and emergency wards are completely unprepared to act as surrogates for all or even most of these functions. The current outpatient and emergency systems of health care for children would simply fail to operate without either consistent parental presence or a massive investment in additional staff trained to act *in loco parentis*.

Hospitalizations: Parents as Communicators, Care Coordinators, and Safety Monitors

On the surface, hospitalizations might seem to provide parents with more scheduling freedom than outpatient or emergency ward visits. Technically, hospitals are required to provide round-the-clock care and supervision for their inpatients. In reality, however, although parent responsibilities shift, they diminish only in certain aspects and often increase in others.

Because many inpatient clinicians care for multiple patients simultaneously, communications are notoriously difficult, limited, and haphazard. Parents often need to spend an entire day waiting in their child's room for a chance at one unscheduled five-minute conversation with a physician.

Figure 2. Patient Regulations from the 1896 Children's Hospital (Now Known as Children's Hospital Boston) Annual Report

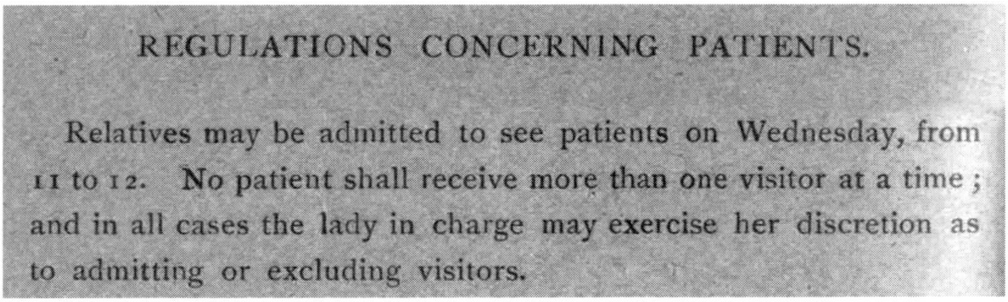

> ## REGULATIONS CONCERNING PATIENTS.
>
> Relatives may be admitted to see patients on Wednesday, from 11 to 12. No patient shall receive more than one visitor at a time ; and in all cases the lady in charge may exercise her discretion as to admitting or excluding visitors.

Source: Courtesy of the Children's Hospital Boston Archives.

During this conversation, parents must be ready to engage fully with the physician in understanding the current clinical status and the anticipated course of illness, ask all the questions they might have, and participate in important health care planning on behalf of their child.

But such planning is only the beginning in an environment that, at the best of times, is confusing and haphazard. A parent who is able to speak with multiple clinicians is likely to find different clinicians saying different and sometimes contradictory things based either on legitimate differences of opinion or on incomplete knowledge or communication. In such instances, parents are often treated as valuable sources of information and care coordination among various clinicians. Moreover, the clinical course of children in the hospital is enormously dynamic. Diagnoses, planned tests and treatments, and prognoses change, sometimes multiple times during a day. Tests are delayed, surgeries are canceled, and emergency situations unfold, often without any timely explanation or warning. In the worst situations, mistakes are made, and mistakes occur frequently.[23] Even with fully staffed nursing and ancillary support from volunteers and child-life

specialists, most hospitalized children spend most of their day with no health care professionals in their room. In such a setting, health care staff fully expect parents to act as an additional, and sometimes essential, line of supervision and safety for their children.

Hospitalizations: Parents as Parents
In addition to fulfilling communication and supervisory roles, parents are also expected to provide emotional support and assistance in ways that health care professionals are simply unable to do. Hospitalized children are often frightened and dependent upon the presence and comfort of their parents. Health care providers often need parents to help their children submit to tests or therapies. This reliance on parental assistance represents a significant shift from hospital policies through the first half of the twentieth century, when parental visiting policies were extremely restrictive.[24] For example, an 1896 policy at Children's Hospital in Boston stated that parents were permitted to visit their children for one hour one day a week (figure 2). This approach to parent visits generally persisted in the United States into the mid-twentieth century.[25] By the 1960s, however, daily visiting hours had become standard in U.S. hospitals, and by the 1980s,

overnight visits had become commonplace—in 1988, 98 percent of hospitals with pediatric residencies allowed parents to stay with their children twenty-four hours a day.[26] This shift was at least partly influenced by a growing body of literature suggesting that child and parent anxiety and emotional distress during hospitalizations may affect how well children recover from their illness.[27]

Family presence during health care procedures decreases anxiety for the child and the parents. Allowing a parent to be present for the induction of mask anesthesia, for example, may minimize the stress pediatric patients experience undergoing a surgical procedure.[28] A study examining whether parental presence during venipuncture altered self-reported distress of the child and parent found that, in the group with parents present, distress scores were lower for both parent and child than they were in the group with absent parents.[29] Another small study was conducted to determine whether allowing parents to be present during invasive procedures reduced the anxiety that parents experienced while their child was in the pediatric intensive care unit, to evaluate whether the parent's presence was helpful to the child and parent, and to determine whether the parent's presence was harmful to the hospital staff. Parental presence significantly reduced parental anxiety related to the procedure. Thirteen of the sixteen parents found their presence helpful to themselves, fourteen found their presence helpful to their child, and fifteen would have repeated their choice to watch. Fifteen of sixteen nurses found parents' presence helpful.[30] Even in critically acute situations, parental presence has not been associated with negative effects on care. A prospective trial showed that family presence for pediatric trauma patients did not prolong the length of time before CT imaging was performed or resuscitation was completed.[31]

Parental presence immediately before and after surgery has also been associated with better outcomes. In a randomized controlled trial evaluating the efficacy of family-centered preparation for surgery (that is, using enhanced presurgical parent-child engagement techniques), parents and children in the family-centered care group exhibited significantly lower anxiety before and during induction of anesthesia compared with other groups.[32] Another study found that children whose mothers were involved in their post-tonsillectomy care recovered faster and were discharged earlier than children whose mothers did not participate in their care.[33] Likewise, a series of quality improvement studies found that children who had undergone surgery cried less, were less restless, and required less medication when their parents were present and assisted in pain assessment and management.[34]

Parent Responsibilities during Care at Home

The communication, coordination, supervision, and emotional support that parents are expected to provide during outpatient and emergency visits and hospitalizations are no less pressing when their children are at home throughout their illness, at home after hospitalization, or at home receiving long-term care. For some tasks—particularly supervision—expectations are often greater at home than they would be in a traditional clinical setting. Parents must also take on the added responsibility of providing most or all of the actual health care services the child needs while at home.

Even for otherwise healthy children, health care services can be substantial and complex.

By routinely accepting intensive responsibilities in order to care for their children at home, parents of children with special health care needs suffer under an enormous burden.

For the growing number of children with serious chronic illnesses, however, parents now provide not only medications, but also oxygen, respiratory treatments, feeding-tube care, intravenous nutrition, physical and occupational therapy, and developmental and behavioral interventions, absorbing an ever-growing portion of health care responsibilities through what amounts to generally unacknowledged shadow care. Since the 1990s families whose children are dependent on technology for their care have also become—initially with home health assistance but now often unassisted—operators of complex and expensive devices such as feeding pumps, suction machines, dialysis machines, or ventilators that were previously restricted to inpatient settings.[35]

A study of families with technology-dependent children found that while the children's health and quality of life benefited from the technology, the time demands of the care routines substantially limited the family's participation in school, employment, and social life in general.[36] The need to use certain medical technologies at night also meant that many family members suffered regular disruptions to their sleep.

The study showed that care related to the devices (or "technical care") was provided mainly by the children's parents, particularly mothers, with varying levels of support from other family members (mainly fathers and older siblings) and formal service providers. Parents and other family members also provided both a large quantity and a wide variety of personal, practical, and other types of care linked to the child's medical condition, in addition to the kinds of care associated with parenting in general.

The technical care involved a range of activities—assisting the child when she or he was using a device; monitoring the child with close visual observation, monitoring devices, or both; managing the equipment (cleaning and preparing it for use, ordering supplies, and managing stocks); maintaining the interface between the device and the body (care of entry and exit sites, placement and replacement of tubes); obtaining technical support from service providers (including hospitals, community services, and companies that supply equipment and consumables); providing technical support to other caregivers through formal or informal training; and preparing equipment for use by other caregivers. These medical tasks had to be performed following strict protocols by parents or other informal caregivers who had been trained in how to manage the devices.

The Parent Burden of Child Illness

By routinely accepting such intensive responsibilities in order to care for their children at home, parents of children with special health care needs face an enormous burden. The additional time and effort they must often devote to finding and managing treatment, attending medical or therapy appointments, and working with day-care providers and schools to find accommodations for their child's complex and challenging needs can create financial problems, marital discord, sibling issues, and problems at work.[37] Across a variety of domains, parental caregivers of children with activity limitations are at a particular disadvantage compared with other parents. They report poorer quality of life, have slightly higher use of sick visits for their own medical issues, and have less favorable employment and financial outcomes.[38]

Families with chronically ill children have high levels of finance-related family problems. About 40 percent of these families, or about 4 million families nationwide, report experiencing financial problems related to their child's condition.[39] Analyses of the 2005–06 national survey of chronically ill children found that 24 percent of their parents reported work loss as a result of their child's health care needs. Greater functional limitations and condition instability were associated with increased odds of family work loss. Illustrating that much of this work loss was in fact illness related, parents reported that having access to a coordinated care system (a medical home, described later) was associated with a 50 percent reduction in the odds of work loss.[40]

A large, nationally representative survey found that children's limitations in taking care of their own personal needs, such as eating, dressing, and bathing, were associated with parents' job changes, income loss, and disruptions in sleep patterns. Functional limitations in mobility and self-care were associated with intensive home-care requirements, leading parents to make various job changes to accommodate these needs. Severe limitations in the child's learning ability greatly increased both job changes and income loss and had a more modest effect on parents' sleep patterns.[41]

A study of families of children requiring a tracheotomy found a correlation between the parental care burden and the child's physical health status, as well as between the parental care burden and increasing economic costs associated with this care. A strong correlation was found between the parental care burden and reduced parental mental health status.[42]

Multiple studies indicate that mothers' careers may be especially affected by caring for children with special health care needs. A study of families with autistic children found that in two-parent households, two-thirds of the parents said the mother's work outside the home was the most affected by their child's autism, with only one-third identifying the father's work or both parents' work as most affected. Three of five mothers had not taken a job because of their child's autism. Of those mothers who were employed, more than half worked fewer hours to care for their child, one-quarter had taken a leave of absence, and nearly as many had turned down a promotion in order to care for their child.[43] Another study found that mothers of children with chronic conditions requiring use of technical devices were much more likely to quit their jobs to care for their child. In addition, single mothers were fifteen times more likely than mothers in two-parent families to quit employment.[44]

An article written by the parent of a medically complex child described a typical day in the life of parents like her: "Physicians struggle to determine Sam's diagnosis; therapists struggle to get Sam to reach for that ball, to turn those knees in, to take an unaided step; but we, as parents of a medically complicated child, struggle with much more. I coordinate Sam's medical records so that every physician knows what every other physician is thinking. Most physicians seem grateful for this. I try to arrange multiple procedures with multiple surgeons on the same day so that Sam will undergo anesthesia as little as possible. Many surgeons seem to want this to happen, but their scheduling staff is not always as accommodating. I consult with our daycare center to determine how Sam can best be served next year in a classroom where everyone is walking but he may not be. I meet with our daughter's teachers to discuss her behavioral problems, possible signs of the stress she feels. I struggle with keeping up with my work when I need to take off so much time to attend medical appointments."[45]

Some partial strategies have been proposed for relieving parents of some of their care coordination responsibilities. One such strategy is enhancing primary care through establishing patient-centered medical homes (also known as PCMHs).[46] These medical homes focus on coordinating care and improving communication among clinicians (primary care providers, specialists, nurses) and between clinicians and parents.[47] This approach relies on an effective referral process and the assignment of clear responsibilities among multiple providers and the patient's family to enable information exchange, facilitate joint decision making, and prevent misunderstandings.[48] Studies have demonstrated that poor care coordination between primary care providers and specialists leads to delayed access to care, inferior quality of care, ineffective use of resources, inflated health care costs, and dissatisfaction among patients and providers.[49] Another strategy is the concept of global payment, in which primary care, subspecialty care, and inpatient care are integrated and payment is "bundled" as a lump sum for each patient or episode of illness. Such systems would require creating networks of primary care providers, specialists, and hospitals that

would benefit from developing close working relationships. Many of the models for "accountable care organizations" envisioned in the Patient Protection and Affordable Health Care Act may incorporate concepts similar to patient-centered medical homes and global payment.

Investing in and enhancing community-based resources, such as school-based health centers, might also help reduce the parental burden of child illness by providing a secondary source of care in a location where children already spend much of their time, thus allowing parents to stay at work occasionally while their child's minor health care needs are addressed (or leave work for less time because they do not have to transport their child between the school and the clinic). Currently, school-based health centers vary widely in the comprehensiveness of the services they provide. If such centers were regularly staffed by some combination of nurse practitioners, physicians, clinical social workers, psychologists, nutritionists, dentists, or dental hygienists, they could potentially provide a variety of routine preventive and minor acute or chronic care services.

The Employer Perspective

Although the child health care burden on parents can be enormous, the burden of parent absences on employers can also be substantial. The costs to employers of unplanned or unscheduled absences by all employees are estimated at 9 percent of payroll, and the total costs, direct and indirect, of all major absence categories average 35 percent of base payroll.[50] Employers, therefore, have clear stakeholder interests in parents' decisions regarding employment and leave.

Employers seek to avoid costly or unnecessary disruptions to essential operations. Even when parent absences are unpaid, they have the potential to create disruptions that can be rectified only by the costly hiring and training of temporary employees or the shifting of work responsibilities to existing employees at the potential expense of less critical but still important activities. Department of Labor estimates suggest that employee absences cost U.S. businesses $100 billion a year in lost productivity.[51] Thus, employers may have an incentive to discourage or prevent parents from leaving work to tend to their child's health care needs. Moreover, workplace benefits are inherently at risk for at least some level of abuse by employees. According to some estimates, only 34 percent of all unscheduled absences are related to employee illness, while 22 percent are related to family issues, such as caring for children or dependent parents.[52] In addition, a survey of 450 human resources professionals found that suspected employee abuse of intermittent leave taken under the FMLA was the primary FMLA-related concern for employers, and that the potential for or suspicion of abuse was reported to cause extreme difficulty in 42 percent of the organizations surveyed.[53] A separate survey showed that 47 percent of employers felt that unjustified intermittent leave posed at least "somewhat of a problem" for their operations.[54] Therefore, employers also have incentives to institute reporting and medical necessity requirements, as well as waiting periods and other restrictions to discourage abuse.

Disruptions to operations can come in several forms. Employers that do not provide parents the opportunity to care for their sick children can find that they permanently lose skilled employees, are unable to recruit highly qualified workers, and suffer a loss to workplace morale, all of which can create serious disruptions. Moreover, evidence is accumulating that employees who continue to work but are distracted by personal issues may create productivity losses of their own ("presenteeism" as opposed to "absenteeism") that may reduce some of the benefit to employers of preventing parent absences in the first place.[55] In this context, employers have some incentive to accommodate parent absences, assuming that employers can find ways to protect themselves from productivity loss or its financial consequences.

What Do Parents and Employers Need?

In a world in which employment and leave benefits could be written *de novo* to best suit parents and their employers, what benefits would best help parents fulfill all of the expectations placed on them with respect to their children's health care needs while limiting negative effects on their employers?

All parents would benefit from some negotiable number of days or portions of days that would allow them to schedule their children for routine preventive care visits assuming adequate advance notice is given. In addition, all parents would benefit from some negotiable number of discretionary days requiring no advance notice that could be used in the event of unpredictable but relatively minor acute illnesses. How employers would accommodate such discretionary days is unclear. Employers are substantially less able to shield themselves from productivity loss when advance notice is impossible than when it is given. Therefore, employers would need some way of insuring themselves against the risk of productivity loss.

Beyond scheduled and discretionary days, however, are two additional scenarios, each of which would not only require a greater investment of resources but also pose greater threats to parent employment—as well as to parent and child health and well-being. First is the scenario in which an otherwise healthy child suffers an acute illness such as severe pneumonia requiring admission to an intensive care unit; the child is expected to recover fully but also to require an extended period of intensive parental caregiving. In this situation, parents would need the ability to take off a large block of time with no advance notice or to shift temporarily to part-time work and transition gradually back to full time without set start or finish dates. Ideally, pay loss during this period would be limited. There would also be some level of guaranteed job retention so that employees could not easily be replaced permanently during extended absences. From the employer standpoint, all of these conditions might generate substantial costs. The need to accept indeterminate start and end dates without advance notice and the need to allow gradual transitions back into a guaranteed-retention position create substantial uncertainty and inefficiency that the employer would need to absorb. Meanwhile, preservation of pay would be a direct additional cost of parent absence. Again, employers would need some way to insure themselves against these risks. In some cases employers might also benefit from help in designing or implementing workflow innovations that could accommodate flexible or alternative schedules and locations.

The second and even more challenging scenario is the one in which a child suffers from a serious chronic illness. It is these situations in particular that would require maximum flexibility. Because children with special health care needs have more scheduled and unscheduled health care encounters, and greater overall care needs at home, than other children, their parents would need access to more time off both with advance

notice and without. In addition, absences for parents of chronically ill children may be brief or extended, continuous or intermittent; may switch from one type to another unpredictably; and are often broken up by periods of relative health. For employers, this scenario would seriously raise the question of whether keeping an employee would be worth any amount of insurance, subsidization, or flexibility. In this case, both parents and employers would have strong incentives for parents to downshift from full-time to part-time work or to simply leave the workforce. Unfortunately, in many cases, these are exactly the same parents who would suffer most from loss of income associated with downshifting or job loss.[56] How employment and leave benefits can be arranged to meet the needs of this population is a critical issue, one for which policy makers and employers have yet to find a comprehensive solution.

Types of Parent Support

Employed parents in the United States tend to rely on a haphazard mix of support to care for their children's health needs, including federal, state, and local leave laws and programs. The extent to which parents can care for their children's health is largely determined, however, by their working conditions, including flexibility in duties, locations, and schedules, as well as other employer-provided benefits. In the United States, where the availability of paid sick leave is limited, parents who have paid sick days are more than five times as likely to be able to care for their sick children themselves as parents who do not have paid sick leave.[57] According to the 2010 National Paid Sick Days Study, about 64 percent of all workers report that they are eligible for paid sick days from their employer (including those receiving "paid time off" days, also known as PTO days, which combine time off for sick leave, vacation, and other reasons).[58] However, only 47 percent of workers receive paid sick days that they can use for sick family members. Without flexible scheduling or paid leave to care for children's health needs, employed parents may forgo disease prevention activities or experience wage and job loss when they take time off to seek or provide care for their children. For example, studies in Haiti, Indonesia, and the United States have found that parents report work schedule conflicts as a significant barrier to getting their children immunized.[59] Among U.S. workers with paid sick days, 14 percent have sent a sick child to school or day care; among those without paid sick days, 24 percent have done so.

Federal Support

The federal government guarantees unpaid leave to some workers but does not mandate paid leave. The federal FMLA provides up to twelve weeks a year of unpaid leave with job protection (that is, protection from being fired) to certain workers to care for themselves or ill family members.[60] The FMLA also requires that an employee's group health benefits be maintained during the leave. Signed into law in 1993, the FMLA was the first federal leave legislation to address the competing demands of work and family. About half (47 percent) of workers are eligible for FMLA leave;[61] eligibility depends on the size of the employer (fifty or more employees), the number of hours worked, and the duration of current employment (at least 1,250 hours for the same employer in the past twelve months). Many employees, however, cannot afford to take unpaid leave. Of the 3.5 million employees who needed but did not take leave in 2000, 78 percent cited inability to afford leave as a reason. Of these, 88 percent said they would have taken leave if they had received either some pay or (if already receiving partial pay) additional pay.[62]

Two pieces of proposed federal legislation, the Healthy Families Act and the Family Leave Insurance Act, would partially address concerns about employees who lack access to paid leave that can be used to care for themselves or family members. The Healthy Families Act would create a new national standard guaranteeing employees one paid hour off for each thirty hours worked and enabling them to earn up to seven paid sick days a year that they could use for the health needs of themselves or family members. It would also be available to more workers than the FMLA is, because it applies to employers with at least fifteen employees and has lower hour requirements. Costs would primarily fall upon employers, who would be responsible for paying employees' wages when they use their sick leave. The Family Leave Insurance Act would create an insurance program, funded through employer and employee payroll tax contributions, to provide up to twelve weeks of paid FMLA benefits. Employees would receive a specified percentage of their daily earnings and be subject to a waiting period of five workdays before receiving benefits. The Family Leave Insurance Act would also have somewhat broader eligibility than the FMLA: it would apply to employers with twenty or more employees (as opposed to fifty or more) and to employees who have worked at least 625 hours for the same employer in the past six months (compared with 1,250 or more in the past twelve months).

Research shows general public support for government-mandated paid sick days. According to a nationally representative study in 2010, across all sociodemographic and political groups, the majority of Americans believe that paid sick leave to care for themselves or for immediate family members

Table 1. Comparison of Federal and State Family Leave Programs

	Federal		State	
Provision	Family and Medical Leave Act	Family Leave Insurance Act (proposed)	California: Paid Family Leave Insurance Program	New Jersey: Family Leave Insurance Program
Length of leave	12 weeks	12 weeks	6 weeks	6 weeks
Leave is paid	No	Yes	Yes	Yes
Benefit structure	n.a.	Specified percentage of daily earnings	55 percent of weekly wage up to a cap	66 percent of weekly wage up to a cap
Maximum benefit (2010)	n.a.	n.a.	$987/week	$561/week
Offers job protection	Yes	Yes	No	No
Employer contribution to pay	No	Yes	No	No
Part-time workers eligible for benefits	Yes*	Yes*	Yes	Yes
Workers in companies with under 50 employees eligible for benefits	No	Yes	Yes	Yes
Waiting period before benefits can be used	No	5 workdays (but no more than 7 calendar days)	7 days**	7 days**

Source: Authors.
n.a. = Not applicable.
*Employees are eligible for FMLA if they have worked at least 1,250 hours for the same employer in the past twelve months. The Family Leave Insurance Act would apply to employees who have worked at least 625 hours for the same employer in the past six months.
**In California and New Jersey the seven-day waiting period refers to seven days of caring for an ill family member. The seven days do not have to be consecutive and can be served regardless of whether the claimant is scheduled to work on those days (weekend days included).

should be a government-guaranteed right for workers.[63] Sixty-nine percent of respondents said that paid sick days were "very important" for workers, and 75 percent favored a law that guarantees paid sick days for all workers.

State or Local Support
In 2004 California attempted to extend the FMLA's approach by instituting the Paid Family Leave Insurance (PFLI) program, which uses a payroll tax to create an insurance pool with broad eligibility that partially funds up to six weeks of leave for a child's (or other immediate family member's) illness or a child's birth or adoption.[64] The PFLI covers most part- and full-time employees at about 55 percent of their salary up to a maximum in 2010 of $987 a week;[65] it does not, however, include job protection. Benefits apply after employees miss one week of work for a given

illness (continuously or cumulatively). A statement signed by a physician or other clinician documenting the illness is required. New Jersey implemented a similar law in 2009. Washington state passed more limited family leave legislation (covering leave only for parents with a newly born or newly adopted child) in 2007 but has yet to implement its program.[66]

In addition, several states, including California, Connecticut, Hawaii, Washington, and Wisconsin, have flexible sick leave laws that entitle all workers who have access to sick leave to use some of their sick days to care for a sick child.[67] A few cities, including San Francisco (2006), the District of Columbia (2008), and Milwaukee (2008), have also passed sick day ordinances that guarantee paid sick days for all or most

Table 2. Comparison of Federal and Local Paid Sick Leave Programs

| Characteristic | Federal | Local | | |
	Healthy Families Act (proposed)	San Francisco	District of Columbia	Milwaukee
Maximum number of paid sick days per year	≥15 employees: 7 ≤14 employees: 0	≥10 employees: 9 ≤9 employees: 5	≥100 employees: 7 25–99 employees: 5 ≤24 employees: 3	≥10 employees: 9 ≤9 employees: 5
Benefit structure	1 hour of paid sick leave for each 30 hours worked	1 hour of paid sick leave for each 30 hours worked	≥100 employees: 1 hour/37 hours worked 25–99 employees: 1 hour/43 hours worked ≤24 employees: 1 hour/87 hours worked	1 hour of paid sick leave for each 30 hours worked
Employer contribution to pay	Yes	Yes	Yes	Yes
Sick days can be used to care for family members	Yes	Yes	Yes	Yes
Part-time workers eligible for benefits	Yes	Yes	Yes	Yes
Workers in companies with under 50 employees eligible for benefits	Yes	Yes	Yes	Yes

Source: Authors.

workers.[68] Legislators in other states and cities are also working on paid leave initiatives, and there are ongoing congressional efforts to pass the Healthy Families Act. Tables 1 and 2 compare the provisions and characteristics of these various laws and proposals.

Employer-Provided Support

Employers, meanwhile, provide a patchwork of formal and informal solutions to support parents, including sick days (often used for children without explicit employer approval, which can place parents at risk for termination); flexible paid time off that combines vacation, sick time, and family leave; telecommuting; and programs that allow employees to donate or share unused paid leave days. Individual supervisors and coworkers also use their discretion to informally enable parents to leave work for hours or days (as in "Just go, and I'll cover for you," or "Just go, and you can make the time up later").

Employees caring for dependent family members face complex challenges in their personal and professional lives. When the dependent is a child with special health care needs, workplace programs can help families more effectively use employee benefits and access public and private resources. Employee assistance and work-life programs are particularly well suited for addressing the needs of these employees and their children. In 2005, for instance, investigators examined how three separate large U.S. employers implemented programs specifically for employees with chronically ill children.[69] Their approaches included establishing a parent network, independently testing and refining the company's employee assistance program/work-life resource and referral service to better serve these parents, helping to guide employees when choosing health plans, and coordinating the company's clinical services with public programs to assist families with chronically ill children. The employers reported a positive impact on employee retention and commitment, improved use of employee benefit programs, and improved promotion of corporate diversity objectives.

International Comparisons

The United States is one of only a few industrialized countries that do not have national laws providing paid leave for children's health needs. At least forty-three countries, including Australia, Canada, France, Japan, Nicaragua, and South Africa, specifically guarantee parents some type of paid leave when their child is ill, and more than half of the forty-three provide full wages.[70] Although length of leave varies, an analysis of thirty-seven countries that offer paid leave for children's health needs found that fourteen guarantee eleven or more days of paid leave, six give seven to ten days, and ten give one to six days.[71] Types of paid leave arrangements also vary. For instance, El Salvador provides up to fifteen days for serious illness or injury of a child, while Norway typically provides ten days annually as a base, fifteen if the employee has more than one child, and twenty if the employee has a chronically ill child. In addition, at least thirty-four countries guarantee discretionary leave (seventeen with pay) that can be used for ill children.[72]

Countries that offer paid leave for children's health needs use different methods of negotiating and administering their paid leave benefits, but cost-sharing between employers and the state is common. For instance, Denmark has traditionally used collective agreements to determine most of the benefits available to workers, with employment laws focused mainly on establishing rules for collective bargaining and enforcing agreements.[73] Lately, however, the Danish government has moved more toward directly applying

statutory requirements to employers. Under most circumstances, the Danish law requires the employer to pay the cost of paid-leave benefits for the first two weeks of a period of absence; any remaining costs are paid by the claimant's residential local authority, a decentralized municipality that imposes taxes and also receives funds from the state.[74] In contrast, Sweden establishes employment standards primarily through laws rather than collective bargaining, despite high levels of unionization.[75] Like Denmark, though, the cost of benefits is divided between employers and the state's social security system, with employers paying during an initial period, and the social security system covering the remainder.[76] The same is true of Poland.[77]

Addressing Gaps in Existing Leave Policies

Current state and federal leave policies in the United States cover some but not all parents and employers, and among those covered, the policies address some but not all of their needs.

FMLA

For parents, the FMLA provides job protection benefits, which parents may need for unscheduled or extended absences, and it allows up to twelve weeks of leave annually, which likely covers the leave needs for parents of all but the sickest children. It also requires that any group health benefits an employee has be maintained during leave. Moreover, the FMLA does not require advance notice (although it does require justification if notice is not given at least thirty days before taking leave), and leave can be taken intermittently, which creates the flexibility that is crucial for parents of children with special health care needs. The FMLA, however, has two critical weaknesses for parents that clearly suppress use. First, eligibility is essentially restricted to long-term, more-than-half-time employees of public agencies and large private employers, a group that includes fewer than half of all employees.[78] Second, the leave is unpaid, which means many parents cannot afford to make use of the benefit.

PFLI

California designed the PFLI program to extend the FMLA's provisions in two important ways. First, it greatly expands eligibility, especially to employees in small organizations. Because the PFLI is tied to the state disability insurance provisions, it covers most employees in the state. Two major exceptions are self-employed individuals and employees covered by collective bargaining agreements that waive disability insurance. Second, the program provides pay, albeit partial, during leave (55 percent of salary up to a maximum of $987 a week in 2010).[79] Moreover, it retains some of the features of the FMLA, including not requiring advance notice and allowing leave to be taken intermittently.

The PFLI, however, like the FMLA, has provisions that discourage uptake. First, the lack of full pay during leave prevents use for many parents.[80] The PFLI is also limited to six weeks rather than the twelve weeks guaranteed by the FMLA. Although it does not require advance notice, it does require one week of missed work (or accrual of seven days if missed intermittently) for an illness during the year before the benefit period can start, which reduces its usefulness for limited absences. It also does not include the FMLA's job protection provision (although FMLA-eligible employees can simultaneously access job protection under the federal law), which raises the risk of job loss for parents who have frequent and extended absences to tend to their chronically ill children. The PFLI does

not require employers to maintain employees' employer-sponsored health benefits during leave, an especially important consideration for parents of children with special health care needs. Finally, the PFLI has far less stringent employee notification requirements than the FMLA and did not benefit from the same kind of aggressive public education roll-out campaign that the FMLA enjoyed. The FMLA was accompanied by a two-year Department of Labor publicity campaign and strong mandatory requirements for dissemination of FMLA information in workplaces. The PFLI was not widely publicized and requires only that employers provide information to new employees and employees who inquire about pay during their leave for a covered purpose. As a result, many employees must either know about the PFLI before requesting it or request it before knowing that they could receive pay. Given these structural limitations and weak dissemination requirements, it is not surprising that awareness of the program among parents of chronically ill children has been low (18 percent about eighteen months after implementation), and use has been almost nonexistent (5 percent).[81] Awareness was only slightly higher for the general California population: 28 percent were aware of the program in 2007.[82]

Despite these limitations, PFLI sets an important and innovative precedent. By using an insurance model to create a benefit funded entirely by employee contributions, the PFLI simultaneously attempts to avoid social stigma associated with welfare benefits and to address one of the key cost concerns of employers—providing pay during leave. It also raises the possibility that, just as employees' contributions to an insurance fund could provide parents with some measure of financial protection in the event of child health-related absences, employer contributions (or even additional employee contributions) to a similar fund could protect employers from other costs of parent absences (such as the cost of a temporary replacement).

What Might a National Paid Family Leave Policy Look Like?

The elements of the FMLA and PFLI that are most useful to parents, as well as innovations designed to protect employers, could be combined to create an outline for a national policy aimed at addressing the needs of both parents and employers. The FMLA has some clear advantages for parents, including job and health insurance protection, twelve-week duration, no advance notice requirement, no waiting period, and the ability to be used intermittently. The PFLI adds much broader coverage and pay. Bringing these strengths together would likely address many parents' most pressing needs across all types of absences, from scheduled limited absences to unscheduled extended ones (although partial pay will remain a disincentive for some). Parents of chronically ill children who are at highest risk of job loss and severe financial consequences could have access to benefits that might protect them from being forced to permanently leave the workforce.

On the employer side, the enhanced benefit would likely need to be balanced by both antifraud protections and financial protections against the costs of employee absences. Strong reporting and illness verification

requirements coupled with the ability for employers to require employees to first use other employer-provided benefits such as paid vacation could provide some protection against abuse. With respect to costs of the absence itself, PFLI benefits in California are entirely funded by employee contributions, with employers absorbing other costs, and a recent study documented little hardship for employers.[83] Thus, some type of cost-sharing between employees and employers would seem reasonable in a national policy framework.

Ultimately, the reasons to implement a national policy reflect multiple perspectives. First, mothers and fathers nationwide might receive a measure of security that could help them to participate more fully in the workforce while also engaging in the care of their children, regardless of their children's health or illness. Second, employers might have fewer disincentives against promoting family-friendly workplace policies, and a strong uniform policy might reduce employer concerns of competitive disadvantage created by an unlevel playing field. Third, the child health care system, operating in conjunction with a standardized system of benefits, might be able to more easily understand and cope with the limitations of the parental shadow system of care upon which it depends. Finally, nearly all children—even those not chronically ill—would surely benefit from having greater parental presence protecting and supporting them in times of need.

Endnotes

1. American Academy of Pediatrics, Bright Futures, "Recommendations for Preventive Pediatric Health Care" (Elk Grove Village, Ill.: 2008); Pamela L. Owens and others, "Annual Report on Health Care for Children and Youth in the United States: Focus on Injury-Related Emergency Department Utilization and Expenditures," *Ambulatory Pediatrics* 8, no. 4 (2008): 219–40.e17.

2. Owens and others, "Annual Report on Health Care for Children and Youth in the United States" (see note 1).

3. Elizabeth Jameson and Elizabeth Wehr, "Drafting National Health Care Reform Legislation to Protect the Health Interests of Children: Children's Health Interests Have Not Been a High Priority with Health Plan Administrators or the Institutional Purchasers of Group Health Coverage," *Stanford Law & Policy Review* 5, no. 1 (1993): 152–76.

4. Stephanie Coontz, "The Family in Upheaval," *Philadelphia Inquirer,* June 19, 2005 (www.stephaniecoontz. com/articles/article17.htm).

5. American Academy of Pediatrics, Bright Futures, "Recommendations for Preventive Pediatric Health Care" (see note 1).

6. Patient Protection and Affordable Care Act, 124 Stat. 119 thru 124 Stat. 1025, H.R. 3590 (2010).

7. American Academy of Pediatrics, Bright Futures, "Recommendations for Preventive Pediatric Health Care" (see note 1).

8. Paul A. Levy, "An Overview of Newborn Screening," *Journal of Developmental and Behavioral Pediatrics* 31, no. 7 (2010): 622–31; Heidi D. Nelson and others, "Screening for Speech and Language Delay in Preschool Children: Systematic Evidence Review for the U.S. Preventive Services Task Force," *Pediatrics* 117, no. 2 (2006): e298–319; E. Honey and others, "Cost Effectiveness of Screening for Chlamydia Trachomatis: A Review of Published Studies," *Sexually Transmitted Infections* 78, no. 6 (2002): 406–12; Evelyn P. Whitlock and others, "Screening and Interventions for Childhood Overweight," *U.S. Preventive Services Task Force Evidence Syntheses,* formerly *Systematic Evidence Reviews,* no. 36 (2005): i-S-1; Evelyn P. Whitlock and others, "Effectiveness of Primary Care Interventions for Weight Management in Children and Adolescents: An Updated, Targeted Systematic Review for the USPSTF," *U.S. Preventive Services Task Force Evidence Syntheses,* no. 76 (2010): i-168; Bridget Wilcken and Veronica Wiley, "Newborn Screening," *Pathology* 40, no. 2 (2008): 104–15.

9. J. F. Hagan, J. S. Shaw, and P. Duncan, "Bright Futures Guidelines for Health Supervision of Infants, Children, and Adolescents," 3d ed. (Elk Grove Village, Ill: American Academy of Pediatrics, 2008).

10. A. Sheiham, "Dental Caries Affects Body Weight, Growth, and Quality of Life in Pre-School Children," *British Dental Journal* 201, no. 10 (2006): 625–26.

11. American Academy of Pediatric Dentistry, "Guideline on Periodicity of Examination, Preventive Dental Services, Anticipatory Guidance/Counseling, and Oral Treatment for Infants, Children, and Adolescents," *American Academy of Pediatric Dentistry 2010–11 Definitions, Oral Health Policies, and Clinical Guidelines,* pp. 93–100 (Chicago: 2010).

12. In some instances, the conditions may result in a child's death. This death can be sudden or prolonged, and raises end-of-life issues for parents that are enormously important but also complex and outside the scope of this paper.

13. Committee on Pediatric Research, "Race/Ethnicity, Gender, Socioeconomic Status: Research Exploring Their Effects on Child Health: A Subject Review," *Pediatrics* 105, no. 6 (2000): 1349–51.

14. J. Currie and W. Lin, "Chipping Away at Health: More on the Relationship between Income and Child Health," *Health Affairs* 26 (2007): 331–44.

15. Committee on Pediatric Research, "Race/Ethnicity, Gender, Socioeconomic Status" (see note 12).

16. Owens and others, "Annual Report on Health Care for Children and Youth in the United States" (see note 1).

17. Barbara Bloom, Robin A. Cohen, and Gulnur Freeman, "Summary Health Statistics for U.S. Children: National Health Interview Survey, 2008," *Vital and Health Statistics*, Series 10, Data from the National Health Survey, no. 244 (2009): 1–81.

18. Merle McPherson and others, "A New Definition of Children with Special Health Care Needs," *Pediatrics* 102, no. 1, pt. 1 (1998): 137–40; Paul W. Newacheck and Sue E. Kim, "A National Profile of Health Care Utilization and Expenditures for Children with Special Health Care Needs," *Archives of Pediatrics and Adolescent Medicine* 159 (2005): 10–17; Ruth E. K. Stein and Ellen J. Silver, "Comparing Different Definitions of Chronic Conditions in a National Data Set," *Ambulatory Pediatrics* 2, no. 1 (2002): 63–70; Ruth E. Stein, Lauren E. Westbrook, and Laurie J. Bauman, "The Questionnaire for Identifying Children with Chronic Conditions: A Measure Based on a Noncategorical Approach," *Pediatrics* 99, no. 4 (1997): 513–21; Christina D. Bethell and others, "Comparison of the Children with Special Health Care Needs Screener to the Questionnaire for Identifying Children with Chronic Conditions—Revised," *Ambulatory Pediatrics* 2, no. 1 (2002): 49–57.

19. John M. Neff and others, "Identifying and Classifying Children with Chronic Conditions Using Administrative Data with the Clinical Risk Group Classification System," *Ambulatory Pediatrics* 2, no. 1 (2002): 71–79; Newacheck and Kim, "A National Profile of Health Care Utilization and Expenditures for Children with Special Health Care Needs" (see note 17); Paul W. Newacheck and others, "An Epidemiologic Profile of Children with Special Health Care Needs," *Pediatrics* 102, no. 1, pt. 1 (1998): 117–23.

20. Health Resources and Services Administration, U.S. Department of Health and Human Services, Maternal and Child Health Bureau, "The National Survey of Children with Special Health Care Needs Chartbook 2005–2006" (Rockville, Md.: 2008).

21. Jeanne Van Cleave and Matthew M. Davis, "Preventive Care Utilization among Children with and without Special Health Care Needs: Associations with Unmet Need," *Ambulatory Pediatrics* 8, no. 5 (2008): 305–11.

22. Nienke P. Dosa and others, "Excess Risk of Severe Acute Illness in Children with Chronic Health Conditions," *Pediatrics* 107, no. 3 (2001): 499–504.

23. Institute of Medicine, *To Err Is Human: Building a Safer Health System*, edited by L.T . Kohn, J. M. Corrigan, and M. S. Donaldson (Washington: National Academy Press, 2000).

24. H. Markel, "When Hospitals Kept Children from Parents," *New York Times,* January 1, 2008 (www.nytimes.com/2008/01/01/health/01visi.html).

25. Ibid.

26. "Children, Families, and Hospitals: Association for the Care of Children's Health Survey," *Children Today* 18, no. 4 (1989).

27. Children, Youth and Women's Health Service, "Parenting and Child Health: Children in Hospital" (www.cyh.com/HealthTopics/HealthTopicDetails.aspx?p=114&np=141&id=1472); Edward A. Mason, "The Hospitalized Child—His Emotional Needs," *New England Journal of Medicine* 272 (1965): 406–14; H. Platt, "The Welfare of Sick Children in Hospital," *The Platt Report* (London: Her Majesty's Stationery Office, 1959).

28. P. A. LaRosa-Nash and J. M. Murphy, "An Approach to Pediatric Perioperative Care. Parent-Present Induction," *Nursing Clinics of North America* 32, no. 1 (1997): 183–99.

29. R. Wayne Wolfram and Edwin D. Turner, "Effects of Parental Presence during Children's Venipuncture," *Academic Emergency Medicine* 3, no. 1 (1996): 58–64.

30. K. S. Powers and J. S. Rubenstein, "Family Presence during Invasive Procedures in the Pediatric Intensive Care Unit: A Prospective Study," *Archives of Pediatrics and Adolescent Medicine* 153, no. 9 (1999): 955–58.

31. Nanette C. Dudley and others, "The Effect of Family Presence on the Efficiency of Pediatric Trauma Resuscitations," *Annals of Emergency Medicine* 53, no. 6 (2009): 777–84.e3.

32. Zeev N. Kain and others, "Family-Centered Preparation for Surgery Improves Perioperative Outcomes in Children: A Randomized Controlled Trial," *Anesthesiology* 106, no. 1 (2007): 65–74.

33. Terri L. Shelton and Jennifer Smith Stepanek, *Family-Centered Care for Children Needing Specialized Health and Developmental Services* (Bethesda, Md.: Association for the Care of Children's Health, 1994).

34. D. K. Fina and others, "Parent Participation in the Postanesthesia Care Unit: Fourteen Years of Progress at One Hospital," *Journal of Perianesthesia Nursing* 12, no. 3 (1997): 152–62.

35. Janet Heaton and others, "Families' Experiences of Caring for Technology-Dependent Children: A Temporal Perspective," *Health & Social Care in the Community* 13, no. 5 (2005): 441–50.

36. Ibid.

37. Cindy K. Goodman, "Caring for an Ill Child: A Challenge for Working Parents," *Miami Herald,* September 14, 2010 (www.miamiherald.com/2010/09/14/1825099/caring-for-an-ill-child.html).

38. Karen Kuhlthau and others, "The Well-Being of Parental Caregivers of Children with Activity Limitations," *Maternal and Child Health Journal* 14, no. 2 (2010): 155–63.

39. Karen Kuhlthau and others, "Financial Burden for Families of Children with Special Health Care Needs," *Maternal and Child Health Journal* 9, no. 2 (2005): 207–18.

40. Megumi J. Okumura and others, "Understanding Factors Associated with Work Loss for Families Caring for CSHCN," *Pediatrics* 124, Suppl. 4 (2009): S392–S98.

41. Michelle L. Rogers and Dennis P. Hogan, "Family Life with Children with Disabilities: The Key Role of Rehabilitation," *Journal of Marriage and Family* 65, no. 4 (2003): 818–33.

42. Christopher J. Hartnick and others, "Final Validation of the Pediatric Tracheotomy Health Status Instrument (PTHSI)," *Otolaryngology—Head And Neck Surgery* 126, no. 3 (2002): 228–33.

43. Dana Lee Baker and Laurie A. Drapela, "Mostly the Mother: Concentration of Adverse Employment Effects on Mothers of Children with Autism," *Social Science Journal* 47, no. 3 (2010): 578–92.

44. Ute Thyen, Karen Kuhlthau, and James M. Perrin, "Employment, Child Care, and Mental Health of Mothers Caring for Children Assisted by Technology," *Pediatrics* 103, no. 6, pt. 1 (1999): 1235–42.

45. Rani Ghose, "Complications of a Medically Complicated Child," *Annals of Internal Medicine* 139, no. 4 (2003): 301–02.

46. Patient Protection and Affordable Care Act (see note 6); Health-Related portions of the Health Care and Education Reconciliation Act, 124 Stat. 1029 thru 124 Stat. 1084, H.R. 4872 (2010).

47. American Academy of Pediatricians, National Center for Medical Home Implementation, (www.medicalhomeinfo.org).

48. K. McDonald and others, *Closing the Quality Gap: A Critical Analysis of Quality Improvement Strategies,* Vol. 7, *Care Coordination,* Technical Review 9 (Rockville, Md.: Agency for Healthcare Research and Quality, June 2007).

49. C. B. Forrest and others, "Coordination of Specialty Referrals and Physician Satisfaction with Referral Care," *Archives of Pediatrics and Adolescent Medicine* 154, no. 5 (2000): 499–506; C. B. Forrest and others, "Gatekeeping and Referral of Children and Adolescents to Specialty Care," *Pediatrics* 104, no. 1 (1999): 28-34; C. J. Stille and others, "Determinants and Impact of Generalist-Specialist Communication about Pediatric Outpatient Referrals," *Pediatrics* 118, no. 4 (2006): 1341–49; C. J. Stille and others, "Generalist-Subspecialist Communication about Children with Chronic Conditions: An Analysis of Physician Focus Groups," *Ambulatory Pediatrics* 3, no. 3 (2003): 147–53; P. Franks and others, "Gatekeeping Revisited: Protecting Patients from Overtreatment," *New England Journal of Medicine* 327, no. 6 (1992): 424–29; M. O. Roland and others, "Improving Care: A Study of Orthopaedic Outpatient Referrals," *BMJ* 302, no. 6785 (1991): 1124–28; T. K. Gandhi and others, "Communication Breakdown in the Outpatient Referral Process," *Journal of General Internal Medicine* 15, no. 9 (2000): 626–31; R. M. Epstein, "Communication between Primary Care Physicians and Consultants," *Archives of Family Medicine* 4, no. 5 (1995): 403–09; R. O. Cummins and others, "Communication Failure in Primary Care: Failure of Consultants to Provide Follow-up Information," *JAMA* 243, no. 16 (1980): 1650–52; S. J. McPhee and others, "How Good Is Communication between Primary Care Physicians and Subspecialty Consultants?" *Archives of Internal Medicine* 144, no. 6 (1984): 1265–68; T. Lee and others, "Impact of Inter-Physician Communication on the Effectiveness of Medical Consultations," *American Journal of Medicine* 74, no. 1 (1983): 106–12.

50. Mercer Inc, "The Total Financial Impact of Employee Absences: Survey Highlights" (Kronos Incorporated, October 2008) (www.kronos.com/absenceanonymous/media/mercer-survey-highlights.pdf).

51. Marcia Carruthers and Vimadalal Nazneen, "Double Whammy of Absence Costs Has Employers Searching for Answers," *Employee Benefit News* (www.ebn.benefitnews.com/news/double-whammy-of-absence-costs-has-employers-searching-for-answers-2672410-1.html).

52. Commerce Clearing House, "CCH 2007 Annual Unscheduled Absence Survey: CCH Survey Finds Most Employees Call in Sick for Reasons Other than Illness" (www.cch.com/press/news/2007/20071010h.asp).

53. WorldatWork, "FMLA Practices and Perspectives" (www.worldatwork.org/waw/adimLink?id=25672).

54. J. Schleifer, "FMLA Intermittent Leave Abuse: 7 Ways to Curb It Now!" *HR Daily Advisor* (www.hrdailyadvisor.blr.com/archive/2007/01/24/Curb_FMLA_Family_and_Medical_Leave_Act_intermittent_leave_abuse.aspx).

55. Ron Z. Goetzel and others, "Health, Absence, Disability, and Presenteeism Cost Estimates of Certain Physical and Mental Health Conditions Affecting U.S. Employers," *Journal of Occupational and Environmental Medicine* 46, no. 4 (2004): 398–412.

56. Lisa Clemans-Cope and others, "Access to and Use of Paid Sick Leave among Low-Income Families with Children," *Pediatrics* 122, no. 2 (2008): e480–e86; S. Jody Heymann, Sara Toomey, and Frank Furstenberg, "Working Parents: What Factors Are Involved in Their Ability to Take Time Off from Work When Their Children Are Sick?" *Archives of Pediatrics and Adolescent Medicine* 153, no. 8 (1999): 870–74.

57. World Adult Labour, "Raising the Global Floor: Adult Labour Leave for Children's Health Needs" (Montreal: McGill Institute for Health and Social Policy) (www.raisingtheglobalfloor.org/policies/policy-selection.php?policy=leavelc).

58. Tom W. Smith and Jibum Kim, "Paid Sick Days: Attitudes and Experiences" (NORC/University of Chicago, 2010).

59. World Adult Labour, "Raising the Global Floor" (see note 56).

60. Ibid.

61. Wen-Jui Han and Jane Waldfogel, "Parental Leave: The Impact of Recent Legislation on Parents' Leave Taking," *Demography* 40, no. 1 (2003): 191–200.

62. David Cantor and others, "Balancing the Needs of Families and Employers: Family and Medical Leave Surveys" (Rockville, Md.: Westat and U.S. Department of Labor, 2001).

63. Smith and Kim, "Paid Sick Days" (see note 57).

64. California Paid Leave Law, S. 1661, 2002.

65. "Paid Family Leave Benefits," California Employment Development Department (www.edd.ca.gov/Disability/PFL_Benefit_Amounts.htm).

66. Family Leave Insurance, New Jersey Senate, S786/A873, 2008; Bill Establishing Family and Medical Leave Insurance, Washington State Senate, S.B.5659, 2007.

67. Jodi Grant, Taylor Hatcher, and Nirali Patel, "Expecting Better: A State-by-State Analysis of Paid Leave Programs," National Partnership for Women and Families (www.nationalpartnership.org/site/DocServer/ParentalLeaveReportMay05.pdf?docID=1052).

68. National Partnership for Women & Families, "State and Local Action on Paid Sick Days as of July 2010" (www.nationalpartnership.org/site/DocServer/Paid_Sick_Days_Tracking_Update_July_2010.pdf?docID=1922); Accrued Sick and Safe Leave Act of 2008, DC Law 17-152.

69. Christina Fluet and others, "Three Workplace Models for Children with Special Needs," *Journal of Workplace Behavioral Health* 23, no. 3 (2008): 245–62.

70. World Adult Labour, "Raising the Global Floor" (see note 56); Jody Heymann, Kate Penrose, and Alison Earle, "Meeting Children's Needs: How Does the United States Measure Up?" *Merrill-Palmer Quarterly* 52, no. 2 (2006): 189–215.

71. Heymann, Penrose, and Earle, "Meeting Chidren's Needs" (see note 69).

72. Ibid.

73. Federation of European Employers, "National Labour Laws, Denmark" (www.fedee.com/natlaw.html).

74. "Danish Consolidation Act on Benefits in the Event of Illness or Childbirth" (www.legislationline.org/documents/action/popup/id/5767); "Economy of the Municipalities" (www.kl.dk/English/Artikler/45802/2008/05/The-Economy-of-the-Municipalities).

75. Federation of European Employers, "National Labour Laws" (www.fedee.com/natlaw.html#sweden).

76. Federation of European Employers, "Sweden: Summary of Social Security and Private Employee Benefits," SPP Livförsäkring AB (www.igpinfo.com/igpinfo/shared/country_info/summaries/sweden.pdf); Invest:Sweden, "Working in Sweden: Employee Guide" (www.investsweden.se/Global/Global/Downloads/Fact_Sheets/Working-in-Sweden--employee-guide.pdf).

77. Practical Law Company, "PLC Cross-Border Labor and Employee Benefits Handbook 2009/10" (www.hg.org/article.asp?id=19416).

78. Han and Waldfogel, "Parental Leave" (see note 60).

79. "Paid Family Leave Benefits" (see note 64).

80. Mark A. Schuster and others, "Awareness and Use of California's Paid Family Leave Insurance among Parents of Chronically Ill Children," *JAMA* 300, no. 9 (2008): 1047–55.

81. Ibid.

82. Ruth Milkman, "New Data on Paid Family Leave" (Los Angeles: California Family Leave Research Project, UCLA Institute for Research on Labor and Employment, 2008).

83. Eileen Applebaum and Ruth Milkman, "Leaves That Pay: Employer and Worker Experiences with Paid Family Leave in California" (Washington: Center for Economic and Policy Research) (www.cepr.net/documents/publications/paid-family-leave-1-2011.pdf).

Families and Elder Care in the Twenty-First Century

Ann Bookman and Delia Kimbrel

Summary

Although most Americans know that the U.S. population is aging, they are far less informed about the reality of providing elders with personal care, health care, and social support. Families—particularly women—have always been critical in providing elder care, but the entry of so many women into the paid labor force has made elder care increasingly difficult.

Ann Bookman and Delia Kimbrel show how changes in both work and family life are complicating families' efforts to care for elderly relatives. Because almost 60 percent of elder caregivers today are employed, many forms of caregiving must now be "outsourced" to nonfamily members. And because elders are widely diverse by race and socioeconomic status, their families attach differing cultural meanings to care and have widely different resources with which to accomplish their care goals. Although the poorest elders have access to some subsidized services, and the wealthiest can pay for services, many middle-class families cannot afford services that allow elders to age in their homes and avoid even more costly institutional care.

Six key groups—health care providers, nongovernmental community-based service providers, employers, government, families, and elders themselves—are engaged in elder care, but their efforts are often fragmented and uncoordinated. All six groups must be able to work in concert and to receive the resources they need. Both employer and government policies must be improved. Although large businesses have taken up the elder care challenge, most small and mid-sized firms still do not offer flexible work arrangements. Social Security and Medicare have provided critical support to families caring for elders, yet both face significant financial short-falls. The Older American Act and the National Family Caregiver Support Program have broadened access to elder services, but need updating to address the needs of today's employed caregivers and elders who want to "age in place." And just over half of the nation's workforce is eligible for the unpaid leave benefits provided by the Family and Medical Leave Act.

The authors close by reflecting on the need for a coordinated, cross-sector movement to create an "aging-friendly" society in the United States—a society that values well-being across the life span and supports citizens from diverse cultures and income levels as they age.

www.futureofchildren.org

Ann Bookman is a visiting scholar and senior lecturer, adjunct, and Delia Kimbrel is a doctoral candidate, at the Heller School for Social Policy and Management at Brandeis University.

For most of the nation's history, caring for the elderly was a family affair carried out largely by women in the home. As the twenty-first century unfolds, however, elder care in the United States is an increasingly complex enterprise, with much personal care "outsourced" to paid nonfamily caregivers. Today elder care is a multisector undertaking with six key stakeholder groups—health care providers, nongovernmental community-based service agencies, employers, government, families, and elders themselves. The six groups, however, often work separately, or even at cross-purposes. They must be better integrated and resourced to ensure that seniors can age with dignity, families can receive appropriate supports, and society can manage the costs associated with geriatric health care and elder economic security.

In this article we examine the changing demographics of elders and families; what it means to engage in care work of an elderly parent or relative; how caregiving varies by race, gender, and socioeconomic status; and institutional responses to the challenges of caregiving from employers and the government. We close with reflections on the need for a coordinated, cross-sector movement to create an "aging-friendly" society in the United States—a society that values well-being across the life course and seeks multi-generational solutions.

Changing Demographics

With the numbers of older Americans rapidly growing ever larger, the landscape of elder care in the United States is changing. During the past century, the population of Americans aged sixty-five and older increased eleven-fold.[1] According to the 2010 census, 13 percent of the population, or 40.3 million individuals, were sixty-five or older.[2] The population share of those aged eighty-five and older, sometimes called the "oldest old," was 1.1 percent. By 2030 approximately 80 million Americans, or 20 percent of the population, are projected to be sixty-five or older, and 2.3 percent of the population will be eighty-five and older.[3]

In addition to its increasing numbers over the coming decades, the elderly population will change in a variety of ways—more people will live longer and healthier lives, the number of older males will grow, and the group's racial and ethnic diversity will increase.[4] But not all trends are positive. Although the poverty rate among the elderly fell from 25 percent in 1970 to 13 percent in 1992, as the real median income of both males and females increased,[5] in 2009, approximately 12.9 percent of people 65 and older still had incomes at the poverty level.[6] The Great Recession that began in 2007 eroded the economic status of moderate-income and middle-class elders, many of whom saw their pensions and 401(k)s decrease, the value of their homes decline, and their other financial investments lose value.[7]

Clearly these changes in the nation's elderly population will present challenges to family members who help provide elder care. And other national demographic shifts—delayed marriage and childbearing for young adults, decreased family size, and changes in family composition and structure—are complicating that challenge. Increased longevity among elders not only extends the years of caregiving by their adult children but may require their grandchildren to become caregivers as well. Married couples may have as many as four elderly parents living; in fact, they may have more parents or relatives in need of care than they have children living at home or on their own. In the past, research on elder care focused on the challenges facing working adults who were caring for both children and elderly parents—the so-called *sandwich generation*—a term coined by sociologist Dorothy Miller to refer to specific generational inequalities in the exchange of resources and support.[8] Miller's research highlighted the stress on the middle generation of employees who are caring for two groups of dependents while receiving little support. The sandwich metaphor, however, is outmoded in several respects: it does not convey that more than one generation may provide elder care or that members of any generational cohort can be both caregivers and care receivers. Nor does the image of static layers do justice to the dynamic interaction between generations, such as transfers of financial aid, sharing residential space, or exchanging personal and emotional care.

Today researchers are increasingly finding that adults may spend more years caring for their parents than caring for their children.[9] And because families today tend to be small, middle-aged adults may have smaller sibling networks to share elder care responsibilities. In short, elder care in the United States is a demanding task, and caregivers, especially the almost 60 percent of family caregivers who are employed, are finding it harder to undertake that task alone.[10]

Care Work and the Dimensions of Elder Caregiving

There is an extensive body of research on family "care work" dating back to the 1960s with a study that challenged the "myth of the abandoned elderly" and showed that families were still caring for elders, but that changes in external conditions in the family, the workplace, and the community were making caregiving more challenging.[11]

One of the contributions of recent care work research is to draw attention to the "work" aspects of caregiving. This framing contradicts personal and cultural ideas about why families care for elders and makes two related arguments: the first is that because family caregiving is largely done by women and is unpaid, it is often devalued; the second is that despite this devaluing, unpaid care work adds huge value to U.S. society in providing much needed care and "services" to the most vulnerable in the nation's population. Some scholars have tried to calculate the monetary value of unpaid care work to strengthen the argument about its value. Estimates vary from $196 billion a year, calculated in 1997,[12] to $257 billion a year based on a subsequent study by the United Hospital Fund in 2004.[13] In either case, the numbers far exceed what the United States spends on home health care and nursing home care, underscoring the importance of family care.

To differentiate the work families provide from the work that professionals and paraprofessionals provide, many studies of caregiving use the terms "informal care" to refer to the care provided by families and "formal care" to refer to that provided by trained health and social service staff. The distinction creates a sharp line between the informal care that is unpaid and takes place in private homes and the formal care that is paid and takes place in institutional and community settings. The distinction, however, has been challenged by some elder care scholars who find that family caregivers of elders provide care in hospitals, rehabilitation facilities, outpatient clinics, and community agencies. Family caregivers are a "shadow workforce" in the geriatric health care system.[14] Some states are piloting "cash and counseling" programs to pay families for the elder care they do, so the paid-unpaid distinction is being challenged in public policies.

Elder care entails a variety of supports and responsibilities, many of which can change in intensity and complexity over time. Cultural differences unique to elders and their families shape their views on what aging, health, and end of life mean and thus affect expectations about who provides care and what is provided.[15] The variations in elder care are numerous, as the following eight dimensions illustrate.

Time Dimension

Elder care takes three forms: short-term, intermittent, and long-term. Elderly parents may, for example, have surgery that immobilizes them temporarily, but restores them to a high level of daily functioning. In such cases the care needed may be fairly intense but of short duration, and so it disrupts the caregiver's job, family, and personal life, but only temporarily. In contrast, the seven in ten care recipients who have chronic health conditions[16] may require intermittent care that entails regular trips to one or more specialists, medication management, and adjustments to household and personal routines. In such cases, the caregiver is needed frequently over a longer period and may be hard pressed to integrate caregiving demands with paid work. In other cases elder care may be long-term, lasting for months or years. Such caregiving may be required on a daily basis and can seriously complicate the caregiver's ability to maintain a job, provide care for other family members, and maintain personal and community involvement.

Since 1987 the American Association of Retired Persons (now called AARP) and the National Alliance for Caregiving (NAC) have conducted several national surveys tracking the time Americans invest in elder care.[17] The most recent survey, in 2009, found intermittent elder care to be the type most commonly

Today researchers are increasingly finding that adults may spend more years caring for their parents than caring for their children.

provided. Caregivers surveyed in that poll report providing such care for an average of 4.6 years; 31 percent report giving such care for more than five years.[18] Half of all of caregivers spend eight hours or less a week, while 12 percent spend more than forty hours. Short-term or intermittent care may evolve into long-term care as an elder's physical or mental function, or both, deteriorates.

Geographic Dimension

The distance between an elder's place of residence and that of the caregiver has a major effect on the type and frequency of care. Because some American families are mobile—about 16 percent of families move each year[19]—adult children sometimes live in different cities, states, or even regions from their elderly parents. According to the most recent AARP-NAC survey data, 23 percent of caregivers live with the elder for whom they are caring (co-residence is particularly common among low-income caregivers) and 51 percent live twenty minutes away.[20]

Long-distance caregiving, however, has been on the rise over the past fifteen years.[21] One study by MetLife finds that at least 5 million caregivers live an hour or more away from the elder for whom they care.[22] Of this group, about 75 percent provide help with daily activities, such as shopping, transportation, and managing household finances. Most long-distance caregivers share responsibilities with siblings or paid caregivers, or both. Several studies document that adult children who live near an elderly relative are most likely to provide the majority of elder care,[23] underscoring the importance of geographic location.

Residential Dimension

To move, or not to move? Many elders struggle with this question, and often turn to family caregivers for help with the answer. Most elders want to live in their own homes and neighborhoods; for some, safety and accessibility require home renovations. Family caregivers may plan, organize, and finance adaptations in an elder's living space. Not all elders and all caregivers are home-owners (some are renters), which can pose particular challenges for all parties.[24] When it is not feasible for elders to adapt their dwelling, moving becomes necessary. In that case, caregivers often research, plan, and organize the move. Some elders move to continuing care retirement communities that provide different types of units for residents of different abilities.[25] Although such communities have grown in popularity, and may relieve families of some responsibilities, the units are expensive to buy, and monthly maintenance fees are costly, thus making this option unaffordable for most elders.

A small share of elders lives in rehabilitation facilities, usually on a short-term basis. Between 5 and 6 percent of elders live in a long-term-care facility or nursing home, with caregivers making regular or intermittent trips to visit and monitor the care being provided. Most elders live in their own homes,[26] which must be constantly assessed for safety and the availability of community services such as transportation, social services, and recreational opportunities. Nongovernmental organizations (NGOs) help maintain more than 10 million elders a day with long-term care supports and services so they can continue to live in their homes independently.[27] To help caregivers assess what is required for independent living, researchers have developed tools that can aid in choosing appropriate housing and support services.[28]

Financial Dimension

The economic resources available to caregiving families vary widely. Upper-middle-class and affluent families usually have adequate funds to pay for elder care services, while poor families are usually eligible for a variety of subsidized services, such as home health care. The hardest-hit families are the working poor and those with moderate incomes, who are too "rich" to qualify for subsidized services but unable to pay for care themselves. Many families caring for elderly relatives encounter this type of "middle-class squeeze."

Researchers who explore the financial dimension of elder care find that cross-generational transfers are fairly common. In a 2005 study, 29 percent of baby boomers provided financial assistance to a parent in the previous year, while about a fifth received financial support from a parent.[29] A recent nationally representative survey of elders over sixty-five offers a slightly different picture: half of these elders say they have given money to their adult children, while about a third say they help their adult children with child care, errands, housework, and home repairs. When asked what their adult children give them, more than 40 percent report receiving help with errands and rides to appointments; about a third, help with housework and home repairs; and about a fifth, help with bill paying and direct financial support.[30] What is striking is that care, time, and money are being exchanged between the generations, going both ways.

Health Dimension

Some caregivers provide help in a short-term acute health care crisis, others care for elders with one or more chronic diseases, and a third group cares for elders with long-term incurable or progressive diseases. Families are a critical resource for the nation's health care system when they care for a relative with a debilitating disease, such as dementia or Alzheimer's, for which paid care is very expensive. Giving such care, however, is a major burden on these families, who frequently find that caregiver training—both how to manage the behavior and symptoms of the elder *and* how to cope with their own feelings—is often not available.[31]

The health status of an elder determines the extent of a caregiver's involvement with personal care, often referred to as activities of daily living, such as eating, bathing, toileting, and dressing, or as instrumental activities of daily living, such as cooking, shopping, and bill paying. The health status of the elder also shapes the extent of caregivers' involvement in medical tasks such as giving medications; dressing wounds after surgery; checking weight, blood pressure, and blood sugar levels; and monitoring medical equipment. A national survey of caregivers found that more than 40 percent helped with one or more medical tasks, even though only one-third reported that they had the training to do so.[32] That finding underscores the "medicalization" of the care work that families are providing for elders.

One elderly cohort that is growing is "frail elders," defined as those sixty-five and older who do not live in nursing homes, but have difficulty with at least one aspect of

independent living or are severely disabled, or both. This group numbered about 10.7 million people in 2002.[33] Analyses of a national data set showed that two-thirds of frail elders receive help—an average of 177 hours a month—with personal care from an unpaid family caregiver. More than half of that help comes from their daughters, most of whom are working.[34]

Legal and Ethical Dimension

When significant declines in physical and mental health compromise elders' ability to manage their own affairs, it is usually the family caregiver who assumes some level of control, decision-making power, and ultimately legal authority such as power of attorney. Studies on the legal issues of elders often focus, particularly when financial resources are involved, on the caregiver as a source of interfamilial conflict and even elder abuse. A recent study of financial elder abuse, however, found that only 16.9 percent of the perpetrators were family members.[35]

Legal issues may also require caregivers to take on complex health-related roles, such as acting as health care proxy or setting up an advance directive or DNR (do not resuscitate) order. These steps can involve complex ethical questions and decisions, such as when to discontinue life supports for a terminally ill parent. Studies on elders at the end of life show the critical role that family caregivers play once palliative care is chosen, including assisting elders with daily living, handling medications, and making medical decisions.[36] Using ethnographic data, a study of one elderly mother and her daughter documents how this family navigated the health care system and brought their own cultural meaning to end-of-life care.[37] Other studies emphasize the high degree of stress on families with terminally ill elders, showing the unresponsiveness of some health care systems, as well as the ways in which community services can ease stress.[38]

Emotional, Moral, and Spiritual Dimension

Much of the research on elder care explores the practical daily routines involved in personal care, health care, and housing. The emotional care that families provide, although essential to the well-being of elders, is less studied and is difficult to define. The medical anthropologist Arthur Kleinman, a caregiver for his wife with Alzheimer's, argues that the emotional part of caregiving is in essence a moral act—"an existential quality of *what it is to be a human being.*"[39]

Attending to the spiritual needs of elders for whom religious experience, practice, and faith have been important is also critical to sustaining their physical and mental health and longevity.[40] For these elders, caregivers' tasks include: spiritual and well-being assessments; using a reminiscence-and-life-review approach; identifying and facilitating contact with religious services, organizations, and clergy; and discussing end-of-life issues.[41] Tailoring these tasks to an individual elder's particular faith tradition is both time-consuming and extremely meaningful.

Outsourcing Elder Care and Care Coordination

When family members cannot provide care, particularly if they are full-time workers or long-distance caregivers, or both, their job is to find an agency close to where the elder lives that will provide services for a fee. It takes time and effort to find an appropriate multiservice or aging service agency,[42] to provide the agency with detailed personal and health information about the elder to ensure a good "client-provider fit," and to

monitor services to be sure that needs are met and the elder is comfortable with the provider. Carrying out all these tasks to find just one type of service is difficult enough; if an elder needs multiple services, the work for the family can be significant.

Many studies have documented the fragmentation in the geriatric health care and social services system, and others have called for greater care coordination to support caregivers.[43] The handoffs between hospitals and families, or between rehabilitation facilities and families, can often be unsafe and unsatisfying, and the need for improved communication is widely documented.[44] Given the cross-institutional complexities, some caregivers hire a geriatric care manager—often a trained social worker—to identify, monitor, and coordinate services. Hiring a care manager requires research by the family caregiver, as well as ongoing monitoring and extensive communication. The work of care coordination is a significant, often unnoticed, aspect of care many families do themselves, either because they cannot afford to hire a geriatric care manager or because they prefer to keep an eye on things themselves.[45]

Elder Caregiving and Diversity

Most studies on aging and elder care treat elders and their caregivers as monolithic groups. But as the nation has become more diverse, so too has the population of elders. Elder caregiving varies by gender, race, and socioeconomic status, and families from African American, Latino, Asian, Native American, and other groups bring their own strengths and needs to the caregiving experience. Although gender, race, and socioeconomic status are treated separately below, it is important to note that these variables often intersect in powerful and important ways in the lives of caregivers. An "intersectionality" approach shows how unequal opportunity over the life course shapes trajectories of advantage and disadvantage for elders and the families who care for them. Future research must explore multiple aspects of diversity in order to develop new policies that address the interaction between socio-economic inequality *and* differences based on gender, race, and culture.

Gender and Elder Care

Elderly women live longer than do elderly men, and despite a lifetime of providing care to others, they are more likely than men to live alone, live in poverty, and lack care themselves when they are elderly.[46] Research on gender and caregiving has two major themes. First, the majority (67 percent) of family caregivers are women,[47] with wives providing care to spouses and adult daughters providing the majority of care to elderly parents. Second, given the persistence of gender inequality in the workforce, including the gender gap in wages, women caregivers are more likely than men to cut back on work hours or quit their jobs because of their caregiving duties and are thus left with less income, small savings, and reduced pensions.

Although women in the general population have greater elder care responsibilities than do men, recent studies reveal that employed women and employed men provide care in roughly equal numbers.[48] But gender differences persist nonetheless: employed women are more likely than employed men to provide family care on a regular basis, they spend more hours providing care, and they spend more time providing direct care such as meal preparation, household work, physical care, and transportation.[49] This finding is consistent with other evidence on gender trends in elder care showing that women tend to perform household and personal care tasks that are physically draining and likely to interrupt daily activities, while men tend to give periodic assistance.[50] Both working and nonworking male caregivers receive more assistance with their caregiving efforts than do women; they also tend to delegate their tasks to others and to seek paid assistance to alleviate some of their caregiving responsibilities.[51]

Despite the growing number of men balancing work and elder care responsibilities, women are particularly vulnerable to negative work-related consequences.[52] Women who are caring for elders generally reduce their work hours, leave the workforce, or make other adjustments that have negative financial or career implications. Some refuse overtime and pass up promotions, training, assignments that are more lucrative, jobs requiring travel, and other challenging but time-consuming job opportunities.[53] Many low-income women and women of color who are employed do not have sufficient flexibility or autonomy in their jobs to be able to take an elderly parent to the doctor or attend to other needs.[54]

Despite feelings of satisfaction from their care, caregivers can sometimes feel burdened, socially isolated, strained, and hopeless. A recent MetLife study of working caregivers, based on a large corporate employer's health risk appraisal database of roughly 17,000 respondents, found that employed women are significantly more likely than employed men caregivers to self-report negative effects on personal well-being.[55] Caregivers in general report more physical and mental health problems than noncaregivers,[56] and more female caregivers (58 percent) report negative health effects than male caregivers (42 percent).[57] In a study assessing gender differences in caregiver health,

Martin Pinquart and Silvia Sörenson found that women had lower scores for subjective well-being and perceived physical health, as well as higher scores for burden and depression than men. The effects for women caregivers indicated a positive and statistically significant relationship.[58]

The growing diversity of the United States makes it important for researchers to consider how race and ethnicity shape aging and the caregiving experience.

Race, Ethnicity, and Elder Care

The growing diversity of the United States makes it important for researchers to consider how race and ethnicity—both socially constructed categories—shape aging and the caregiving experience. The nation's legacy of racial oppression and structural inequality has created socioeconomic inequities in education, health, housing, income, and wealth. Many low-income men and women of color enter old age after a lifetime of cumulative disadvantage, during which limited access to economic opportunity has obstructed efforts to accumulate savings for retirement and limited access to health care has led to poorer health.

Few families from racial and ethnic minority groups use paid or outsourced care, and those who do can sometimes face structural barriers in accessing them. Although most Americans refrain from putting their elderly kin in nursing homes, Latinos, African Americans, and Asians are least likely to do so.[59] Even elders of color with greater care needs, such as those afflicted with dementia or chronic illnesses, are more likely than whites to receive care from their children and live in the community with them.[60]

Many studies show that families of color rely on extended kin networks and friends for financial assistance, material goods, domestic duties, and other supports.[61] African Americans, especially, rely on networks of neighbors, friends, and fellow congregants. Language and cultural barriers often lead Chinese American and Puerto Rican caregivers to use ethnically oriented organizations in their communities for support.[62]

Extensive social support may partially explain why racial and ethnic minority groups tend to have more favorable attitudes toward caregiving and higher caregiving satisfaction.[63] Studies suggest that many groups of color value mutual exchange, reciprocity, filial responsibility, and interdependence, whereas Western European and white ethnic groups value self-reliance and independence. Using well-established positive appraisal scales and coping questionnaires, several studies find a significant "race" effect, with caregivers of color such as African Americans and Latinos showing the highest appraisals of positive aspects of caregiving and higher scores on well-being measures.[64]

Among some Latino groups, the extended family is expected to provide care to older relatives,[65] and Native Americans strongly value giving back to those who have provided for them, reinforcing the value of reciprocity in their culture.[66] White caregivers report greater depression and view caregiving as more stressful than do caregivers of color.[67] Studies that have addressed racial and ethnic differences among caregivers generally have not focused on working caregivers. One that does finds that employed white caregivers report significantly higher work demand and strain than Latino and black working caregivers.[68]

Although research consistently reveals significant differences in caregiver outcomes by race, findings may vary because of differences in recruitment strategies, in criteria for inclusion and exclusion, in construct measurement, in research instruments, and in statistical techniques. The studies also vary in sample size and sampling strategy and rarely use random assignment or national probability sampling to posit any causal relationships between variables. To strengthen generalizability, accuracy of statistical findings, and comparability across studies, researchers will have to use more diverse and random sampling strategies as well as experimental and mixed qualitative and quantitative methodologies.[69]

Socioeconomic Status and Elder Care

Although researchers do not often explore the implications of socioeconomic status—defined by education, occupational status, family income, net worth, and financial assets—for elder care, it can nevertheless have important effects on elders' quality of life and the kind of care their families can provide.

In the first place, many low-income elders have insufficient resources. More than half of all senior households (54 percent) cannot meet their expenses even using their combined financial net worth, Social Security benefits, and pension incomes.[70] Among older persons reporting income in 2008, 20.3 percent had less than $10,000.[71] Such economic challenges often increase the financial

burden, hardship, and strain on their families. Many studies do show that families with higher socioeconomic status tend not to provide physical care themselves, and instead tend to purchase elder care services, provide financial gifts, buy alternative lodging, and remodel homes to accommodate an elder.[72]

A scarcity of resources makes working poor and working-class caregivers more likely to provide direct care themselves rather than to hire professional care managers. When low-income families do purchase formal services, they use them only for short periods. Middle-class and higher-income caregivers hire elder care assistance for longer periods or until their resources run out.[73]

Responses from Employers and Government

Researchers have also investigated how employers and government are responding to the challenges families face in providing elder care. Are employers, for example, providing working caregivers of elders with "family-friendly" benefits and policies? Are federal, state, and local governments meeting the needs of elders and caregivers with public policies? We explore the adequacy of their responses to the needs of both elders and family caregivers to gain insight into what policy changes may be needed in the future.

Responses from Employers

Given the aging of the population and the high rate of female labor force participation, the share of elder caregivers who are employed has been growing over the past thirty years and is expected to continue, nearing the percentage of employees with child care responsibilities. One of the earliest national estimates, based on data from the 1982 National Long-Term Care Survey and its companion National Informal Caregivers

Survey, was that 15.8 percent of elder caregivers were employed,[74] 9 percent had quit their jobs because of elder care responsibilities, and 20 percent were experiencing conflict between work and elder care.[75] Surveys conducted in the late 1980s and 1990s found the share of employed caregivers rising significantly, up to 64 percent in 1997.[76] One 2010 study found that six in ten family caregivers are employed;[77] another found that considered as a group, 50 percent of employed caregivers of elders work full time, and 11 percent work part time. In the coming years, employers will need to respond to the elder care needs of their workforce lest they compromise the performance of their firms and the retention of some of their most valued employees.

Research on work and family conflict is extensive, and many studies focus on work and elder care for employees.[78] Beyond general feelings of role conflict, working caregivers in one study report using their own sick leave or vacation hours to accommodate elder care needs (48 percent), cutting back on hours or quitting their job (37 percent), taking an additional job or increasing their hours to get funds for elder care expenses (17 percent), taking unpaid leave (15 percent), and leaving their job for a different one (14 percent).[79] Many studies report negative health consequences for employed caregivers, including increased risk of stress and depression, diabetes, hypertension, and even premature death.[80] If caregivers cut back work hours, take unpaid leaves, or leave their jobs, the negative effects can go beyond the individual caregivers themselves to include whole families. For example, a MetLife study documented negative financial repercussions for families from short-term income losses, long-term losses of retirement savings, and lost opportunities for career advancement.[81]

Researchers are also examining the policies and programs of employers to address their employees' elder care needs; rough estimates are that from 25 to 50 percent of employers offer these programs.[82] Large firms are more likely than small companies to have elder care programs, and a 2003 study estimates that 50 percent of large corporations offer such programs.[83] For small and mid-sized firms, the estimate was 26 percent in 2006 and 22 percent in 2007.[84] Studies on how the recent recession affected elder care programs are just now becoming available; one, for example, shows that most employers are maintaining workplace flexibility, although reduction of hours may translate into reduction in pay, so increased flexibility entails both costs and benefits.[85]

Elder Care Assistance Programs, introduced by companies during the late 1980s, have grown in scope. The early programs—paralleling those developed to support workers with young children—included resource and referral services to locate elder care services in the elder's community, and flexible spending accounts for putting aside funds on a pre-tax basis to cover elder care expenses.[86] During the 1990s, some companies expanded elder care benefits through Employee Assistance Programs or new "work-life programs" to include flexible work arrangements (58 percent), personal or sick leaves (16 percent), and access to short-term emergency backup care when a paid caregiver was unexpectedly absent (4 percent).[87]

During the mid-1990s, some researchers began exploring the question of whether employees made use of elder care benefits. Early studies found that use rates were low, although the range was fairly wide—from 2 to 34 percent—with use by employees in private-sector firms lower than use by public-sector employees.[88] Most scholars and human resource managers hypothesize that rates were low because employers had not publicized the programs that were available. A 2007 survey of human resource managers at Fortune 500 companies found that flexible work arrangements and leave programs were the most highly utilized and had the best use-to-cost ratio.[89] Emergency short-term home care had the lowest use rates and highest cost, and thus the worst use-to-cost ratio. In open-ended questions, respondents focused on the need for better communication about elder care programs; the importance of supervisors actively encouraging the use of these programs; and the difficulty of countering negative perceptions about these programs.[90] Although elder care benefits appear to boost employee recruitment and retention, that link has not been conclusively demonstrated.[91]

To date, the needs of employed elder caregivers far exceed the employer response, and elder care assistance tends to be offered only by the largest employers. Some studies about "family-responsive" workplaces do not even mention elder care as a benefit needed by families,[92] and the findings of studies that do focus on elder care have less than encouraging findings. The 2009 Age and Generations study found that employees who are caring for elders had less access to flexible work arrangements than did employees who were caring for their children or who had no dependent care responsibilities, that employees in the sandwich generation were less likely to be included in new projects based on teamwork than workers with no elder care demands,[93] and that employees who provide elder care had lower job security than other groups.[94] Elder care programs are still less frequently offered than child care programs, and a 2006 study found that although almost three-quarters of employers offered some child care assistance, only one-third offered elder care assistance.[95]

What accounts for employers' lag in offering elder care assistance? And how can workplaces make elder care a key component of the work-family or work-life agenda? Elder care may have received less attention than child care because ageism and denial about aging is deeply entrenched in U.S. culture. As Muriel Gillick, a palliative care physician, argues, "Contemporary Americans are eager to prevent, obliterate, or at least conceal old age…in keeping with the belief that we can control our destiny."[96] This denial can lead employers to ignore or minimize the elder care needs of their workforce, using arguments about high costs and low utilization to justify having few elder care programs.

Some work-family scholars argue that developing a family-friendly workplace is a long-term process with three distinct stages. In the first stage the goal is to promote the recognition of a particular work-family issue as a visible, legitimate need. In the second stage the goal is to implement and then refine specific programs, including effective communication and supervisor training. The third stage involves institutionalizing the new work-family programs into the culture of the workplace to heighten program reach and effectiveness.[97] In this evolutionary paradigm, different percentages of companies are at different stages in responding to elder care. Many private-sector firms and the majority of small and mid-sized firms are still in the first stage, struggling to recognize elder care programs as a legitimate need of the workforce. Roughly a third of firms are in the second stage, starting, developing, and retaining elder care programs. Only a minority of firms—mainly large companies—are in

Table 1. Institutional Responses to Aging and Elder Care from Government

Name of policy	Year started	Basic goal	Eligibility	Source of funds
Social Security Act	1935	Provide income for people who have retired from paid employment	Work in a Social Security-covered job for 10 years or more, can start collecting at age 62 up to age 70, widow(er)s at 60, disabled at 50	Payroll taxes and self-employment contributions, paid into Social Security Trust Fund by employees and employers
Medicare	1965	Coverage of health care costs, including Part A: hospital care, Part B: outpatient care, and Part D: prescription drugs	People 65 and older, who had Medicare-covered employment, not linked to income earned	Employers and employees pay taxes for Part A, funds from SSI checks cover Part B, and Part D paid for by Medicare plus private insurance
Medicaid	1965	Cover health care costs for low-income children and families, long-term care for elderly and/or disabled	Pregnant women, children, teens, elders, blind, and disabled with low incomes	Means-tested, funded by state and federal funds, managed by states
Older Americans Act (OAA)	1965	Promote the delivery of social services to aging population via Administration on Aging (AoA) and state agencies	National Elder Locator for all families, some meal programs, housing, and services for low-income elders	Taxes and other government funds, most funding for social service programs, rest goes to jobs program, research, and training
Family and Medical Leave Act	1993	Twelve weeks of job-protected unpaid leave with continuation of health benefits for own serious health condition, and/or care of seriously ill parent, child or spouse, and child rearing	Workers at firms with 50 or more employees within 75-mile radius, who worked 1,250 hours and 12 consecutive months	Payroll tax in California and New Jersey, otherwise unpaid. Administrative costs funded by states and U.S. Department of Labor
National Family Caregiver Support Program	2000, under OAA reauthorization	Referrals for services/respite care, information, counseling, training, and support groups for family caregivers	Persons of any age who serve as unpaid caregivers for persons 60 years or older	Funds from Older Americans Act, Title III E

the third stage. Making the "family-friendly workplace" an "elder-care-friendly workplace" remains an unrealized project for many employers.

Responses from Government

During the nineteenth and twentieth centuries the United States gradually transferred responsibility for elder care from the family to the government, from the private sphere to the public sphere.[98] But despite landmark twentieth-century legislation, it can be argued that the United States lacks the full range of public policies needed to address the aging of the population, and that families still bear the primary responsibility.

Table 1 briefly summarizes six public policies that are key to the well-being of elders and their family caregivers. Some have enhanced health and income security for elders; others have enhanced the supports available to both employed and nonemployed family caregivers. We briefly address the strengths and weaknesses of some of these policies to suggest possible areas for policy expansion.

Social Security is critical to providing a basic level of financial support and security to elders. Several issues, however, weaken its effectiveness. Initially the system strengthened intergenerational ties because those who retired—only 5.2 percent of the population was sixty-five or older in 1930—were reaping benefits based on the productivity of younger workers. But in the decades ahead, more people will be needing retirement income, and fewer young workers will be available to replenish Social Security funds, thus putting pressure on the younger generation and creating tension between generations.[99] In addition, because Social Security is based on wages in the paid labor force, women who delayed work, interrupted work, or never entered the workforce because of family caregiving responsibilities have smaller benefits in old age than men (though at the death of her spouse, a woman is eligible to collect a "survivor" Social Security benefit).

Medicare, a second foundational piece of economic security for elders, ensures coverage of many health care costs. It, too, however, is problematic. Originally enacted to cover the costs of acute care and hospitalization, Medicare does not provide adequate insurance for chronic illnesses, those common to most elders. Medicare does not reimburse hospitals fully for the care they provide, so many hospitals have shortened patient stays, creating difficulties for caregivers when an elder is prematurely discharged to rehab or to home. Medicare will cover a stay in a skilled nursing facility only if daily nursing or rehab services are needed, and will cover ten hours a week of home care only if skilled nursing care is required. Finally, Medicare does not cover the cost of long-term care.

Medicaid, the third key government policy, is the largest source of payment for nursing home care, and it will become increasingly important as the nation's population ages. In 2008, nearly 41 percent of the nation's nursing facility care was paid by Medicaid, averaging nearly $30,000 for each beneficiary.[100] In most states, Medicaid also pays for some long-term

care services at home and in the community. Although eligibility varies from state to state, those elders who are eligible for Medicaid assistance must have limited assets and incomes below the poverty line. They also must contribute all or most of their available income toward the cost of their care. Many elderly who enter nursing homes pay for their own care initially. Once their resources have been depleted, however, they are covered by Medicaid. According to a study by Brenda Spillman and Peter Kemper, 16 percent of Medicaid users began by paying their own way in long-term nursing facilities, exhausted their resources, and converted to Medicaid; 27 percent were covered by Medicaid when they were admitted to the nursing home.[101]

Despite their many provisions for elder support, Medicaid and Medicare leave significant gaps in coverage.

Medicaid often provides supplemental services to fill gaps left by Medicare. The Centers for Medicare and Medicaid Services estimated that Medicaid provided some additional health coverage for 8.5 million Medicare beneficiaries in 2009.[102] In addition, Medicare and Medicaid jointly fund a model program called PACE (Program of All-Inclusive Care for the Elderly), in which an interdisciplinary team, consisting of professional and paraprofessional staff, assesses participants' needs, develops care plans, and delivers all services (including acute care services and nursing facility services when necessary), which are integrated for a seamless provision of total care. The program is available to individuals fifty-five and older who are certified by the state as nursing home eligible and meet the income and assets requirements to qualify for Medicaid.[103]

Despite their many provisions for elder support, Medicaid and Medicare leave significant gaps in coverage. The new Patient Protection and Affordable Care Act of 2010 should ease some of the burdens by expanding drugs covered by Medicare Part D, the prescription drug program, improving prevention benefits such as free annual wellness visits, and changing the cost of Medicare Advantage plans. Mechanisms to control or reduce Medicare spending may or may not benefit elders, and a new Medicare and Medicaid Innovations Center holds promise of testing new payment and service delivery models that could benefit elders and their families.

A fourth important policy with implications for elder care is the Older Americans Act (OAA), passed as part of Lyndon Johnson's "Great Society" reforms and the first public policy to recognize the importance of community-based NGOs in the elder care system. Although the OAA signaled a significant effort to systematize and broaden access to elder services, studies evaluating its effectiveness have had mixed findings. For example, studies of home care programs have found that although providers have had some success in managing the daily practical needs of elders, they have been less successful in dealing with emergencies or significant health issues or levels of impairment.[104] Studies have shown that home care is more effective than inpatient care and reduces the length of hospital stays, but little data are available on how OAA programs affect measures of quality of life for elders or caregivers.[105] A book on

OAA's Long-Term Care Ombudsman Program summarizes a number of issues cited in studies of other OAA programs. These include: a misalignment of resources and goals, which compromises program effectiveness; a lack of coordination between OAA programs and resources, which diminishes program effectiveness; and a lack of elder or caregiver empowerment to take control of elders' health care or make positive programs more sustainable and cost-effective.[106]

The Family and Medical Leave Act (FMLA) is the only law that deals specifically with the challenges of working and providing elder care. A bipartisan commission that conducted two nationally representative random-sample surveys to study the impact of the FMLA on employers and employees reported to Congress in 1996 that the law was not the burden to business that some had anticipated.[107] In terms of ease of administration and impact on productivity, profitability, and performance, the law was found either to have "no noticeable effect" or, in some cases, to produce cost savings. On the employee side, the FMLA was found to be a boon to families in their caregiving roles. Most leaves were short, and concerns that employees would abuse the law and use it for recreational time off proved unwarranted. In fact, some "leave-needers" did not take advantage of the law because they could not afford an unpaid leave. The surveys were repeated in 2000 with largely comparable results for employers and employees.[108] The major complaint from the employer community was the difficulty of administering "intermittent leaves," although employees find that type of leave useful for chronic health problems. Between the 1995 and 2000 surveys there was a statistically significant increase in the use of FMLA for elder care.[109]

From a policy perspective, the FMLA is like a minimum labor standard. It provides valuable protections to workers, but has limitations that hamper its effectiveness. Access to FMLA, for example, is restricted to about 55 percent of the workforce because of eligibility requirements for firms and employees. The definition of "family" is limited to parent, child, and spouse, depriving many elderly relatives such as grandparents or aunts and uncles, as well as those who are members of the lesbian, gay, bisexual, and transgendered (LGBT) community or who are not legally married, of coverage. And because the leave provided is unpaid, it is difficult for low-income workers to use. Recently two states, California and New Jersey, passed laws to establish paid leave programs, and a new study of the California law yields useful information about the applicability of these models for other states.[110] These new state policies are contemporary examples of the historical research of sociologist Theda Skocpol, who showed that federal policy is often driven by demands from local citizen associations and the actions of state legislatures.[111]

Finally, the National Family Caregiver Support Program (NFCSP) is the first federal law to acknowledge fully the needs of caregivers regardless of their employment status. Preliminary studies have shown that the program is expanding caregivers' access to elder care information and providing needs assessments, support groups, and stress reduction programs.[112] Although NFCSP offers many excellent services, such as respite care, counseling, and training for family caregivers, the funds available to deliver them are limited, particularly in the area of respite care.[113] As with many OAA programs, the goals of the statute are not matched by the resources needed for nongovernmental agencies to carry them out. Although the

NFCSP has brought greater attention and supports to families caring for elders, particularly resources to promote caregiver health and prevent caregiver burnout, inadequate resources impair its effectiveness. Proposals for tax-based supports for caregivers or programs to pay family caregivers are appearing in state legislatures, but have yet to gain traction in Congress.

When government and employers cannot provide adequate support for elder care, family caregivers often rely on nongovernmental organizations, such as health care providers and community-based aging service agencies. Although NGOs are often created and funded by government, they are not direct policy-making organizations, and their role is beyond the scope of this article. Caregivers do, however, receive significant support, information, and services from these groups, including faith-based organizations, neighborhood centers in communities of color, LGBT advocacy organizations, and educational organizations. Because so many elder caregivers are employed, NGOs that provide services for elders and their caregivers must take the needs of employees into account.

Creating an Aging-Friendly Society

The challenges faced today by elders and their family caregivers are enormous and will continue to increase during the twenty-first century as the population ages. Families alone cannot provide elder care, employers alone cannot provide all the supports employed caregivers need, and the government alone cannot provide or fund all the elder policies required. A large-scale, cross-sector initiative is needed to coordinate efforts at the national, state, and local level and to support all citizens from diverse cultures and income levels as they age.

Public policies must move in a universal direction, like Social Security and Medicare, to help transform U.S. communities and make housing, transportation, and open space accessible to all elders. There is a pressing need to better integrate nongovernmental organizations in the health care and social service sectors and to ensure they are culturally responsive. Employers must be encouraged to give employees in both professional and hourly jobs access to flexible work arrangements including part-time work, paid leave policies, paid sick days, and other "elder-friendly" workplace benefits. Overall, these groups must work together to create a culture in which aging is seen as a natural part of the life course and caregiving is seen as a multigenerational enterprise of great value to children, adults, elders, and society.

Elders themselves and their family caregivers, as well as the public and private sectors, must build support for social investment in the next generation. Today's children will be the workers, citizens, and family caregivers who will care for the growing U.S. elderly population tomorrow. Focusing on children's healthy development and education will build their capacity to provide supportive care for the elders of future generations.

Endnotes

1. Frank B. Hobbs, "Population Profile of the United States: The Elderly Population," U.S. Census Bureau (www.census.gov/population/www/pop-profile/elderpop.html).

2. Census 2000 Brief, C2KBR/01-12, U.S. Census Bureau (2001).

3. Jennifer Cheeseman Day, *Population Projections of the United States by Age, Sex, Race, and Hispanic Origin: 1993–2050,* Current Population Reports, P25-1104, U.S. Census Bureau (1993); Administration on Aging, Table 12, "Older Population as a Percentage of the Total Population, 1900–2050" (www.aoa.gov/aoaroot/aging_statistics/future_growth/future_growth.aspx#age).

4. U.S. Census Bureau, "Age: 2000," Census 2000 Brief, October 2001 (www.census.gov/prod/2001pubs/c2kbr01-12.pdf).

5. Wan He and others, "Sixty-Five Plus in the United States," *Current Population Reports, Special Studies,* Series P23-209 (Washington: December 2005).

6. U.S. Census Bureau, Current Population Survey, Annual Social and Economic Supplements (www.census.gov/hhes/www/poverty/histpov/hstpov5.xls); U.S. Census Bureau, Historical Poverty Tables, table C, "Poverty Rates for Elderly and Non-Elderly Adults, 1966–2009."

7. The percentage of homeless adults fifty and older appears to be increasing, particularly in cities. M. William Sermons and Meghan Henry, "Demographics of Homelessness Series: The Rising Elderly Population," National Alliance to End Homelessness (April 2010).

8. Dorothy A. Milller, "The 'Sandwich' Generation: Adult Children of the Aging," *Social Work* 26, no. 5 (September, 1981): 419–23.

9. Leslie Foster Stebbins, *Work and Family in America: A Reference Handbook* (Santa Barbara, Calif.: ABC-CLIO, 2001), p. 40.

10. National Alliance for Caregiving and AARP, *Caregiving in the United States* (Washington: 2009), p. 53.

11. E. Shanas and G. F. Streib, eds., *Social Structure and the Family: Generational Relations* (Englewood Cliffs, N.J.: Prentice-Hall, 1965).

12. Peter S. Arno, Carol Levine, and M. N. Memmott, "The Economic Value of Informal Caregiving," *Health Affairs* 18, no. 2 (1999): 182–88.

13. Carol Levine, ed. *Always on Call: When Illness Turns Families into Caregivers* (Vanderbilt University Press, 2004), p. 5.

14. Ann Bookman and Mona Harrington, "Family Caregivers: A Shadow Workforce in the Geriatric Health Care System?" *Journal of Health Policy, Politics and Law* 32, no. 6 (2007): 1026.

15. Carol Levine and Thomas H. Murray, eds., *The Cultures of Caregiving: Conflict and Common Ground among Families, Health Professionals and Policy Makers* (Johns Hopkins University Press, 2004).

16. *Family Caregiving in the U.S.: Findings from a National Survey* (Washington: National Alliance for Caregiving and the American Association of Retired Persons, 1997).

17. Donna Wagner, *Comparative Analysis of Caregiver Data for Caregivers to the Elderly, 1987 and 1997* (Bethesda, Md.: National Alliance for Caregiving, June 1997).

18. National Alliance for Caregiving, *Caregiving in the U.S.*, National Alliance for Caregiving in collaboration with the AARP (November 2009), p. 5.

19. "What Moves Americans to Move?" Census 2000, U.S. Census Bureau (http://usgovinfo.about.com/library/weekly/aa060401a.htm).

20. National Alliance for Caregiving, *Caregiving in the U.S.* (see note 18), p. 14.

21. Linda K. Bledsoe, Sharon E. Moore, and Lott Collins, "Long Distance Caregiving: An Evaluative Review of the Literature," *Ageing International* (New York: Springer Science, 2010); Beverly Koerin and Marcia Harrigan, "P.S. I Love You: Long Distance Caregiving," *Journal of Gerontological Social Work* 40, no. 1/2 (2003): 63–81.

22. MetLife, *Miles Away: The MetLife Study of Long-Distance Caregiving* (Westport, Conn.: MetLife Mature Market Institute, July 2004).

23. S. H. Matthews and T. T. Rosner, "Shared Filial Responsibility: The Family as the Primary Caregiver," *Journal of Marriage and the Family* 50, no. 1 (1998): 278–86; E. P. Stoller, L. E. Forster, and T. S. Duniho, "Systems of Parent Care within Sibling Networks," *Research on Aging* 14, no. 1 (1992): 472–92.

24. E. Fuller-Thompson and M. Minkler, "Housing Issues and Realities Faced by Grandparent Caregivers Who Are Renters," *Gerontologist* 43, no. 1 (2003): 92–98.

25. Continuing care retirement communities include "independent living" units for those who can still care for themselves; "assisted living" units for those who need some daily help with personal care; and "long-term-care" beds for those who are no longer able to take care of themselves.

26. National Alliance for Caregiving, *Caregiving in the U.S.* (see note 18), p. 14.

27. National Council on Aging, "Long-Term Services and Supports" (www.ncoa.org/independence-dignity/long-term-services-supports.html).

28. J. Keefe and others, "Caregivers' Aspirations, Realities, and Expectations: The CARE Tool," *Journal of Applied Gerontology* 27, no. 3 (2008): 286–308.

29. Pew Research Center, "From the Age of Aquarius to the Age of Responsibility: Baby Boomers Approach Age 60, A Social Trends Report" (2005), pp. 10–13.

30. Pew Research Center, *Growing Old in America: Expectations vs. Reality*, A Social and Demographic Trends Report (June 2009), p. 11.

31. E. Papastavrou and others, "Caring for a Relative with Dementia: Family Caregiver Burden" (JAN Original Research, Blackwell Publishing, Ltd., 2007).

32. Karen Donelan and others, "Challenged to Care: Informal Caregivers in a Changing Health Care System," *Health Affairs* 21, no. 4 (2002): 222–31 (http://content.healthaffairs.org/cgi/content/full/21/4/222).

33. R. Johnson and J. Wiener, *A Profile of Frail Older Americans and Their Caregivers*, The Retirement Project, Occasional Paper 8 (Washington: Urban Institute, 2006).

34. Ibid, p. 24.

35. MetLife, *Broken Trust: Elders, Family, and Finances* (Westport, Conn.: MetLife Mature Market Institute, 2009), p. 12.

36. Joshua Hauser and Betty Kramer, "Family Caregivers in Palliative Care," *Clinics in Geriatric Medicine* 20, no. 4 (November 2004): 671–88.

37. Luisa Margulies, *My Mother's Hip: Lessons from the World of Elder Care* (Philadelphia: Temple University Press, 2004).

38. Kevin Brazil, Daryl Bainbridge, and Christine Rodriguez, "The Stress Process in Palliative Cancer Care: A Qualitative Study on Informal Caregiving and Its Implication for the Delivery of Care," *American Journal of Hospice and Palliative Medicine* 27, no. 2 (2010): 111–16.

39. Arthur Kleinman, "On Caregiving: A Scholar Experiences the Moral Acts That Come Before—and Go Beyond—Modern Medicine," *Harvard Magazine* (July–August 2010): 27.

40. David O. Moberg, ed., *Aging and Spirituality: Spiritual Dimensions of Aging Theory, Research, Practice, and Policy* (Binghamton, N.Y.: Haworth Press, 2001).

41. M. Crowther and others, "Spiritual and Emotional Well-Being Tasks Associated with Elder Care," *Geriatric Care Management Journal* 13, no. 1 (Winter/Spring 2003): 15–21.

42. The Administration on Aging has a website to help families find an agency near where their elderly relative lives (www.eldercare.gov/Eldercare.NET/Public/Home.aspx).

43. T. Semla, "How to Improve Coordination of Care," *Annals of Internal Medicine* 148, no. 8 (April 15, 2008): 627–28.

44. Grif Alspach, "Handing Off Critically Ill Patients to Family Caregivers: What Are Your Best Practices?" *Critical Care Nurse* 29, no. 3 (2009): 12–22.

45. Bookman and Harrington, "Family Caregivers" (see note 14).

46. Laura Katz Olsen, *The Not-So-Golden Years: Caregiving, the Frail Elderly, and the Long-Term Care Establishment* (Lanham, Md.: Rowman & Littlefield Publishers, Inc., 2003), p. 98; Nancy R. Hooyman, "Research on Older Women: Where Is Feminism?" *Gerontologist* 39, no.1 (1999): 115–18.

47. National Alliance for Caregiving and AARP, *Caregiving in the U.S.: A Focused Look at Those Caring for Someone Age 50 or Older* (Washington, 2009), p. 22.

48. Kerstin Aumann and others, *Working Family Caregivers of the Elderly: Everyday Realities and Wishes for Change* (New York: Families and Work Institute, 2010), p. 2.

49. Ibid.

50. Lynn M. Martire and Mary Ann Parris Stephens, "Juggling Parent Care and Employment Responsibilities: The Dilemmas of Adult Daughter Caregivers in the Workforce," *Sex Roles* 48, no. 3/4 (2003): 167–73.

51. Olsen, *The Not-So-Golden Years* (see note 46).

52. Margaret B. Neal and Donna L. Wagner, "Working Caregivers: Issues, Challenges, and Opportunities for the Aging Network," *National Family Caregiver Support Program Issue Brief* (2002): 1–31.

53. Susan C. Eaton, "Eldercare in the United States: Inadequate, Inequitable, but Not a Lost Cause," *Feminist Economics* 11, no. 2 (2005): 37–51; MetLife Mature Market Institute, *Employer Costs for Working Caregivers* (Washington: MetLife Mature Market Institute and National Alliance for Caregivers, 1997).

54. Karen Bullock, Sybil L. Crawford, and Sharon L. Tennstedt, "Employment and Caregiving: Exploration of African American Caregivers," *Social Work* 48, no. 2 (2003): 150–62.

55. MetLife, *MetLife Study of Working Caregivers and Employer Health Costs* (Westport, Conn.: National Alliance for Caregiving and MetLife Mature Market Institute, February 2010).

56. Peter P. Vitaliano, Jianping Zhang, and James M. Scanlan, "Is Caregiving Hazardous to One's Physical Health? A Meta-Analysis," *Psychological Bulletin* 129, no. 6 (2003): 946–72.

57. Martin Pinquart and Silvia Sörensen, "Gender Differences, Caregiver Stressors, Social Resources, and Health: An Updated Meta-Analysis," *Journals of Gerontology Series B: Psychological Sciences & Social Sciences* 61, no. 1 (2006): 33–45.

58. Ibid.

59. Sara Torres, "Barriers to Mental-Health Care Access Faced by Hispanic Elderly," in *Servicing Minority Elders in the Twenty-First Century*, edited by Mary L. Wykle and Amasa B. Ford (New York: Springer, 1999), pp. 200–18.

60. Sarah J. Yarry, Elizabeth K. Stevens, and T. J. McCallum, "Cultural Influences on Spousal Caregiving," *American Society on Aging* 31, no. 3 (2007): 24–30.

61. James Jackson, "African American Aged," in the *Encyclopedia of Aging*, 2nd ed., edited by George L. Maddox (New York: Springer, 1995), pp. 30–80; Sharon L. Tennstedt, Bei-Hung Chang, and Melvin Delgado, "Patterns of Long-Term Care: A Comparison of Puerto Rican, African-American, and Non-Latino White Elders," *Journal of Gerontological Social Work* 30, no. 1/2 (1998): 179–99.

62. Sue Levkoff, Becca Levy, and Patricia Flynn Weitzmann, "The Role of Religion and Ethnicity in the Help Seeking of Family Caregivers of Elders with Alzheimer's Disease and Related Disorders," *Journal of Cross-Cultural Gerontology* 14, no. 4 (1999): 335.

63. Martin Pinquart and Silvia Sörensen, "Associations of Stressors and Uplifts of Caregiving with Caregiver Burden and Depressive Mood: A Meta-Analysis," *Journals of Gerontology Series B: Psychological Sciences & Social Sciences* 58B, no. 2 (2003): 112; D. W. Coon and others, "Well-Being, Appraisal, and Coping in Latina and Caucasian Female Dementia Caregivers: Findings from the REACH Study," *Aging & Mental Health* 8, no. 4 (2004): 330–45.

64. W. E. Haley and others, "Well-Being, Appraisal, and Coping in African-American and Caucasian Dementia Caregivers: Findings from the REACH Study," *Aging & Mental Health* 8, no. 4 (2004): 316–29; Coon and others, "Well-Being, Appraisal, and Coping in Latina and Caucasian Female Dementia Caregivers" (see note 63).

65. Tennstedt, Chang, and Delgado, "Patterns of Long-Term Care" (see note 61).

66. Catherine Hagan Hennessey and Robert John, "American Indian Family Caregivers' Perceptions of Burden and Needed Support Services," *Journal of Applied Gerontology* 15, no. 3 (1996): 275–93.

67. Martin Pinquart and Silvia Sörensen, "Ethnic Differences in Stressors, Resources, and Psychological Outcomes of Family Caregiving: A Meta-Analysis," *Gerontologist* 45, no. 1 (2005): 90–106; M. R. Janevic and M. C. Connell, "Racial, Ethnic, and Cultural Differences in the Dementia Caregiving Experience: Recent Finding," *Gerontologist* 41, no. 3 (2001): 334–47.

68. Karen I. Fredriksen-Goldsen and Nancy Farwell, "Dual Responsibilities among Black, Hispanic, Asian, and White Employed Caregivers," *Journal of Gerontological Social Work* 43, no. 4 (2004): 25–44.

69. Peggye Dilworth-Anderson, Ishan Canty Williams, and Brent E. Gibson, "Issues of Race, Ethnicity, and Culture in Caregiving Research: A 20-Year Review (1980–2000)," *Gerontologist* 42, no. 2 (2002): 237–72.

70. Tatjana Meschede, Thomas M. Shapiro, and Jennifer Wheary, *Living Longer on Less: The New Economic Insecurity of Seniors* (Institute on Assets and Social Policy and Demos, 2009).

71. Administration on Aging, *A Profile of Older Americans: 2009* (www.aoa.gov/AoAroot/Aging_Statistics/Profile/2009/docs/2009profile_508.pdf).

72. Deborah M. Merrill, *Caring for Elderly Parents: Juggling Work, Family, and Caregiving in Middle and Working Class Families* (Westport: Auburn House, 1997), pp. 13–15.

73. Ibid.

74. Rachel F. Boaz, "Full-Time Employment and Informal Caregiving in the 1980s," *Medical Care* 34, no. 6 (1996): 524–36.

75. Robyn Stone, Gail Lee Cafferata, and Judith Sangl, "Caregivers of the Frail Elderly: A National Profile," *Gerontologist* 27, no. 5 (1987): 616–26.

76. Wagner, *Comparative Analysis of Caregiver Data for Caregivers to the Elderly, 1987 and 1997* (see note 17), p. 2.

77. MetLife, *MetLife Study of Working Caregivers and Employer Health Costs* (see note 55).

78. Margaret B. Neal and others, *Balancing Work and Caregiving for Children, Adults, and Elders* (Newbury Park, Calif.: Sage, 1993); Urie Bronfenbrenner and others, *The State of Americans: This Generation and the Next* (New York: Free Press, 1996); J. L. Gibeau, J. W. Anastas, and P. J. Larson, "Breadwinners, Caregivers, and Employers: New Alliances in an Aging America," *Employee Benefits Journal* 12, no. 3 (1987): 6–10; Andrew E. Scharlach, "Caregiving and Employment: Competing or Complementary Roles?" *Gerontologist* 34, no. 3 (1994): 378–85.

79. Evercare, *Family Caregivers—What They Spend, What They Sacrifice* (Minnetonka, Minn.: 2007), p. 21.

80. R. Schutltz and S. Beach, "Caregiving as a Risk Factor for Mortality: The Caregiver Health Effects Study," *Journal of the American Medical Association* 282, no. 23 (1999): 2215–19; R. Schutlz,, P. Visintainer, and G. M. Williamson, "Psychiatric and Physical Morbidity Effect of Caregiving," *Journal of Gerontology* 45, no. 5 (1990): 181–91.

81. National Alliance for Caregiving and the National Center for Women and Aging at Brandeis University, *The MetLife Juggling Act Study: Balancing Caregiving with Work and the Costs Involved* (New York: The MetLife Mature Market Institute, 1999).

82. Society for Human Resource Management (SHRM), *2007 Employee Benefits Survey* (Alexandria, Va.: 2007).

83. Hewitt Associates, *Work/Life Benefits Provided by Major U.S. Employers in 2003–2004* (Lincolnshire, Ill.: 2003)

84. SHRM, *2007 Employee Benefits Survey* (see note 82).

85. Ellen Galinsky and James T. Bond, *The Impact of the Recession on Employers* (New York: Families and Work Institute, 2009), p. 7 (www.familiesandwork.org/site/research/reports/Recession2009.pdf).

86. Allarde Dembe and others, "Employer Perceptions of Elder Care Assistance Programs," *Journal of Workplace Behavioral Health* 23, no. 4 (2008): 360.

87. SHRM, *2007 Employee Benefits Survey* (see note 82).

88. Donna Wagner and Gail Hunt, "The Use of Workplace Eldercare Programs by Employed Caregivers," *Research on Aging* 16, no. 1 (March 1994): 69–84.

89. Dembe and others, "Employer Perceptions of Elder Care Assistance Programs" (see note 86), p. 371.

90. Ibid., p. 373.

91. Terry Bond and others, *The National Study of Employers: Highlights of Findings* (New York: Families and Work Institute, 2006).

92. J. L. Glass and A. Finley, "Coverage and Effectiveness of Family Responsive Workplace Policies," *Human Resources Management Review* 12, no. 3 (Autumn 2002): 313–37.

93. Marcie Pitt-Catsouphes, Christina Matz-Costa, and Elyssa Besen, *Age and Generations: Understanding Experiences at the Workplace* (Chestnut Hill, Mass.: Boston College, 2009), p. 17.

94. Ibid.

95. Bond, *The National Study of Employers* (see note 91).

96. Muriel Gillick, *The Denial of Aging: Perpetual Youth, Eternal Life, and Other Dangerous Fantasies* (Harvard University Press, 2006), pp. 4, 6.

97. Ellen Galinsky, Dana Friedman, and C. Hernandez, *The Corporate Reference Guide to Work-Family Programs* (New York: Families and Work Institute, 1991).

98. Tamara Haraven, "The Changing Patterns of Family Life as They Affect the Aged," *Families and Older Persons: Policy Research and Practice,* edited by G. K. Maddox, I. C. Siegler, and D. G. Blazer (Durham, N.C.: Duke University Center for the Study of Aging and Human Development, 1980), pp. 31–41.

99. Nancy Folbre, *The Invisible Heart* (New York: The New Press, 2001), p. 102.

100. Centers for Medicare and Medicaid Services, "National Health Accounts" (http://cms.hhs.gov/statistics/nhe).

101. Brenda Spillman and Peter Kemper, "Lifetime Patterns of Payment for Nursing Home Care," *Medical Care* 33, no. 3 (1995): 280–96.

102. Centers for Medicare and Medicaid Services, Brief Summaries of Medicare and Medicaid, 2010 (www.cms.gov/MedicareProgramRatesStats/downloads/MedicareMedicaidSummaries2010.pdf).

103. Carol Levine, ed., *Always on Call: When Illness Turns Families into Caregivers* (New York: United Hospital Fund, 2004), p. 137.

104. L. W. Kaye, "The Adequacy of the Older Americans Act Home Care Mandate: A Front Line View from Three Programs," *Home Health Care Service Quarterly* 5, no. 1 (Spring 1984): 75–87.

105. T. Burns and others, "Home Treatment for Mental Health Problems: A Systemic Review," *Health Technology Assessment* 5, no. 15 (2001): 1–139.

106. Jo Harris-Wehling and others, *Real Problems, Real People: An Evaluation of the Long-Term Care Ombudsman Programs of the Older Americans Act* (Washington: Division of Health Care Services, Institute of Medicine, 1995).

107. Commission on Leave, *A Workable Balance: A Report to Congress on Family and Medical Leave Policies* (Washington: U.S. Department of Labor, May 1996).

108. David Cantor and others, *Balancing the Needs of Families and Employers: Family and Medical Leave Surveys* (Bethesda, Md.: Westat, 2001).

109. Jane Waldfogel, "Family and Medical Leave: Evidence from the 2000 Surveys," *Monthly Labor Review* 124, no. 9 (September 2001): 17–23.

110. Ruth Milkman and Eileen Applebaum, "Leaves That Pay: Employer and Worker Experiences with Paid Family Leave in California" (Center for Research on Economic Policy, January 2011), pp. 1–36.

111. Theda Skocpol, *Protecting Soldiers and Mothers: The Political Origins of Social Policy in the United States* (Harvard University Press, 1992), pp. 46–47.

112. Stephanie Whittier, Andrew Scharlach, and Teresa S. Dal Santo, "Availability of Caregiver Support Services: Implications for Implementation of the National Family Caregiver Support Program," *Journal of Aging and Social Policy* 17, no. 1 (2005): 45–62.

113. In 2006, Congress passed the "Lifespan Respite Care Act" (Public Law 109-442), but no funds have been allocated for implementation.

Workplace Flexibility: From Research to Action

Ellen Galinsky, Kelly Sakai, and Tyler Wigton

Summary

Ellen Galinsky, Kelly Sakai, and Tyler Wigton explore the "time famine" among American workers—the continuing sense among employees of not having enough time to manage the multiple responsibilities of work and personal and family life. Noting that large shares of U.S. employees report feeling the need for greater workplace flexibility to enable them to take better care of family responsibilities, the authors examine a large-scale community-engagement initiative to increase workplace flexibility voluntarily.

Using the 2008 National Study of the Changing Workforce as a primary source of data, the authors begin with an overview of the prevalence of flexibility in today's American workplace. They track which categories of employees have access to various flexibility options, as well as the extent to which employees with access to various types of flexibility use those options. Findings from the study indicate that the majority of employees want flexibility but that access to it varies, with more advantaged employees—those who are well educated, have high salaries, and work full time, for example—being doubly advantaged in having greater access to flexibility.

A number of employers, say the authors, tend to be skeptical of the value of workplace flexibility and to fear that employees will abuse it if it is offered. But the study data reveal that most employees use flexibility quite conservatively. When the authors use their nationally representative data set to investigate correlations between access to workplace flexibility and a range of workplace outcomes especially valued by employers—employee engagement, job satisfaction, retention, and health—they find that employers as well as employees can benefit from flexibility.

Finally, the authors discuss When Work Works, a large, national community-based initiative under way since 2003 to increase voluntary adoption of workplace flexibility. The authors detail the conceptual basis of the project's design, noting its emphasis on flexibility as one component of effective workplaces that can benefit employers, employees, and communities alike. Galinsky, Sakai, and Wigton conclude by drawing lessons learned from the project and briefly discussing the implications of using research to bring about workplace change.

www.futureofchildren.org

Ellen Galinsky is the president and co-founder and Kelly Sakai and Tyler Wigton are program managers at Families and Work Institute, a nonprofit, nonpartisan research organization in New York City that studies the changing workforce, the changing family, and the changing community.

Ellen Galinsky, Kelly Sakai, and Tyler Wigton

The recurrent feeling of so many American employees that there simply are not enough hours in the day has been called many things, but one phrase—a "time famine"—captures the feeling especially well.[1]

Employees experience the time famine in different ways (figure 1). Women, in particular, feel the effects of the time squeeze on their psychological well-being.[2] Almost all employee groups of parents feel that they have insufficient time with their children. Employed fathers and mothers, for example, feel similarly deprived of time with their children. Differences begin to appear in other areas of time deprivation. Parents, full-time employees, more highly educated employees, managers and professionals, higher paid, and younger employees are the most likely to feel deprived of time with their husbands, wives, or partners. The gap between parents (73 percent) and nonparents (52 percent) in that respect is particularly striking. The disparity between parents (72 percent) and nonparents (50 percent) is similarly large when it comes to feeling deprived of time for themselves. Women, full-time employees, managers and professionals, unionized employees, salaried employees, employees living with a spouse or partner, employees making between $25,000 and $39,999 annually, and more highly educated employees are the most likely to feel starved for time to spend on themselves.

In recent years, researchers have focused their attention on the effect of the time strain on women. Women, particularly mothers, face challenges in the workplace that men and childless women are less likely to experience. Workplace evaluations, for example, seem to hold mothers to higher standards (in terms of commitment to work, punctuality, and competence) than they hold their childless counterparts.[3]

Access to Workplace Flexibility

A logical remedy to employees' sensation of being famished for time is workplace flexibility —allowing employees to have flexible work

Figure 1. Feelings of a "Time Famine" among Wage and Salaried Employees

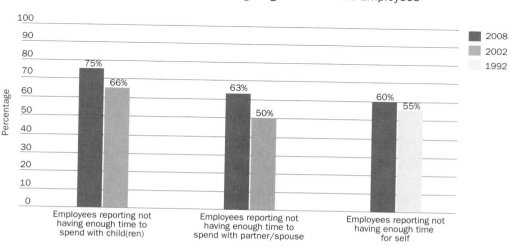

Source: Families and Work Institute, 1992, 2002, and 2008 editions of the National Study of the Changing Workforce.

National Study of the Changing Workforce

The primary source of data for this article is Families and Work Institute's National Study of the Changing Workforce (NSCW), a comprehensive, nationally representative, ongoing study of American employees' lives on and off the job. Originally conducted as the U.S. Department of Labor's Quality of Employment Survey (QES), it was discontinued in 1977. It was then adopted by Families and Work Institute in 1992 and continues to be conducted every five to six years.

Technical Background on the National Study of the Changing Workforce

Primary sources to inform this article were the Families and Work Institute's 1992, 1997, 2002, and 2008 National Study of the Changing Workforce (NSCW) surveys. The NSCW builds directly on the 1977 Quality of Employment Survey (QES) conducted by the Institute for Social Research at the University of Michigan with funding from the U.S. Department of Labor. Both the NSCW and QES are based on random samples of the U.S. workforce.

Total samples of the NSCW include wage and salaried employees who work for someone else, independent self-employed workers who do not employ anyone else, and small business owners who do employ others. The overall sample size of the 2008 NSCW is 3,502; this article, however, is based on 2,769 wage and salaried employees. All NSCW samples are adjusted to (that is, weighted to) reflect recent U.S. Bureau of the Census statistics on the total U.S. population to adjust for any sampling bias that might have occurred. The response rates for all NSCW surveys are above 50 percent, applying the conservative method of calculation recommended by the American Association for Public Opinion Research. In 2008 the response rate was 54.6 percent and the completion rate was 99 percent. The estimated maximum sampling error for the total wage and salaried sample is approximately plus or minus 1 percent.

schedules that enable them to better manage work and personal or family life. According to the latest (2008) edition of Families and Work Institute's ongoing nationally representative study, the National Study of the Changing Workforce (NSCW), a large majority of employees—87 percent—report that having workplace flexibility would be "extremely" or "very" important if they were looking for a new job. Employee access to such flexibility, however, is limited, and even when employees do have access, they may worry about using the offered flexibility—often for good reasons, as several studies show.

Jennifer Glass, for example, found that mothers who used flexibility policies offered by their employer experienced wage depression, missed promotions, and other negative consequences, even when the policies used were employer-sanctioned. The long-term effect of flexibility policies on mothers' wages depended on the type of flexibility used, the occupation, and continuity with the employer.[4] Similarly, Michael Judiesch and Karen Lyness studied 11,815 managers and found that those who took leaves were more likely to receive smaller salary increases and negative performance evaluations, and less likely to be promoted. They did not find gender differences in the penalties for leaves of absence.[5] In addition, a study by Scott Schieman and Paul Glavin found that increased use of flexibility can lead to "work-home blurring."[6] Because workers were available to their employers anytime, anywhere, they reported "receiving work-related contact outside of normal work hours" and found themselves working during designated family time.

Table 1. Access to Flexibility among All Employees

Type of flexibility	Percentage of employees with access
Choices in Managing Time	
Allowed complete or a lot of control over their work schedule	37
It is very true that their schedule or shift meets their needs	62
Flextime and Flexplace	
Allowed traditional flextime (can choose own start and end schedules)	45
Allowed daily flextime (able to make short-notice schedule changes)	84
Allowed to work compressed workweek some of the time	36
Allowed to work some regular paid hours at home	16
Reduced Time	
Full-timers who could arrange to work part time in their current position if desired	37
Part-timers who could arrange to work full time in their current position if desired	92
Could arrange to work part year	23
Time Off	
It's not hard at all to take time off during the workday for personal or family matters	35
Receive at least five paid days for personal illness a year	62
Receive at least five paid days for sick child(ren) a year	48
Able to take time off for elder care without fear of losing income	53
Able to take time off for elder care without fear of losing job	70
Have paid vacation days	78
Average days of annual paid vacation days allowed	15
Receive paid holidays	77
Able to volunteer during work time without losing pay	32
New mothers (with children under the age of six) with access to parenting leave	99
New mothers (with children under the age of six) with access to parenting leave with partial or full pay	48
New fathers (with children under the age of six) with access to parenting leave	94
New fathers (with children under the age of six) with access to parenting leave with partial or full pay	56
Culture of Flexibility	
Strongly or somewhat disagree that they have to choose between advancing in their jobs or devoting attention to their family or personal lives	58
Strongly or somewhat disagree that employees who ask for flexibility are less likely to get ahead in their jobs or careers	61
Supervisor support (summary of five questions on a scale from 1=low to 4=high)	3

Source: Families and Work Institute, 2008 National Study of the Changing Workforce.

The 2008 edition of the NSCW investigated, for the first time, workers' access to, use of, and demand for flexibility. The 2008 survey explored twenty-eight different aspects of workplace flexibility, which can be grouped into five categories (the categories are aligned with the labels used by business leaders). The first category, Choices in Managing Time, includes feeling control over one's schedule and agreeing that the schedule or shift meets one's needs. The second, Flextime and Flexplace, includes traditional flexibility (control over when the workday begins and ends), daily flexibility (short-notice schedule changes), compressed workweeks, and working at home. Reduced Time, the third category, includes, for full-timers, being able to work part time in their current position, and, for part-timers, being able to work full time in their current position, as well as to work part year. The fourth option, Time Off, includes being able, without difficulty, to take time for personal or family matters, at least five paid days off for personal illness, at least five paid days off to care for sick children, time off for elder care without fear of losing one's job, paid vacation time, paid holiday time off, time off for volunteering without the loss of pay, and maternity and paternity leave. The final category, Culture of Flexibility, includes not having to choose between advancement and devoting attention to family life, not jeopardizing advancement by asking for flexibility, and having overall supervisor support when work-life issues arise. Table 1 presents an overview of how many employees have access to each of these five types of flexibility.

In the following subsections we break down the overall employee responses from the 2008 NSCW, making comparisons within the following employee groups: men and women; parent and nonparents; employees of different ages—Generation Y (born between 1980 and 1995), Generation X (born between 1966 and 1979), Baby Boomers (born between 1946 and 1965), and Matures (born between 1922 and 1945); employees with different levels of education (high school or less, some postsecondary education, four-year college degree or more); employees with full- and part-time jobs; employees from different industries (goods-producing and service industries); employees who are managerial and professional and those who are not; unionized and nonunionized employees; hourly and salaried employees; employees who are married or living with spouse or partner and those who are not; and employees from various annual wage groups (less than $25,000, $25,000–$39,999, $40,000–$64,999, and $65,000 and more).[7]

Choices in Managing Time

Only 37 percent of employees overall report having "complete" or "a lot" of control over their work schedules. Perhaps surprisingly, no differences exist between the responses of men and women and between the responses of parents and nonparents in schedule control, but there are differences among other groups. Older employees, more educated employees, part-time employees, employees working in the service sector, nonunionized employees, managers and professionals, and those with higher wages report having the greatest schedule control.

Employees are more likely to feel that their schedule or shift meets their needs (62 percent) than they are to feel that they have control over their schedule (37 percent). Age matters here. Matures (76 percent) clearly experience a better fit in their schedule or shifts than Generation Y employees (56 percent), as do managerial employees, non-union employees, and those living in a couple relationship.

Flextime and Flexplace

Overall, 45 percent of employees report having access to traditional flextime, defined as being able to choose one's own starting and ending times for work. Men (48 percent) are more likely to have access to traditional flextime than women (41 percent), as are more highly educated employees. Those with a college degree or higher have much greater access (57 percent) than those with a high school degree or less (37 percent). Employees working in the service sector, salaried employees, employees in managerial positions, and employees with higher wages have greater access to traditional flextime than other groups, but the gap in access is particularly large between nonunionized (49 percent) and unionized employees (27 percent).

A far smaller share of employees (16 percent) is allowed the option of flexplace, defined as working some regularly scheduled paid hours at home. Men, older employees, more highly educated employees, full-timers, employees in the service sector, managers, nonunion employees, salaried employees, those living with their spouse or partners, and those with the highest wages are the most likely to have access to flexplace. Particularly large is the gap between employees with the highest wages (41 percent) and those with the lowest (4 percent).

In addition to asking about traditional flex-time and flexplace, the 2008 NSCW asked employees whether they can make changes to their starting and quitting times when last-minute problems arise and found that 84 percent had such access. The groups with the most access to this short-notice daily flex-ibility are managers, nonunionized employ-ees, salaried employees, better-educated employees, and higher-income employees. Certainly, education affects the kind of jobs that employees have—and certain jobs lend themselves more easily to flexibility than others—but, as becomes clear when we discuss other types of flexibility, less advan-taged employees are also less advantaged in having access to workplace flexibility in many respects, although they may in fact have the greatest need for it. Experience at Families and Work Institute reveals that more jobs lend themselves to flexibility than employers might initially imagine.

Compressed workweeks are defined as work-ing a full-time schedule, but shifting some of those hours into longer days to be able to take more time off on other days—such as being able to work four ten-hour days a week instead of five eight-hour days or for all or part of the year. Some employers allow compressed workweeks during the summer months, calling them "summer hours." Thirty-six percent of the total work-force reports having access to compressed workweeks. The only difference in access is between nonunionized and unionized employees (37 percent and 31 percent, respectively).

Reduced Time
In investigating access to reduced time, the 2008 NSCW asked part-timers whether they believe they could work full time in their same position and full-timers whether they believe they could work part time in their position if they wished to. The question raises a variety of constraints, including whether employees could afford such changes in workload and time commitments. Only 37 percent of the full-time employees (who make up 82 percent of the study sample) report that they could arrange to reduce their hours to part time in their same position, if they wanted to, with women (41 percent) more likely than men (34 percent) to feel this way. Overall, because part-time jobs are more likely to be filled by women (63 percent) than men (37 percent), it may not be surprising that women might also take jobs where reducing their time is a possibility.

Part-time work is sometimes referred to as a part-time ghetto from which escape is difficult. But according to the 2008 NSCW survey, 92 percent of the part-time employ-ees (who make up 18 percent of the study group) report that they can move into a full-time schedule and maintain their current position if they want to.

The 2008 NSCW also asked full-time employ-ees if they would prefer to work a part-time schedule, and part-time employees if they would prefer a full-time schedule. A greater

As becomes clear when we discuss other types of flexibility, less advantaged employees are also less advantaged in having access to workplace flexibility in many respects, although they may in fact have the greatest need for it.

share of part-time employees (37 percent) report an interest in working a full-time schedule than vice versa (20 percent). With 37 percent of part-time employees wanting to move to a full-time schedule and more than nine in ten reporting being able to do so, it is unclear why more part-timers don't increase their hours. Obviously, other factors must explain this discrepancy. Interestingly, data from Families and Work Institute's most recent nationally representative study of employers, the 2008 National Study of Employers, show that 44 percent of employers allow at least some of their employees to move back and forth between full- and part-time positions while remaining at their same level.[8] Thus employees may also be more optimistic about being able to make these changes than employers are.

In exploring access to part-year work, the 2008 NSCW asked whether employees could arrange to work for only part of the year in their current job and found that 23 percent have such access. Part-time employees are more likely than full-time employees to be able to work part year (36 percent and 20 percent, respectively). Other employees who are most likely to be able to work part year are those in the service industry, hourly employees, employees not living with a spouse or partner, and employees in jobs with the lowest wages.

Time Off

Overall, 35 percent of employees report that it is "not at all hard" to take time off during the workday for personal or family matters. Mature employees (51 percent) have much greater access to this kind of flexibility than do Generation Y employees (29 percent). The kind of trust that permits time off during the day appears to be earned by a longer tenure in the workforce. Employees who live with a spouse or partner (38 percent) also have greater access to time off during the workday than those who do not (30 percent).

The 2008 NSCW asked employees who were providing elder care if they were able to take the time off they needed without fear of losing income as a result. Overall, 53 percent report being able to do so, with men, full-time employees, and those living with a spouse or partner having more access to this flexibility than their counterparts. Seventy percent of employees who have elder care responsibilities report being able to take time off to perform such care without fear of losing their job. Women and older employees report having the greatest such access.

Asked the extent to which their employers support their contributing to their communities by volunteering, 32 percent of employees report that they are able to volunteer during work time without losing pay. Three differences emerge among groups: men (36 percent) have greater access to paid leave for volunteering than women (28 percent), nonunion employees (35 percent) have more access than unionized employees (19 percent), and salaried employees (42 percent) have more access than hourly employees (26 percent).

The 2008 NSCW also asked employees with a child under the age of six about their experiences in taking time off after birth or adoption (although these employees may not have worked for their current employers when the child was born). Nearly all women with children under the age of six (99 percent) report having access to some maternity leave, which could also include the time off for medical disability. The only significant differences in access are between full-time (100 percent) and part-time (95 percent) employees and between those in the service industries (100 percent) and the goods-producing industries (92 percent). When asked whether either partial or full pay was provided during this leave, the share reporting access drops to 48 percent. Those most likely to receive pay during leave are better-educated, full-time, and salaried employees and those who already have higher wages.

Men and women with children under the age of six have similar access to caregiving leave. Overall, 94 percent of fathers have some access to leave after the birth or adoption of a child. The only difference is between men who live with a spouse or partner (95 percent) and men who don't (76 percent). Overall, 56 percent of fathers report being given some pay during leave, with older, better-educated, and salaried employees and those with higher wages more likely to have access to payment during leave than others. It is likely, however, that men are using personal or vacation time for wages during caregiving leaves rather than paid paternity leave.

For the most common forms of paid time off, large differences exist among different groups of employees. For example, 62 percent of all employees report having at least five paid days off for personal illness, but the share of full-timers (68 percent) with access to paid sick time is much larger than the share of part-timers (37 percent). Parents (67 percent) are more likely to have paid sick time than nonparents (59 percent)—perhaps because parents look for jobs that provide this option. In addition, employees who are in the Baby Boomer generation, in service industries, salaried, living with their spouse or partner, and who have higher wages are the most likely to have paid sick time. One particular difference—that between union and nonunion employees—is interesting. Nonunionized employees have greater access to unpaid flexibility, but unionized employees have greater access to paid time off. For example, 72 percent of unionized employees have at least five paid sick days, compared with 60 percent of nonunionized employees.

More advantaged employees have the greatest access to paid sick days—only 55 percent of employees with a high school degree or less have access compared with 76 percent of college-educated employees. Managers and professionals, as well as employees with higher wages, are also more likely to have access to paid sick days than do less well-paid employees.

A smaller share of employees has at least five paid days for their children's illnesses (48 percent) than has such leave for their own illnesses (62 percent). The pattern of access is similar to that for paid sick time, with more highly educated employees, full-timers, employees in the service industries, managers and professionals, unionized employees, salaried employees, and higher wage earners having the greatest access.

Overall, 78 percent of employees have access to paid vacation days. Men (82 percent) have greater access than do women (73 percent). Employees in the middle years (Generation X and Baby Boomers) have greater access than those who are younger and older. Parents, better-educated employees, full-timers, managers and professionals, salaried employees, employees living with a spouse or partner, and higher wage earners have the greatest access.

On average, employees have 15.4 days of paid vacation time a year. As has been the pattern, more advantaged employees have access to longer vacations. As an example, the highest-paid employees average 18.9 vacation days, compared with 10.3 days for the lowest-paid employees.

Similarly, 77 percent of the workforce has access to paid holidays. Those most likely to have paid holidays are men, parents, better-educated employees, full-timers, managers and professionals, salaried employees, employees living with their spouse or partner, and higher-wage employees.

Culture of Flexibility

Some employees who have access to flexibility believe that they would pay a price if they used it. To determine how widespread such views are, the 2008 NSCW investigated the extent to which employees think that they put their jobs in jeopardy if they use the flexibility they are offered.

Asked how strongly they agree or disagree with the statement that they have to choose between advancing in their jobs or devoting attention to their family or personal lives, 58 percent of employees disagree strongly or somewhat. Thus, about two in five employees feel that they must make a choice between work and family life. Interestingly, those least

likely to feel the need to make that choice are less well-educated employees, full-timers, and nonmanagers. In other words, the higher employees climb within their organizations, the more likely they are to believe that they have had to make tough choices.

Asked if they agree or disagree with the statement that employees who ask for flexibility are less likely to get ahead in their jobs, 61 percent disagree strongly or somewhat. The employees who are most likely to disagree are older employees, better-educated employees, employees in the service industries, managers and professionals, salaried employees, employees living with a spouse or partner, and employees with higher wages.

To measure the final item in the Culture of Flexibility—support that supervisors give employees regarding work-life issues—we created a scale of supervisor support that combines five variables.[9] The scale runs from 1 to 4, with 1 representing low support and 4, high support. Among all employees, the average "score" for supervisor support is 3.3. The only significant difference in support received from supervisors is between managers and professionals (3.4) and employees in other positions (3.2).

How Widespead Is the Use of Flexibility?

Employers' assumptions about the use of workplace flexibility can be negative and strongly entrenched. Firm managers voice concerns about flexibility at employer conferences and events, typically saying that if they offer workplace flexibility, their employees will take advantage of them by abusing it. "If you give them an inch, they'll take a mile" and "There will be nobody here when we need them" are oft-repeated comments in such discussions.

The 2008 NSCW is one of the first studies to investigate the usage of flexibility nationwide. Asked if they "sometimes" use a variety of types of flexibility, 79 percent of employees with access to traditional flextime report that they sometimes use it; 46 percent of those with access to compressed workweeks report that they sometimes use it; and 64 percent of those allowed to work some of their paid hours at home report that they sometimes do so. These types of arrangements, once adopted, can become predictable so that employers and employees can know when and where employees are working. The study finds that employees make less use of short-notice flextime: 19 percent never use it, 70 percent use it once a month or less, and only 11 percent use it regularly. Likewise, only 3 percent of those allowed to work mainly at home do so, and 23 percent of those who could work part year adopt that schedule.

Likewise employees take less time off than they are allowed. For example, although they are offered, on average, 15.4 days of paid

vacation time, they take 12.9 days on average. Only 60 percent of employees use all of the vacation time available to them in a year. Employees who receive at least five paid days off a year for personal illness on average took 1.9 days for personal illness over the past three months. Eighty-nine percent are satisfied with the amount of time they are given.

Employees who are allowed to volunteer during some of their paid hours spend 4.8 hours a week on these activities—or the equivalent of half a workday (though the 2008 NSCW measure does not indicate whether these hours are on-the-job hours). Finally, among employees who have given birth to or adopted a child in the past six years, mothers take 14.4 weeks off on average, and fathers take 5.4 weeks (though these totals likely include personal and vacation time).

In sum, although a small number of employees may take advantage of their employers by abusing the flexibility they are offered, most appear to use it quite conservatively,

Figure 2. The Relationship between Job Engagement and Access to Flexibility*

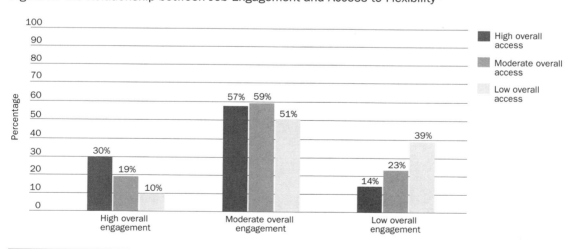

Source: Families and Work Institute, 2008 National Study of the Changing Workforce.
*This figure shows that the relationship between having access to flexibility and an employee's level of engagement would occur by chance 1 in 1,000 times.

indicating that employers' fears about high usage and abuse are largely unfounded.[10]

Does Access to Flexibility Make a Difference in the Workplace?

Findings from the 2008 NSCW indicate that employees want flexibility; that access to it varies, with more advantaged employees being doubly advantaged in that they have greater access; and that overall usage is modest. To what extent do the NSCW data address the larger issue: does access to flexibility matter—both for employers and for employees? Though correlations do not indicate causation, we believe our findings can lead the way to other studies that do assess causation. Several studies are now under way to assess employee outcomes such as job engagement, retention, physical health, and well-being before and after employees are offered greater access to supportive supervisors and flexibility (such as the studies funded by the National Institutes of Health and conducted by the Work, Family, and Health Network).[11]

To explore whether access to flexibility makes a difference in the workplace, we used a global measure of access to thirteen types of flexibility included in the 2008 NSCW.[12] We conducted a series of analyses to determine how access to flexibility affects four workplace outcomes of interest to employers and employees: job engagement, job satisfaction, job retention, and employee health. Our focus was on access to, rather than use of, flexibility, because analyses reveal that access has a greater impact on workplace outcomes than usage. It appears that flexibility functions like an insurance policy—just knowing that flexibility is there for them, should they need to use it, appears to be reassuring to employees.

Job Engagement

One workplace outcome about which employers are deeply concerned is job engagement—which they see as a proxy measure for productivity and business success.[13] As figure 2 shows, flexibility and engagement are positively linked.[14] For example, 30 percent of employees with high access to flexibility are highly engaged in their jobs, compared with 19 percent of those with moderate access and only 10 percent of those with low overall access. Similarly, 39 percent of employees with low access to flexibility have low overall job engagement, compared with 23 percent of those with moderate access and 14 percent with high access. Interestingly, the relationship between high, moderate, and low access to flexibility and moderate job engagement is less systematic, a finding that warrants further investigation by other researchers.

Job Satisfaction

Job satisfaction is also positively linked to access to flexibility (figure 3).[15] Sixty percent of employees with high access to flexibility are highly satisfied with their jobs, compared with 44 percent of those with moderate access and only 22 percent of those with low access.

Retention

Overall, according to the 2008 NSCW, 17 percent of employees are very likely and 23 percent are somewhat likely to make a concerted effort to find a new job in the coming year. As the national economy slowly recovers, many employers know that they need to retain their best talent to thrive. Among employees with high access to flexibility, 71 percent are very unlikely to try to find a new job in the coming year, compared with 61 percent of those with moderate access and 45 percent of those with low access (figure 4).[16]

Figure 3. The Relationship between Job Satisfaction and Access to Flexibility*

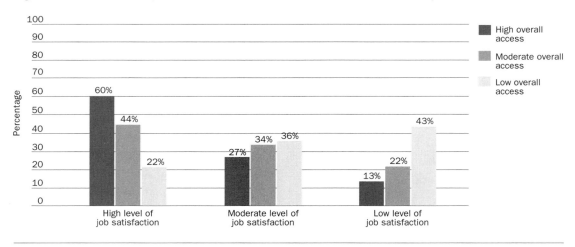

Source: Families and Work Institute, 2008 National Study of the Changing Workforce.
*This figure shows that the relationship between having access to flexibility and an employee's level of job satisfaction would occur by chance 1 in 1,000 times.

The inhospitable nature of an inflexible work environment has led some mothers to leave successful jobs in a number of fields and return home to raise their children. In *Opting Out? Why Women Really Quit Careers and Head Home*, Pamela Stone chronicles the experiences of women who quit their jobs because of a one-size-fits-all work environment and the unwillingness of corporations and managers to help women create other options.[17] Only a few of these women had originally planned to leave the workforce to raise children; most had expected to continue with their careers while raising their families, but found it very difficult to do. Phyllis Moen and Patricia Roehling similarly call attention to how the mystique "that Americans give their all to paid labor in order to 'make it'" is at odds with the expectations of women today. In their book, *The Career Mystique*, they illuminate the clash between the expectation that employees will devote their entire lives to their employer and the reality of life among dual-earner families today.[18]

Employee Health

As escalating health care costs take a rising toll on employers' bottom line, the overall health of the U.S. workforce is in decline.[19] On average, less than one-third of employees (28 percent) say their overall health is "excellent"—a 6-percentage-point drop since 2002. For that reason, the link between employee health and access to flexibility (figure 5) is of particular concern, particularly because of the cost implications. Among employees with high access to flexibility, 39 percent report being in excellent health, compared with 29 percent of those with moderate access and only 20 percent of those with low access. Again, however, these relationships are complex and warrant further investigation.

An Experiment to Increase Access to Flexibility

The findings reported above as well as those from other articles in this volume reveal that workplace flexibility can have positive benefits for employers, employees, and children.

Figure 4. The Relationship between Job Retention and Access to Flexibility*

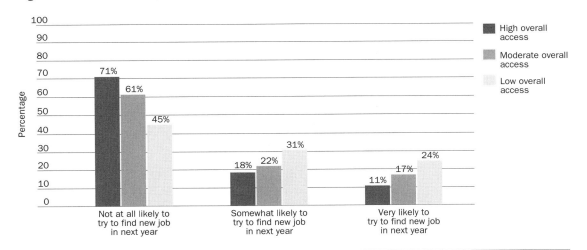

Source: Families and Work Institute, 2008 National Study of the Changing Workforce.
*This figure shows that the relationship between having access to flexibility and an employee's likelihood of leaving his or her job in the next year would occur by chance 1 in 1,000 times.

So the question is how to increase flexibility. There are two broad alternatives: a *mandated* approach, where change is required by law, and a *voluntary* approach, where employers recognize their own self-interest in offering workplace flexibility and thus increasingly provide it.

In 2003, the Alfred P. Sloan Foundation challenged Families and Work Institute to create and evaluate an experiment to increase the voluntary adoption of workplace flexibility. The resulting project, called When Work Works, was launched later that same year with funding from the Sloan Foundation. The project, based on a strategy of community involvement, was directed by Families and Work Institute in partnership with the Institute for a Competitive Workforce (an affiliate of the U.S. Chamber of Commerce) and the Twiga Foundation. In 2011 the Society for Human Resource Management partnered with Families and Work Institute to expand the project in new ways.

Eight Principles of the Theory of Change

The conceptual basis of When Work Works is a theory of change developed by Families and Work Institute after extensive consultations with scholars and practitioners who have successfully carried out change experiments. Eight principles inform this theory of change.

The change theory's first principle is to proceed in stages. Social and business change takes time and requires a long-term strategy that unfolds slowly, with each stage containing within itself the seeds of the next. The first stage is raising awareness; the second, changing behaviors; and the third, engaging people in action.

The second principle is to understand how the public frames the issue. Knowing in advance how people see the issue helps target change for maximum effectiveness. It also ensures against the inadvertent use of language or issues that trigger unnecessary opposition or backlash.

Figure 5. The Relationship between Overall Health and Access to Flexibility*

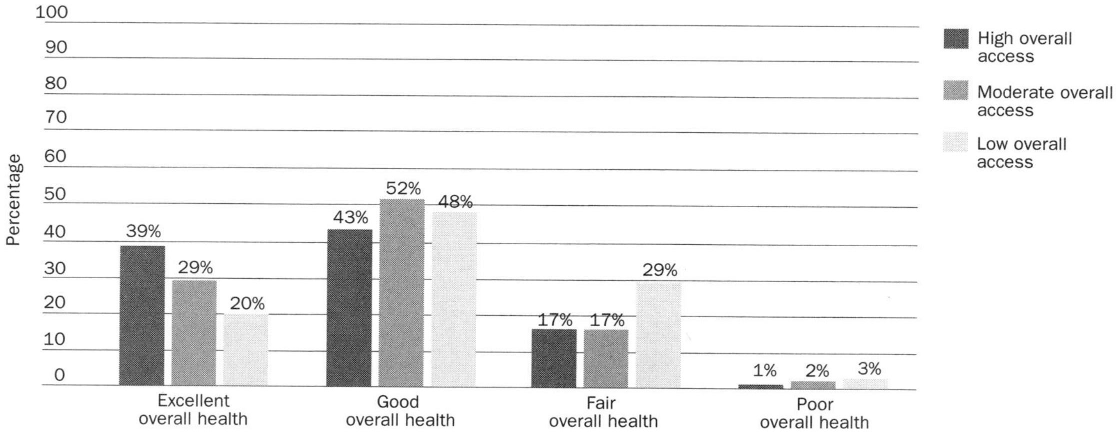

Source: Families and Work Institute, 2008 National Study of the Changing Workforce.
*This figure shows that the relationship between having access to flexibility and an employee's health would occur by chance 1 in 1,000 times.

The third principle of the theory of change is to focus on action. Changing attitudes is not enough. It is important to be able to specify concrete steps when people say, "I get it. What do you want me to do?"

The fourth principle, that messages are critical, incorporates several ancillary lessons. One is that unexpected messages can get people's attention. An unexpected message causes people to take in information precisely because it is unexpected. Another related lesson is that the message should be based on solid research that spells out not only the benefits of change, but also the costs of no change—of not taking action. People change their opinions or actions when they see that the benefits of change can outweigh the costs of no change. This kind of cost-benefit analysis is what employers call "making a business case." A third related lesson is the need for messages to project into the future. It is easier for people to think about the present in new ways and to move beyond everyday realities

and opinions when they are looking into an unknown future. The final lesson is the importance of tailoring different messages for different groups. One size does not fit all.

The fifth principle is that unexpected messengers also make a difference. Hearing messages from the usual messengers (for example, advocates talking about the importance of their advocacy issue) is predictable and easy to dismiss as self-interest. Hearing messages from unexpected messengers creates increased attention and involvement.

The sixth principle is to target the people who have the power to bring about change—to recognize, connect with, and assist them. It is essential first to define both the decision makers and those who influence them and then to target both groups—typically, public policy makers, businesses, professionals, the media, citizens, families, and employees—and finally to develop strategies to reach them effectively. Enabling people in diverse sectors to feel connected to a large change initiative and to learn from their successes and failures can be very sustaining.

The seventh principle of change is to take advantage of opportunities as they arise. The release of a new study or some event that captures the public's attention could lead to unexpected opportunities. It is critical to take advantage of an issue that has already engaged the public or key constituencies to show how it relates to the change effort.

The final principle of the theory of change is to plan in detail what outcomes to expect and to assess results and make adjustments all along the way. Goals should be built into the process from the very beginning. Continuing to assess progress in reaching these goals allows for ongoing mid-course corrections and a greater likelihood of achieving what is hoped for and expected.

The Strategy of Change

To reach small and mid-sized employers (where most U.S. employees work) as well as large employers from all sectors—public, private, for-profit, and not-for-profit—When Work Works took a local and worksite, or community involvement, strategy. The strategy was chosen before the analyses from the 2008 NSCW became available, but in retrospect it could hardly have been better suited to the survey results. In detailing who has most access to workplace flexibility, the 2008 NSCW survey described, again and again, the more advantaged worker[20]—men, parents, married employees, employees who are better educated, who are salaried, who are managers and professionals, full-timers, employees in the service industries, and those with higher wages. To reach less advantaged employees, who do not yet have and who most need access to flexibility, the

project would have to do extensive outreach within communities.

When Work Works was launched as a pilot effort in eight communities in 2005. Having a pilot year made it possible to get the kinks out before expanding—as the project has done every year thereafter. In 2011, the project is ongoing in twenty-eight communities and statewide in five states. Each of these communities and states is asked to take a series of strategies, which grow out of the eight principles of the theory of change.

Strategy 1: Create a Coalition of Community Leaders

Community leaders serve as champions for workplace flexibility. This strategy targets the people who have the power to bring about change with the aim of recognizing, connecting with, and assisting them. Coalitions of leaders involve local "movers and shakers" who represent diverse constituencies, such as local and state government, business councils and employer groups, media, nonprofits, and workforce development. The When Work Works project provides these local leaders with information, tools, and resources to be champions for creating better workplaces in their communities so that they, in turn, can become expected and unexpected spokespersons for change.

Strategy 2: Provide Educational Events within the Community

This strategy speaks to the principle of moving in stages from changing awareness to changing behavior to engaging people in action. The lead organization, in partnership with its coalition of community leaders, hosts a minimum of two educational events on effective *and* flexible workplaces. This business-to-business strategy integrates workplace flexibility with existing business topics and presents it as a stand-alone live or webinar event. The national When Work Works team has supported this educational effort by providing and suggesting resources and services that can be customized to meet the issues and needs of a particular community or audience.

Strategy 3: Provide Media Outreach within the Community

This strategy is linked to the principle of knowing ahead of time how the public sees this issue. When the When Work Works initiative was launched in 2003, workplace flexibility was seen largely as a benefit either for employees—a perk that was given to an individual (often a woman)—or for employers—a strategy to help businesses manage the ebbs and flows of demand by having "on call" employees who have little certainty about their work schedules.

The challenge has been to reflect solid research—that flexibility can be a component of effective workplaces that can benefit employers, employees, and communities alike. When Work Works has tackled this challenge by sharing research data on the potential links between workplace flexibility and employers, employees, and communities.

The partner communities provide a gateway to local media outlets for targeted efforts, especially because members of the local business media often belong to the leader coalitions and because the communities are responsible for outreach to local media. The When Work Works national team provides support for these efforts and continues to release research that keeps these issues in the news.

Since When Work Works first went into operation, overall media attention to workplace

flexibility has grown, and the issue is now being reported less as a "nice-to-have" benefit in human-interest stories, and more as a necessary business tool in hard-news stories.

Strategy 4: Implement the Sloan Awards

This strategy speaks to the principle of knowing what you want people to do. At the center of When Work Works are the Sloan Awards. Worksite-based awards make it possible for organizations to be evaluated on their effective and flexible programs and policies as well as their organizational culture. The Sloan Awards also allow When Work Works to evaluate its progress in bringing about change.

Employers are eligible to apply for the Sloan Awards if they have been in operation for at least one year and have at least ten employees who work from or report to the applying worksite. Employers can reapply every year, whether or not they win. The application process takes place in two rounds. In Round I, *employers* self-nominate by completing a questionnaire about their worksite's flexibility practices, policies, and the supportiveness of its work culture. Responses to the questionnaire are then measured against norms that have been derived from Families and Work Institute's ongoing nationally representative study, the National Study of Employers. To qualify for Round II, employers must rank in the top 20 percent of employers nationally.

In Round II *employees* are asked about their access to and use of flexibility, the aspects of the workplace culture that support their ability to work flexibly, whether they experience "jeopardy" when working flexibly, and their access to other ingredients of an effective workplace. Of those surveyed, a minimum of 40 percent must respond (the average response rate is 52 percent).

On the basis of both the employer and employee questionnaires, an overall score is computed, with two-thirds of the score based on employees' responses. There is no minimum or maximum number of award recipients. All applying companies have access to technical assistance and receive an individualized benchmarking report that compares their responses on the surveys with those of employers nationally, of applicant companies, and of winners. If they participate in Round II, their benchmarking report also compares their employee data with the 2008 NSCW. All winning companies are written up in an annual *Guide to Bold New Ideas for Making Work Work*, which describes and promotes best practices in workplace flexibility.

Strategy 5: Specify Outcomes and Measure Results

The principle of detailing expected outcomes, assessing results, and making changes informs this strategy. Every year, When Work Works sets goals and measures itself against them, making changes as necessary.

Lessons Learned

Through the When Work Works project we have learned important lessons about when workplace change is most likely to occur.

The first lesson is that key community leaders across different sectors (business, media, government) must direct the effort locally. A well-functioning coalition of key community leaders can ensure that the initiative is informed by diverse constituents; that it taps into networks that can lead to new opportunities and synergies; and that it maintains a continuum of support, keeping change going during times of transition. By securing the commitment of influential leaders, including unexpected messengers, partner communities build a broad-based foundation of local support, sowing the seeds for a sustainable grassroots movement for workplace change.

Houston, Texas, for example, promoted workplace flexibility as a community solution to ease traffic congestion and lessen pollution under the leadership of former Mayor Bill White. By moving even a relatively small number of people off the roads during peak congestion times, Flex in the City was able to improve commuting time, reduce traffic congestion and pollution, and help employers improve productivity as well. The mayor's office worked with the city's mass transit and Commute Solutions programs, local employers, chambers of commerce, and the When Work Works national team. This community approach served the program well and ensured its continuity after the mayor left office. Although no longer housed by the city government, the initiative, now called Flexworks, continues to operate as a division of TCT Enterprises, LLC, a management consulting firm, and is poised to expand to other areas of Texas.

The second lesson is that change is most likely when community leaders are committed to improving workplaces to meet an important community challenge. For local efforts to take root and succeed, workplace flexibility must be framed not just as an employer issue that can yield business benefits, but also as a community issue—such as reducing traffic congestion and air pollution, becoming green, attracting younger workers, retaining older workers and helping them live better as they age, and responding to economic challenges. One role of the leadership coalition is to help define the community case for the initiative.

In Dayton, Ohio, for example, flexibility is framed as a way for the community to address its economic challenges. Located in the nation's "Rust Belt," the Dayton region is transitioning from a manufacturing-based to a knowledge-based economy. Effective and flexible workplaces are part of the community's overall workforce development strategy to recruit and retain talent. Michigan, a state-wide When Work Works partner, likewise focuses on flexibility as a strategy for attracting new businesses to the state.

The third lesson is that flexibility does not stand alone but should be viewed as one component of an effective workplace. Research from Families and Work Institute has found that flexibility is one element—albeit an essential one—of an effective workplace that benefits employers and employees. Analysis of 2008 NSCW data has identified six criteria of effective workplaces: job challenge and learning, a climate of respect, autonomy, work-life fit and flexibility, economic security, and supervisor task support.

Because employers know that flexibility alone will not solve all their problems, flexibility has much more resonance in the context of other more accepted components of an effective workplace. In effect, making flexibility one component of an effective workplace reflects the principle in the theory of change that action should be based on solid research evidence. It also builds on a cost-benefit strategy. When employers' own company research shows that certain components of an effective workplace enhance their employee engagement and productivity, they can begin to see flexibility in a similar light.

The fourth lesson is that the effectiveness of the Sloan Awards grows out of the respect they earn from the employer community by providing quality assurance and by being based on a rigorous application process.

When Work Works uses the Sloan Awards to assess—rigorously and comprehensively—workplace flexibility programs, policies, practices and culture, and the components of an effective workplace. The award program, one of the few such evidence-based programs in the country, draws on information about effective and flexible workplaces from Families and Work Institute's nationally representative studies of employers and employees. The award is unique in being worksite-based and reaching employers of all sizes and industries—from mom-and-pop shops to global companies. It also reaches employers with varying ethnic groups and income levels, as well as companies where people have said flexibility is "not possible," such as call centers or manufacturers.

The application process is reviewed annually by subject-matter experts and modified to address emerging concerns. The criteria for the awards evolve in response to changing conditions so that there is always "something new." In 2009 new questions included how employers were helping employees manage the recession; in 2010, how to help employees increase their education and improve their skills. In 2011 surveys are addressing the flexibility needs for members of the military and their families.

The fifth lesson is that workplace awards alone are not sufficient to bring about change. The awards' effectiveness is magnified because they are part of a continuing process that includes education, technical assistance, and employer-to-employer communication about promising practices and how-to techniques. Applicants for a Sloan Award receive, in essence, a comprehensive tutorial on the different types of programs and policies that employers might use to create effective and flexible workplaces. Upon completing the process, all applicants receive a custom benchmarking report, which compares their employer and employee responses to other Sloan Award applicants and winners as well as to nationally representative data. An annual publication, the *Guide to Bold New Ideas for Making Work Work*, compiles promising practices from all of the award winners and is a useful resource for any employer, manager, or employee interested in innovative workplace initiatives.

Finally, what we have learned as these lessons have been absorbed and the change experiment has matured is that workplace flexibility has increased. When Work Works is not a controlled experimental study, in which subjects are randomly assigned to different conditions and cause and effect can be rigorously determined. Many conditions beyond the project's control—not least, the local, national, and global economy—affect what happens to flexibility. Another complication is that the employers involved in the project are self-selected and thus do not represent a random group of employers within the population. These limitations make it impossible to draw causal conclusions about whether and how the When Work Works project has increased flexibility. That said, however, flexibility has increased over time among participants in the project. Analysis of the data to try to explain that increase more narrowly has been inconclusive. The length of time that communities are involved with this initiative,

for example, is not consistently linked with increased employer flexibility. For four years there was a consistent link between increases in workplace flexibility and repeated applications for the Sloan Awards. That correlation made sense, on the hypothesis that the process itself—the benchmarking reports, technical assistance, and the best-practice guide—helps reapplying employers improve. Then, in 2009–10 all applicant companies, not just repeat applicants, saw an overall increase. We hope other researchers will investigate the possibilities, as we will.

In Conclusion

When Work Works has offered Families and Work Institute and its partners an unprecedented opportunity to explore the conditions under which workplaces can be improved by providing employees with greater access to workplace flexibility. Initial data reveal that increased flexibility can make work "work" for increasing numbers of employers, employees, employees' families, and communities.

A perennial issue in research is how it can be applied to practice. And a perennial issue in practice is how to bring successful pilot projects to scale and make them sustainable. Now in partnership with the Society for Human Resource Management and poised to spread even further, we believe that When Work Works offers many lessons that can be adapted to other research-based change experiments.

Endnotes

1. Ken M. Nomaguchi, Melissa A. Milkie, and Suzanne M. Bianchi, "Time Strains and Psychological Well-Being: Do Dual-Earner Mothers and Fathers Differ?" *Journal of Family Issues* 26, no. 6 (2005): 756–92.

2. Ibid.

3. Shelley J. Correll, Stephen Benard, and In Paik, "Getting a Job: Is There a Motherhood Penalty?" *American Journal of Sociology* 112, no. 5 (2007): 1297–1338.

4. Jennifer Glass, "Blessing or Curse? Work-Family Policies and Mothers' Wage Growth over Time," *Work and Occupations* 31, no. 3 (2004): 367–94.

5. Michael Judiesch and Karen Lyness, "Left Behind? The Impact of Leaves of Absence on Managers' Career Successes," *Academy of Management Journal* 42, no. 6 (1999): 641–51.

6. Scott Schieman and Paul Glavin, "Trouble at the Border? Gender, Flexible Work Conditions, and the Work-Home Interface," *Social Problems* 55, no. 4 (2008): 590–609.

7. Because our initial analyses reveal that having elder care is not predictive of the outcomes we look at in this article, we exclude it from our analyses.

8. The 2008 National Study of Employers surveyed a representative national sample of 1,100 for-profit (77 percent of the sample) and nonprofit employers (23 percent of the sample) with fifty or more employees by telephone interviews with human resource directors. Representatives of Harris Interactive conducted the thirty-minute interviews from April 19 through August 13, 2007. Employers were selected from Dun & Bradstreet lists using a stratified random sampling procedure in which selection was proportional to the number of people employed by each company to ensure a large enough sample of large organizations. The response rate for the study was 43 percent. The maximum sampling error (margin of error) for the study in describing the total sample is approximately 2 percent.

9. The five variables included in the supervisor support measure are: 1) My supervisor or manager is fair and doesn't show favoritism in responding to employees' personal or family needs; 2) My supervisor or manager is responsive to my needs when I have family or personal business to take care of; 3) My supervisor or manager is understanding when I talk about personal or family issues that affect my work; 4) I feel comfortable bringing up personal or family issues with my supervisor or manager; and 5) My supervisor or manager really cares about the effect that work demands have on my personal and family life.

10. We analyzed the data for demographic differences in use, but there were few significant findings, so they are not included in this report.

11. E. Kossek and J. Michel, "Flexible Work Schedules," in *Handbook of Industrial-Organizational Psychology*, vol. 1, edited by S. Zedeck (Washington: American Psychological Association, 2011), pp. 535–72.

12. The thirteen types of flexibility included in the global measure are: traditional flextime, short-notice flextime, flexplace, compressed workweek, lack of difficulty in taking time off, advance notice for overtime, at least five paid sick days for oneself, at least five paid sick days for one's child, part-time work if full time or full-time work if part time, part-year work, overall schedule flexibility, a schedule or shift that meets one's needs, and lack of career jeopardy for using flexibility.

13. Steve Bates, "Getting Engaged," *HR Magazine* 49, no. 2 (February 2004): 44–51.

14. This measure of job engagement asks employees how much they agree with the following statements: "I look forward to going to work," "I feel I am really a part of the group of people I work with," and "When I'm at work, time passes very quickly." We also ask, "How often do you think about good things related to your job when you're busy doing something else?" Answers are averaged and then converted into a three-point scale in which low overall engagement represents the bottom 25 percent of scores (bottom quartile), moderate overall engagement represents the middle 50 percent of scores (quartiles 2 and 3), and high overall engagement represents the top 25 percent of scores (top quartile).

15. Our measure of job satisfaction includes three items: all in all, how satisfied are you with your job? knowing what you know now, if you had to decide all over again to take the job you now have, what would you decide? and if a good friend of yours told you that he or she was interested in working in a job like yours for your employer, what would you tell your friend? Job satisfaction was measured with an index scale, which was converted into a three-point scale (low is the bottom 25 percent; moderate is the middle 50 percent; high is the top 25 percent of scores).

16. Turnover intent was measured with one item (not at all likely, somewhat likely, very likely to look for a new job with a new employer in the next year).

17. Pamela Stone, *Opting Out? Why Women Really Quit Careers and Head Home* (University of California Press, 2007).

18. Phyllis Moen and Patricia Roehling, *The Career Mystique* (Oxford: Rowman & Littlefield Publishers, Inc., 2005), p. 6.

19. Kerstin Aumann and Ellen Galinsky, *The State of Health in the American Workforce: Does Having an Effective Workplace Matter?* (New York: Families and Work Institute, 2009).

20. Joan Williams, *Unbending Gender: Why Family and Work Conflict and What to Do about It* (New York: Oxford University Press, 2000).

The Role of the Government in Work-Family Conflict

Heather Boushey

Summary

The foundations of the major federal policies that govern today's workplace were put in place during the 1930s, when most families had a stay-at-home caregiver who could tend to the needs of children, the aged, and the sick. Seven decades later, many of the nation's workplace policies are in need of major updates to reflect the realities of the modern workforce. American workers, for example, typically have little or no control over their work hours and schedules; few have a right to job-protected access to paid leave to care for a family member.

Heather Boushey examines three types of work-family policies that affect work-family conflict and that are in serious need of repair—those that govern hours worked and workplace equity, those that affect the ability of workers to take time off from work because their families need care, and those that govern the outsourcing of family care when necessary. In each case Boushey surveys new programs currently on the policy agenda, assesses their effectiveness, and considers the extent to which they can be used as models for a broader federal program.

Boushey looks, for example, at a variety of pilot and experimental programs that have been implemented both by private employers and by federal, state, and local governments to provide workers with flexible working hours. Careful evaluations of these programs show that several can increase scheduling flexibility without adversely affecting employers.

Although few Americans have access to paid family and medical leave to attend to family needs, most believe that businesses should be required to provide paid leave to all workers. Boushey notes that several states are moving in that direction. Again, careful evaluations show that these experimental programs are successful for both employers and employees.

National programs to address child and elder care do not yet exist. The most comprehensive solution on the horizon is the universal prekindergarten programs offered by a few states, most often free of charge, for children aged three and four.

www.futureofchildren.org

Heather Boushey is a senior economist at the Center for American Progress.

Laws and regulations—at all levels of government—play an important role in creating the setting in which families and workers manage work-family conflict.[1] Although public policies can help ease work-family conflicts, they can also exacerbate them, particularly if the policies are based on an outdated set of assumptions about how families live and work.

Most American workers today have family responsibilities that can create conflict with paid employment. Yet paid employment is critical to family well-being. Families who earn less than $100,000 a year typically derive 80 percent of their income from employment.[2] Most workers are breadwinners or cobreadwinners, and when a worker is unemployed or cannot be at work and has no access to paid leave, his or her family loses a significant portion of its income.[3] The typical U.S. middle-class family relies especially heavily on the earnings of a breadwinner or cobreadwinner because it has little in savings. In 2007, just before the onset of the Great Recession, less than a third (29.4 percent) of middle-class families had at least three months of income in savings.[4]

Given the economic importance of work and the reality that most workers are also bread-winners or cobreadwinners, finding ways to manage work-family conflicts is at the top of the agenda at kitchen tables all across the nation. American workers typically have little or no control over their work hours and schedules, and few have a right to job-protected access to paid leave to care for a family member. The workers most likely to have some control over their schedules and to have access to paid leave are disproportionately those at the top of the wage distribution.

For the most part, the foundations for the federal policies that affect the intersection of work and family in the United States today were laid by President Franklin Roosevelt and Secretary of Labor Frances Perkins during the 1930s. During that era most families had a stay-at-home caregiver, usually a mother, who could provide full-time care for children, the aged, and the sick. Few women worked outside the home, although some, disproportionately women of color and recent immigrants, always have had relatively high labor force participation.[5] But despite remarkable changes in both women's labor supply and family structure over the decades, especially since the 1970s, the wage-and-hours regulatory system and the social insurance infrastructure put in place by Roosevelt and Perkins have not been systematically expanded to address specifically the dual role that most workers play as workers and caregivers today.

The patchwork of work and family policies that has evolved over the years typically does not cover everyone. Overtime regulations, for example, tend not to apply to the highest-paid workers, leaving them subject to long workweeks. And family and medical leave are available to only about half of all workers, leaving a disproportionate share of low-wage workers with no access at all to job-protected leave. Further, when employers voluntarily implement such policies, they are under no requirement to cover all their employees and so tend to offer benefits as "perks" to high-status workers.

Government has for many years intervened in the nation's labor market to address a wide array of issues, setting, for example, basic labor standards, such as the minimum wage, and social insurance for workers who cannot work or are unemployed. In today's society—one in which adults are expected and encouraged to work—government also has a clear role to protect the welfare of children, the elderly, and the sick by setting standards to ensure that workers can meet their familial commitments.

Empirical evidence points to a failure of the market to come to grips with this issue on its own. Economists hypothesize—based on the theory of "compensating wage differentials" —that workers who need or value workplace flexibility will choose jobs that offer flexibility and will be willing to trade off higher wages in exchange.[6] But researchers have found that many workers appear to have limited ability to bargain for these benefits. The workers who most need workplace flexibility report having the least access to it, and the workers who have the greatest access to flexibility are those who are well paid.[7] Researchers have also found that mother-hood itself, beyond time out of the labor force or the practice of taking advantage of family-friendly policies, entails a wage penalty, although there is evidence that workers who take advantage of flexible hours may see slower wage growth over time.[8]

One reason why the market may not be able to produce greater workplace flexibility is that so few U.S. workers today are covered by collective bargaining agreements that address wages, hours, and workplace flexibility. Unions have made progress in getting those issues into their contracts, but with fewer than one in ten private-sector U.S. workers belonging to a union today, those contracts do not help many working families.[9] With unionization falling sharply over the past half-century, from nearly one in three workers in 1948 to 11.9 percent in 2010, broad union coverage is no longer the norm.[10]

My discussion focuses on three work-family issues: employees' ability to have some control over their hours of work, their ability to take time off from work to tend to their families' care, and their ability to find suitable options for outsourcing family care when necessary. Accordingly I examine three types of policies that shape the interaction between the labor market and family life—those that govern hours worked and workplace equity, those that provide income support when workers cannot be at work because their families need care, and those that govern the existence of and access to care for families who do not have a stay-at-home caregiver. I also examine how and how well the market is managing these issues and the appropriate role for government intervention.

The first large set of work-family policies involves what happens at work and how work intersects with the need to provide family care. The cornerstone is the 1938 Fair Labor Standards Act (FLSA), which first set out the nation's regulatory wage-and-hours frame-work. Congress enacted the FLSA following earlier state action to limit hours worked by women and children. Although the FLSA was not designed to address work-family conflict, it limited the hours of work for some workers and established the minimum wage, both of which affect the ability of workers to reserve time to care for families. Because the assumption underlying the FLSA is that workers are employed full time—in that era, commonly ten to twelve hours each day—the law did not deal with or encourage workplace flexibility.

Another issue at work is whether an employer can treat workers differently based on their status as caregivers or on family relationship. Until the 1950s, for example, many employ-ers refused to hire married women or mothers, because women were presumed to belong in the home.[11] Title VII of the 1964 Civil Rights Act took a giant first step toward ensuring that work performance, not a worker's personal characteristics, determined employment and pay, but large gaps remained—and remain still—for workers with care responsibilities.

The second large set of work-family policies addresses the need for income support when a worker cannot be at work because a family member requires care. The cornerstone of this set of policies is the Social Security Act of 1935, which established Old Age and Survivors Insurance, unemployment insurance, and income assistance to mothers and children. Because the law was grounded in the assumption that men were breadwinners and women were caretakers, it left a legacy of gaps in coverage and eligibility for today's families. Policy makers have since tried to fill many of these gaps, but inequalities that affect caregivers remain, perhaps most notably the failure of the law to cover caregiving leave. In two states, California and New Jersey, state-level programs provide social insurance to workers for family leave, but the United States remains the only developed nation that does not provide some type of paid leave to new parents nationwide.[12]

The third broad set of policies involves the need for families to provide care when potential caregivers are either working or in school and training for work. Because the United States does not provide a system of care for the young, the ill, or the aged, families must patch together various, mostly private, solutions. The subsidies available to help pay for this care are typically available only to the poor, while tax relief is available to middle- and upper-class citizens who pay

for care.[13] One key reason for the absence of a unified system of care is the deeply held belief that mothers belong in the home, not the workplace.

I examine each of these three sets of policies in turn: those that regulate work, those that provide income support for those who cannot be at work, and those that help provide care for workers' family members while their caretakers are at work. I conclude each section with an analysis of proposals now on the policy agenda.

At Work, but Needing Flexibility and Equity

Most American workers today are also caregivers. In 2008, among mothers of children under age eighteen, 71 percent participated in the workforce, which means most families no longer have a full-time stay-at-home parent; among all workers, both male and female, 42 percent reported that they had cared for an elderly person within the past five years.[14] Workers with care responsibilities may be able to perform their jobs fully, but may also need some flexibility from their employers to manage work-family conflicts; such flexibility would include, for example, being allowed to negotiate, have input into, or control their hours or location of work, without fear of discrimination or penalty. For professional workers and those subject to mandatory overtime, the problem is most often too much work; for low-wage workers, it is more often too few hours and unpredictable schedules.[15] Many higher earners, whether they are professionals tied to their BlackBerrys or nurses struggling to comply with mandatory overtime on little or no notice, would like to work fewer hours, while many low-wage workers can find only part-time work, or none at all, and often have highly unpredictable schedules.[16]

Several surveys confirm that employees see control over their hours of work as critical for managing day-to-day quality-of-life issues. A recent poll conducted by the Rockefeller Foundation and TIME, Inc., for *The Shriver Report: A Woman's Nation Changes Everything* asked, "Which of these things, in particular, would need to change in order for working parents to balance evenly their job or business, their marriage, and their children?" In response to the four broad options given— longer school hours or school years, more flexible work schedules, more paid time off, or better and more day-care options—half (51 percent) of those polled picked more flexible work schedules.[17] In a poll conducted for the Heartland Alliance, "Millennials" (members of the generation born during the last quarter of the twentieth century) reported that workplace flexibility was almost as important to them as wages; they also ranked workplace flexibility as more important than strong benefits or intellectually interesting work.[18] Workers caring for an elder family member too report that they would like to see greater schedule flexibility and options for managing time at work.[19]

Although workers report needing and wanting some flexibility in terms of hours or location of work, the nation's wage-and-hours regulatory structure, based on outdated models of who works and who gives care, provides little guidance to help employers deal with the realities of today's workforce. The FLSA, which lays out the national regulatory structure on hours, remains grounded in assumptions about work and family that are no longer valid—and in fact were never valid for large numbers of workers. Although many employers do address workplace flexibility issues, wide gaps exist regarding which workers have access to flexibility. Further, a growing body of research suggests that mothers and caregivers often experience explicit discrimination because of their roles as caregivers and their need for workplace flexibility.

> *A growing body of research suggests that mothers and caregivers often experience explicit discrimination because of their roles as caregivers and their need for workplace flexibility.*

The Fair Labor Standards Act

The 1938 Fair Labor Standards Act is the foundation of the nation's regulatory structure governing hours of work. The FLSA sets overtime thresholds by defining a regular workweek as being forty hours and requiring that workers covered by the law be paid 150 percent of the usual hourly wage for any hours worked above that threshold. When Congress passed the FLSA, its intent was to encourage employers to curtail the long hours of their current employees and to put more people to work. The law specifies that workers who need protection in terms of hours of work are those employed full time at regular jobs. The legislation was passed following decades of state efforts to restrict excessive work hours, at least for women and children.[20] The FLSA initially excluded some groups of workers, but was gradually extended from the 1940s through the 1980s to include almost every worker except employees of state and local government and small farms, as well as some domestic workers.[21]

The FLSA's overtime provisions do not apply to all workers; indeed, they cover only the six in ten workers who are paid hourly wages.[22] Salaried workers who earn at least $23,600 a year, who are paid on a salary basis with a "guaranteed minimum," and who perform exempt job duties are not protected by the FLSA's overtime provisions.[23] No statutory limit governs the number of hours that salaried (known as "exempt") employees can be asked to work in a given week. In 2004, the Bush administration increased the share of workers who are categorized as exempt by expanding the definition of "executive, administrative, and professional" workers. At the time, analysts estimated that the redefinition would make 8 million more workers (about 6 percent of the total employed workforce) ineligible for overtime pay.[24] The FLSA's failure to provide universal coverage thus creates conditions of overwork for exempt employees.

To the extent that the FLSA limits overtime for covered workers, it may help them better manage work-family conflict. In addition, its overtime provisions have improved the take-home pay of millions of lower- and middle-class families who benefit from overtime pay. But it places no limit on overtime work. Many workers must often work overtime with little or no notice, a practice that not only exacerbates the work-family conflict but is also a frequent source of contention between managers and employees.[25]

Because the FLSA was never targeted at the problem of underwork, it does not address part-time parity, sufficient hours of work, or scheduling. A careful analysis by Susan Lambert and Julia Henly of the scheduling issues facing low-wage workers documents how low-wage employees often experience "fluctuating and reduced work hours and unpredictable work schedules that can compromise their job performance and their

ability to earn an adequate living."[26] The authors find that "employers can and do vary workers' hours," making it hard for workers to coordinate work schedules with a family's need for care. The FLSA offers no guidance on these issues.

Private-Sector Responses to the Need for Scheduling Flexibility

The gaps in FLSA worker protections leave a great deal of room for private-sector employers to experiment with flexible schedules to address work-family conflict. The FLSA itself allows workers and employers great leeway in how and where hours are worked.[27] Employers can allow any employee—whether covered by or exempt from the FLSA overtime provisions—to vary arrival and departure times, days worked, and shift arrangements, or to take time off during the day so long as covered workers put in no more than forty hours in a given week if the employer wants to avoid paying overtime. Employers have even more flexibility regarding the hours of exempt workers. For example, exempt employees can have compressed workweeks over two-week intervals, working nine-hour days each week Monday through Thursday, then, every other Friday, alternating between working eight hours and taking the day off.

Whether compensatory time (a program, known as "comp time," that allows employees to work more hours than usual and bank them to use later to compensate them for the extra work) or flexibility programs are helpful for employees struggling to resolve work-family conflict hinges on how they are implemented. A review of litigation history on comp time found that even within the public sector, where comp time is less contentious than it is in the private sector, employers limit their employees' ability to use comp time at their own discretion.[28] In the private sector, which is less regulated and less unionized than the public sector, employees are likely to be even less able to make use of their comp time when it suits them.

Firms that experiment with workplace flexibility often allow employees to make requests for flexibility, thus beginning a process of negotiation over how the schedule will help both employees and employers to meet their needs.[29] Few workers, however, have access to workplace flexibility, and those that do are still too often "mommy tracked." Only about a quarter of employees report having some kind of flexibility, although from about half to most of all employers report offering flexibility of some kind.[30] Workers with the least access to predictable work schedules are disproportionately low-wage workers, women, and workers of color.[31]

Some firms offer comp time to their salaried employees who are exempt from the overtime provisions of the FLSA. In the private sector, this policy is available only to workers exempt from the FLSA's overtime provisions; about a third (36 percent) of employers offer comp time to some workers and one in five (18 percent) makes it available to all workers.[32]

Firms that voluntarily implement flexibility do so because they see it as good for their bottom line. A growing body of empirical research suggests that these policies enhance productivity by improving retention and reducing turnover. In 2010, the Council of Economic Advisers reviewed evidence on the economic value of adopting workplace flexibility and concluded that the "costs to firms of adopting these kinds of management practices can also be outweighed by reduced absenteeism, lower turnover, healthier

workers, and increased productivity."[33] In a review of research in *The Shriver Report*, Brad Harrington and Jamie Ladge cite several studies showing that when firms allow workers flexibility and managers implement it, the benefits are considerable.[34]

New Ideas for Workplace Flexibility

Government policy has a clear role in workplace flexibility. Although the government has been setting basic labor standards pertaining to hours of work for nearly a century, workers today both need and want better policies. Generally, to be considered effective at addressing workplace flexibility, new policies must work for employees as well as employers and give them some control over the hours or location of work so they can address their work-family conflicts. Further, participation should be at the worker's discretion and should not entail disparate pay or promotion penalties; it may entail pay cuts commensurate with reduced hours, but not penalties over time. Finally, new policies should not exacerbate the gaps left by the FLSA or undermine its protections.

Alternative Schedules and Compressed Workweeks. Federal, state, and local governments have experimented with several innovative programs to increase scheduling flexibility that could provide a model for policy makers. Since the late 1970s, for example, federal employees have had some access to two kinds of alternative work schedules, a "flexible work schedule" and a "compressed work schedule."[35] In 2010, the Office of Personnel Management launched a pilot program called Results-Only Work Environment that allows employees to work whenever and wherever they want, as long as they complete their tasks. Initial results from the evaluation of the federal pilot found greater employee satisfaction, a shift in focus among both employees and employers to output instead of hours worked, and improved perception of leadership.[36]

State and local governments have also implemented alternative schedules. In 2008 Utah Governor Jon Huntsman moved most state employees to a four-day workweek by executive order.[37] Although the primary goal of the reform was to reduce energy expenses, a Brigham Young University study found that implementing compressed schedules in Utah reduced work-life conflict and improved productivity.[38] In 2006 Houston Mayor Bill White began a Flexible Workplace Initiative Program to encourage companies to implement flexible work-scheduling policies. In an annual Flex in the City program, participating Houston area employers "adopt new flexible workplace policies for two weeks." City government surveys of both employees and employers found that the flexible scheduling reduced traffic congestion, lowered commute costs, and increased productivity.[39]

Right-to-Request. The United Kingdom, New Zealand, and Australia have implemented policies that give workers the right to request a flexible schedule without fear of retaliation.[40] Because many U.S. workers are subject to being disciplined for even asking about flexibility or predictability, the right to request could be a very important addition to the U.S. work-family policy framework.[41] The new policies implemented abroad require employers to set up a process to discuss and negotiate workplace flexibility and permit them to turn down the requests only for certain business reasons. In the United Kingdom, for example, employers may refuse the request for flexibility only for such reasons as the burden of additional costs, negative effects on meeting customer demand or on business quality and performance, or the

inability to reorganize the existing staff to make it work.[42]

Right-to-request legislation has increased the number of workers in the United Kingdom with flexible schedules.[43] Only 10 percent of requests have been turned down since the law was enacted. And although the law applied originally only to workers with a child under the age of six, the business community joined with workers to lobby to extend it gradually to workers with caregiving responsibilities for disabled or ill adults or for children under age eighteen by April 2011.[44]

Making the right-to-request model work in the United States would require careful analysis of how to adapt it to fit the U.S. legal and institutional structure. For example, the right to request would have to be made available to workers across the income distribution.[45] Employees would have to be assured a right to request a schedule that works for them, as well as their employer, even in the absence of a union setting. For right-to-request to be effective in the United States, it should also be used to help workers who do not want to (or cannot) work overtime, who want to place limits on their hours, and who need help in addressing the issue of scheduling predictability. Right-to-request legislation, in the form of the Working Families Flexibility Act, was introduced in the 111th Congress by Carolyn Maloney in the House of Representatives and Robert Casey in the Senate. So far, New Hampshire is the only state where such legislation has been introduced.[46]

Equal Rights in the Workplace

The foundation for equitable treatment at work in the United States is laid out in Title VII of the 1964 Civil Rights Act. As originally passed, Title VII protected individuals against employment discrimination on the basis of sex, race, color, national origin, and religion; it has been amended to include pregnant women, and other legislation has expanded the rights of the disabled. Although the Civil Rights Act ensures that all employees have an equal opportunity within the existing workplace structure, it does not require an employer to make changes to the workplace to address specific protected class issues. And although having broad protections from unfair treatment certainly helps some caregivers address discrimination in the workplace, nevertheless, as Ann O'Leary and Karen Kornbluh note, "Equal protection laws are only as good as the nature and quantity of benefits the employer provides to other workers."[47]

In 1978 the Pregnancy Discrimination Act amended Title VII to prohibit discrimination on the basis of pregnancy. The Pregnancy Discrimination Act has helped normalize a pregnant woman as a still-functioning employee,[48] but it does not mandate that employers take any specific positive actions; they must only offer pregnant women the same benefits that they offer any other worker.[49] For example, a company may fire an employee for breast feeding too often, making the argument that breast feeding is part of child care and not part of pregnancy.[50] The Patient Protection and Affordable Care Act of 2010 now requires employers with more than fifty employees to provide appropriate breaks and locations so that working mothers covered by FLSA can pump breast milk.[51]

The Americans with Disabilities Act (ADA) of 1990 prohibits discrimination on the basis of disability in employment, as well as in other areas such as public services, public accommodations, transportation, and telecommunications.[52] For employees with disabilities, the ADA provides workplace flexibility by requiring employers to provide "reasonable accommodations" that enable employees to perform their jobs. An employer is not required by the ADA to provide a reasonable accommodation if doing so would create an "undue hardship"—defined as "significant difficulty or expense." The ADA also covers caregivers for the disabled.

Evidence is growing that workers with care responsibilities experience discrimination in the workplace and that government policy has a role in ensuring workplace equity. Joan Williams, at the Center for WorkLife Law, has coined the phrase "family responsibility discrimination" to describe disparate treatment at work of "pregnant women, mothers and fathers of young children, and workers with aging parents or sick spouses or partners." She notes that these workers "may be rejected for hire, passed over for promotion, demoted, harassed, or terminated—despite good performance—simply because their employers make personnel decisions based on stereotypical notions of how they will or should act given their family responsibilities."[53] Sociologists Shelley Correll, Stephen Benard, and In Paik have found that among two groups of job candidates with identical credentials, the group identified as mothers was perceived to be less competent, less promotable, less likely to be recommended for management, and less likely to be recommended for hire, and that the mothers had lower recommended starting salaries than nonmothers.[54]

Employment discrimination is particularly problematic in the United States, where most workers have no explicit employment contract and thus can be fired for any reason not explicitly prohibited through judicial or statutory exceptions.[55] Workers with care responsibilities may need to request flexible work arrangements, but may have no job-protected mechanism even for asking their employer to help them resolve their work-family conflict.

New Ideas to Address Family Responsibilities Discrimination

In 2007, the Equal Employment Opportunity Commission (EEOC), the enforcement agency for the Civil Rights Act, laid out how the laws that establish workplace fairness also provide protections for workers with family responsibilities. Although no one law specifically addresses the dual role that most workers now play as workers and caregivers, a framework based on the growing body of case law is emerging. The EEOC's caregiver guidance outlines how, based on current law, workers cannot be subject to a hostile work environment or treated differently once they develop caregiver responsibilities, or be held to stricter standards (for example, about requesting leave or timeliness) than other workers. It also highlights difficulties in the workplace for women who are pregnant or have young children, as well as for men, when they request flexible schedules, and what treatment constitutes discrimination for them.[56] The guidance, however, does not provide a framework that would give workers the time and flexibility to take care of caregiving obligations and not be discriminated against as a result.

For the future, one possibility would be to transform the EEOC caregiver guidance into legislation. The Australian state of New South Wales has done something similar, implementing protection for employees against discrimination based on care responsibilities, and requiring employers to affirmatively provide reasonable, flexible work schedules unless doing so would cause them undue hardship.[57]

With a Job, but Needing Paid Time Off to Give Care

Because the vast majority of American families now have no one at home to provide care, workers occasionally need paid time off from work to tend to loved ones with serious illnesses or to bond with a new child. Most families receive the bulk of their income from employment, making access to paid time off critical for family economic well-being. U.S. social insurance programs provide income support when a family member cannot work because of retirement, unemployment, or disability, but they do not cover a worker's need for short-term or extended time off to provide care for a new child or a sick family member.

Two related, but conceptually separate, issues create work-family conflict in this area. The first is whether workers can take extended time off work to care for a seriously ill family member or to care for a new child. Such time off, which I call family and medical leave, can often but not always be planned in advance. The second issue is whether workers can miss up to a few days of work to care for a family member who has a relatively minor illness, such as a cold or flu. The need for this second type of leave, which I call sick days, is often unexpected.

Although few American workers have paid family and medical leave and paid sick days, most would like to have both. Nationwide, 77 percent of Americans believe that businesses should be required to provide paid family and medical leave for every worker who needs it. And support cuts across the political spectrum —including 64 percent of conservatives and 89 percent of liberals.[58] Support for paid sick

U.S. social insurance programs provide income support, but they do not cover a worker's need for short-term or extended time off to provide care for a new child or a sick family member.

days is also robust. In a nationally representative survey conducted in 2010 by the National Opinion Research Center, 75 percent of Americans voiced support for a law that would give all workers paid sick days.[59]

The Social Security Act

The Social Security Act of 1935 established Old Age, Survivors, and Disability Insurance, commonly known as Social Security. The new law established social insurance, whereby workers pay into funds through payroll taxes and then, having demonstrated sufficient labor market attachment, become eligible for benefits upon retiring or becoming unemployed. The law also established a program of income support for women and children without a breadwinner. In 1954, the federal government added Social Security Disability Insurance for workers who become disabled; in 1972, it added Supplementary Security Income for disabled and blind people regardless of work history.[60] The income support program for women and children—called Aid to Dependent Families in the original legislation—was designed for widows who had lost their male breadwinner and needed funds to help them support their children. The program is means-tested—that is, available only to mothers with income up to a certain

limit—and reforms during the mid-1990s tied eligibility for benefits to work or job search activities.[61]

Some of the fundamental assumptions underlying the Social Security Act were that individuals were either caregivers or breadwinners, but not both; that married couples typically stayed married for life; and that most families had a stay-at-home parent, usually a mother, to provide care for children, the sick, and the elderly.

Eligibility for the retirement and disability benefits of Social Security depends on a history of employment and payment into the system by the recipient or his or her spouse. Social Security resembles insurance, because workers' income risks are pooled and payments into the system (that is, insurance premiums) are paid based on expected benefits.[62] To qualify for retirement benefits, a worker must accumulate at least forty credits (approximately ten years of work).[63] Adults and younger people qualify for disability or survivor benefits with proportionally fewer credits appropriate to their age and potential labor market experience. Most Americans are eligible for both the retirement and disability benefits. In 2009, 89.7 percent of those aged sixty-five and older received Social Security benefits.[64] Caregivers, however, are less likely to be eligible for benefits in their own right, because they are likely to have spent less time in the workforce. Spousal benefits provide a married woman with as much as half of her husband's benefit if she has no work history. In 2008, 56 percent of women received Social Security benefits that depended wholly or in part on their husband's benefits.[65]

The Social Security Act also established an unemployment insurance system that is administered by the states, but this system too leaves out some workers with care responsibilities. Although all workers (except some domestic and agricultural workers) are covered by the program, eligibility depends on reaching certain thresholds of earnings and hours worked in the period preceding unemployment. Up until 2009, much of the nation's unemployment insurance system did not cover part-time workers and did not allow workers to receive unemployment benefits if they quit their job because of problems with child care or if they had to leave because their spouse found a job in another location. Such rules made it less likely that caregivers would be able to receive unemployment benefits if they lost their job. Some of these issues were addressed in the Unemployment Insurance Modernization Act, which was implemented as a part of the American Recovery and Reinvestment Act in 2009, but not all states have put the reforms into effect.[66]

The Family and Medical Leave Act

By the 1980s, although increasingly fewer families had a stay-at-home caregiver, much of the social insurance infrastructure continued to assume that they did. In 1993, to address the issues of care and work, Congress passed and President Bill Clinton signed the Family and Medical Leave Act (FMLA), the first piece of legislation in U.S. history to give workers a right to job-protected leave for caregiving. The FMLA provides up to twelve weeks of unpaid leave a year for employees who need time off to care for a new child (newborn or adopted), to recover from a serious illness, or to care for a seriously ill family member. To be eligible for FMLA leave, an employee must put in at least 1,250 hours of work a year at a large company (one with fifty or more employees) and must have worked at that company for at least a year, although not necessarily consecutively.[67]

The FMLA gave approximately 44 million workers (out of a workforce of more than 128 million) the right to job-protected unpaid family and medical leave.[68] Among all U.S. workers, 16.5 percent took FMLA leave between mid-1999 and 2000 (the latest survey data available). Of that total, 17.9 percent took leave to bond with or care for a new child, 7.8 percent took leave for maternity or disability, 47.2 percent for their own illness, and 27.1 percent to care for a seriously ill family member.[69]

The FMLA, however, has two major shortcomings. The first is that the leave it provides is unpaid. Unlike programs that offer leave for other reasons, such as a short-term disability or unemployment, the FMLA is not a social insurance program; rather, it provides job protection when workers take the leave. Unpaid leave, however, is not adequate to the needs of low- and moderate-income families. For them, the right to job-protected leave is nice, but not enough.[70] The FMLA's second shortcoming is that it excludes about half the labor force, many of whom are the workers who may need coverage the most.

By covering only workers in firms with fifty or more employees, the law leaves out about a third of all U.S. workers—those who tend to earn less, and to be less likely to have access to paid benefits, than their counterparts in larger companies.[71] Furthermore, even workers in covered establishments are eligible for FMLA leave only if they meet other requirements that fit the traditional model of employment—which no longer captures many of the realities of the modern workforce. Tying workers' eligibility to a minimum number of hours worked, for example, fails to acknowledge that many people work part time for caregiving reasons. And because part-time workers are more likely than full-time workers to have more than one job, tying FMLA eligibility to time with a single employer limits their eligibility. Requiring workers to undergo a waiting period each time they switch jobs ignores the reality that young workers change jobs often during the first few years of their career and thus harms many young parents, disproportionately those of color. Among workers aged eighteen to twenty-five with a small child at home, 43.3 percent of women, 31.2 percent of men, 38.5 percent of whites, 48.0 percent of blacks, and 31.5 percent of Hispanics have been at their job less than a year.[72] Finally FMLA eligibility requirements do not acknowledge the reality that workers today typically do not enjoy lifetime employment with a single employer, especially workers in emerging industries such as the technology sector. According to the Bureau of Labor Statistics, between 1979 and 2008, a typical worker aging from eighteen to forty-four held an average of 11.0 jobs and held more than two-thirds of those jobs (7.6) between the ages of eighteen and twenty-seven, the ages at which many workers start families.[73] Requiring workers to hold jobs for at least a year may also lead some workers to stay in unsuitable jobs to retain eligibility for benefits.

The Market Response to the Need for Paid Time Off for Caregiving

Thus far, the market on its own has not filled the need for paid time off for caregiving. Employers do not typically offer extended leave to care for a new child or for an ill family member, and when they do, they tend to offer it only to higher-wage, higher-status workers, thus flying in the face of the compensating-wage model. And employers who do provide paid leave, unlike those who offer pensions and health insurance, face no government requirements that policy be uniform within the firm.[74] Thus, even within a

Employees least likely to get family and medical leave are low-wage workers who are most likely to need workplace flexibility because they cannot afford paid help to care for loved ones.

given firm, not all employees may have access to the same paid family and medical leave benefits.[75] Employees least likely to get family and medical leave are low-wage workers who are most likely to need workplace flexibility because they cannot afford paid help to care for loved ones.[76] The U.S. Census Bureau reports that 60 percent of new mothers with a bachelor's degree or higher received any kind of paid maternity leave, compared with only 22 percent of those without a high school degree.[77]

Further, the leave that exists is a patchwork available to employees for their own illness or for childbirth with very little available for caregiving or bonding with a new child. About 40 percent of all workers are covered by private temporary disability insurance programs that provide benefits for maternity and an employee's own illness.[78] Such insurance, however, does not address the work-family conflicts that arise when no stay-at-home family member is available to provide care for others who are ill or for a new child. New fathers, who are ineligible for disability leave for childbirth, are typically offered little or no paid leave, and employees who have sick days and deplete them must hope that they—or their new children—do not get sick later on. Further, because there is no government requirement that the programs be universally applied, many low-paid workers may not be offered the benefit even if higher-paid workers are.

New Ideas for Paid Time Off for Caregiving

Nearly every developed country in the world except the United States uses the social insurance model to provide extended time off for family and medical leave.[79] The American model—which is to rely on individual firms to pay for these leaves—disproportionately burdens firms that have staff who are prone to serious health problems, who have ailing family members who need their care, or who are of childbearing age.

There is no need, however, for the United States to set up a social insurance infrastructure to provide workers with paid sick days. The costs of sick day benefits are minimal and therefore should be borne by individual employers, who also stand to reap gains from not having workers with contagious diseases show up at work, make their colleagues ill, and reduce overall firm productivity. Paid sick days are now guaranteed by law in several U.S. localities—San Francisco, the District of Columbia, and Milwaukee—but not nationwide.

Building on State Temporary Disability Insurance Programs. Five states (California, Hawaii, New Jersey, New York, and Rhode Island) have long-standing Temporary Disability Insurance (TDI) programs that provide workers with coverage for non-work-related disabilities. Over the past decade, California and New Jersey have expanded their TDI programs to cover caregiver leave for new parents or for workers who need to care for a seriously ill family

member. In 2002 California extended its TDI program to offer six weeks of family leave (with only partial wage replacement), for which every private-sector California worker is eligible.[80] New Jersey passed similar legislation in 2008.[81] In 2007, Washington became the first state to pass legislation establishing a new, stand-alone program for paid parental leave (although the financing mechanism remains to be worked out).[82]

Of the three other states with TDI—Hawaii, New York, and Rhode Island—New York is actively considering expanding its program to include family leave.[83] The prospect of passage in the states without TDI programs may be limited, although Oregon and New Hampshire are looking into paid family and medical leave. Experimentation is important, and policy makers should support it. When states pass laws giving more generous benefits than federal laws provide, they can provide a model for an eventual federal law, as happened during the early decades of the twentieth century with minimum wage laws.

So far, the experimentation at the state level shows that paid family and medical leave can be a successful policy for both employers and employees. Eileen Appelbaum and Ruth Milkman's evaluation of California's family leave insurance program found that, contrary to opponents' warnings, it was not a "job killer" and in fact had no discernible effect on overall employment. Their survey of employers found that the program had either no effect or positive effects; 89 percent of employers said it had no effect or a positive effect on productivity and 87 percent reported no increase in their costs. The survey of employees also revealed positive effects. It found that 26 percent of paid family leave claims are now filed by fathers who wish to bond with a new child, up from

17 percent when the program first began in 2004. And 82.7 percent of workers in low-quality jobs who used the leave returned to their jobs, compared with 73.9 percent of those who did not use the leave.[84] (Individuals may not have used leave because they either did not know they were eligible or did not want to risk losing their job because the leave is paid, but not job-protected, for all workers.)

Congress and the Obama administration have recently advanced proposals that support such state experimentation. The Family Income to Respond to Significant Transitions Act (H.R. 2339), sponsored by Representative Lynn Woolsey (D-CA), would provide start-up funds to states that want to implement paid family leave programs. Similarly, President Barack Obama's fiscal year 2011 budget included $50 million to help states set up their own paid family and medical leave programs. Congress is also considering a bill to provide paid family and medical leave. The Family Leave Insurance Act (H.R. 5873), introduced recently by Representative Pete Stark (D-CA), and a companion bill introduced during the last Congress by Senator Christopher Dodd (D-CT) would establish a national family leave insurance program.

Another approach is to implement paid family and medical leave nationwide and administer it through the Social Security Administration,[85] with individuals paying into a new trust fund that would support paid family and medical leaves. Such an approach would resemble the extensions to Social Security for long-term disabilities implemented during the 1950s. The approach has a variety of advantages: it would reduce start-up costs for a new program; everyone would be covered because Social Security coverage is now nearly

universal; and the lifetime employment rules of Disability Insurance could be used to determine adequate employment history and benefit level, thus covering young and intermittent workers.

Paid Sick Days. The market has not on its own developed an effective system of paid sick days to provide care for a sick child or family member. In a recent National Opinion Research Center poll, 64 percent of workers said they could access paid sick time for their own illness, while 47 percent said they had paid sick days that they could use both when they were ill and when they needed to care for a sick family member.[86] Some observers have argued that workers who have paid vacation or other personal leave are really "covered" for sick time, but many workers cannot take such leave without giving their employer advance notice, making it impossible to use when a child wakes up with the flu or other urgent care needs arise.[87] Other research found that nearly two-thirds (63 percent) of workers (both full time and part time) do not have access to paid sick leave to care for a sick child.[88] The share of employees without paid leave for their own or a child's illness rises to 84 percent in construction and nondurable manufacturing and to 94 percent in accommodations and food services, an industry that disproportionately employs women.[89]

Advocates are conducting active campaigns for paid sick days at both the federal and state level. As of 2010, workers have the right to job-protected paid sick leave in only two places: San Francisco (as of 2007) and Washington, D.C. (as of 2008). Voters in Milwaukee passed a paid-sick-days ballot initiative in 2008, but it is being held up by a court injunction. The Healthy Families Act, sponsored in the House by Representative Rosa DeLauro, which would give workers the

Having access to affordable child care and, increasingly, help with elder care, is important to Americans, most of whom agree that the government or businesses should provide more funding for child care to support parents who work.

right to earn up to seven paid sick days a year, has been introduced, but not acted on, in the past few Congresses.

Caring While Working

Working families need access to safe, affordable, and enriching care for children, the elderly, and the ill while family members are at work. Workers cannot be in two places at once, and the decline in the number of stay-at-home parents has been matched by a decline in the share of adults who have the time to care for an ailing family member, whether on a day-to-day basis or occasionally helping drive an elder to the doctor or deal with a health emergency. More than 15.3 million U.S. children under age six need care while their parents are at work, and some 9 million Americans over age sixty-five, a number that is projected to grow to 12 million by 2020, need long-term care.[90] Women continue to care for family members more than men do, and, because of changing demographics, those caring for elderly parents are more likely to be working and caring for children at the same time.[91]

The challenge for many families is twofold: finding safe and enriching care and being able to afford it. Care work is by definition done by people, and, even if the ratio of care-givers to those being cared for is relatively high, the reality is that without subsidies of some kind most families cannot afford to pay reasonable salaries for such workers. Most families need care support for finite periods when their children are young and when a family member is elderly or ailing, but the high cost over even a few years can be out of reach, especially for young workers in their early earning years. A clear role for government policy is to smooth the costs of that care across workers and across workers' lifetimes, as government already does with the public school system.

Having access to affordable child care and, increasingly, help with elder care, is important to Americans, most of whom— 68 percent—agree that the government or businesses should provide more funding for child care to support parents who work. Support is weaker among conservatives, at 50 percent, than among liberals, at 85 percent.[92] In qualitative research about what families would like to see to help them with elder care, respondents reported that they wanted a "more user-friendly and easily navigable health care system, especially with respect to managing cost and insurance issues."[93]

The model for government assistance in this area has involved assistance of two kinds: helping families reduce the cost of providing care to dependents through tax credits and providing direct care for poor and low-income families.

Tax Relief

Families typically rely on a variety of child- and elder-care options. Roughly one-third of both low- and middle-income families—34 percent and 30 percent, respectively—and one-quarter, or 24 percent, of professional-managerial families rely primarily on relatives other than the parents themselves for child care. Among higher-income families, 37 percent rely on child-care centers, as do 30 percent of low- and middle-income families. Low-income families are more likely to rely on the parents themselves for child care—26 percent, compared with 20 percent of middle-income families and 14 percent of professional families. Less than 4 percent of families in all three groups rely on sitters or nannies.[94]

Care for elders is equally varied. According to the Department of Health and Human Services, 70 percent of the elderly receive all of their care from family and friends, rather than professionals.[95] A 2010 survey by the Families and Work Institute found that 17 percent of workers were providing elder care and that those caregivers were employed forty-five hours a week on average on top of caregiving, an hour more each week than noncaregivers.[96]

Both child and elder care are quite expensive. The Department of Health and Human Services advises families to spend no more than 10 percent of their income on child care, but many families do. In 2009, a year of full-time center-based care for a four-year-old ranged from an average of $4,056 in Mississippi to $13,158 in Massachusetts.[97] Not surprisingly, lower-income families spend a far higher share of their income on care than do higher-income families. An analysis that I conducted with Joan Williams found that, in March 2009 dollars, low-income families pay around $2,300 a year in care for each child under age six—about 14 percent of their income. Families in the middle average

$3,500 a year—6 percent to 9 percent of their income. Professional families pay about $4,800 a year—3 percent to 7 percent of income.[98] Among working elder-caregivers, almost half helped cover the cost of caring for a parent; of those, nearly half (44 percent) reported that their financial contributions were at least "somewhat" burdensome.[99]

Two types of tax relief are available to families for care-related expenses. The Child and Dependent Care Tax Credit is a nonrefundable credit of up to 35 percent of qualifying expenses to tax filers to help cover the cost of child or dependent care.[100] The care must be for a child under the age of thirteen or for a mentally or physically handicapped spouse or dependent.[101] The requirement that the person in care be a dependent of the person taking the tax credit puts the deduction out of reach of the millions of families who provide occasional support to an ailing or elder family member who is not a dependent, as well as extended families who share the financial and emotional costs of caring for an ailing family member, but cannot share the credit. Some employees also have access to Flexible Spending Accounts for Dependent Care to set aside up to $5,000 pre-tax dollars a year to pay for child or dependent care. Families can choose whether to use the tax credit or the flexible spending account; they cannot use both.

Both of these tax benefits disproportionately benefit higher-income families. As is common with nonrefundable tax credits, the tax credit goes primarily to middle- and higher-income workers and families because it is available only to families in which parents—both parents if it is a married couple—have earnings, are in school, or are disabled. Further, because the tax credit is nonrefundable, low-income families who do not earn enough to pay taxes cannot receive the credit. Flexible Spending Accounts must be set up by employers and thus mostly go to professional-managerial families.[102] Although both these tax benefits certainly help some families, they provide fairly small benefits relative to the cost of care and do not touch many of the neediest families.[103]

The tax-based programs, which assume that the market provides sufficient options for families to find adequate—ideally, safe and enriching—care, have no direct effect on the quality of care available. Yet high-quality and affordable care seems to be in short supply. In addition to providing tax relief for higher-income workers, the government also, as I note in the next section, provides some direct subsidies to lower-income workers. What it does not provide is any national public program, either for child care or for elder care.

Direct Subsidies to Care Providers

The federal government provides direct subsidies for some lower-income families to make child care more affordable through the Child Care Development Block Grant Fund and also provides funds for child care from the Temporary Assistance for Needy Families program. States also help families with child-care expenses.[104] In addition, Head Start programs often are incorporated into child-care programs, although because the goal of the former is primarily educational, the care provided does not necessarily fit with a parent's work schedule. The American Recovery and Reinvestment Act pumped an additional $2 billion into the Child Care Development Block Grant Fund on top of the $2.1 billion of discretionary funding for 2009 authorized by the regular federal budget appropriations process, but these extra dollars were temporary.[105]

Child Care Development Block Grant funds are targeted to low-income families and administered by the states, which have considerable leeway in setting provider payment levels, parent co-payment levels, and income eligibility requirements, and also in regulating the programs. Typically, for a family to be eligible for child-care subsidies, its earnings must fall below the state's median income, but the threshold varies widely.[106] An analysis of eligibility rules in ten states found that in Texas the income of a single-parent family with two children could not exceed 85 percent of the federal policy threshold, or about $1,176 a month, while in the District of Columbia a family's income could reach 250 percent of that threshold, or $3,458 a month. Most families who are eligible do not receive the benefit. In the same ten-state analysis, in no state did more than half of those eligible receive the subsidy.[107] Subsidies, then, are available only for low-income families and are scarce and sporadic even for them. About 30 percent of low-income families using center-based care and 16 percent using an in-home care center for a child under age six receive subsidies, while the share of middle-income families receiving subsidies is negligible—about 3 percent for an in-home care center.[108]

Unlike families needing care for small children, most families with elder-caregiving needs do not receive services from a paid caregiver. According to the Families and Work Institute, a paid caregiver helps a quarter of family caregivers with a significant amount of daily care.[109] Medicare—which provides health insurance coverage for more than 46 million Americans, including people sixty-five and older, some people with disabilities, and people with end-stage renal disease—covers skilled nursing home expenses for up to 100 days, as well as assistance for those who need part-time health services and are homebound. It does not cover help with activities of daily living.[110] Medicaid provides insurance for those with limited finances and are sixty-five or older or disabled; it can be used to help pay for residential or nursing home care for elderly people who meet income and asset requirements set by the program.[111] The Families and Work Institute survey on elder care reports that most (60 percent) of the funding for costs associated with elder care comes from Medicare, followed by private medical insurance (44 percent), elders themselves (34 percent), and Medicaid (8 percent).[112]

Because of increasing demand by workers who need help with care of children and ailing family members, the Bureau of Labor Statistics predicts that employment will grow faster in the care sector than in most other occupations. The Bureau of Labor Statistics predicts that the number of home health aides will rise by 50 percent between 2008 and 2018, while the number of child-care workers will rise by 10.9 percent.[113] The low subsidy levels for both child and elder care, however, limit not only the availability of affordable care options for families, but also the pay and benefits of the care providers. These jobs, held disproportionately by women and often women of color, typically pay relatively low wages.[114]

New Ideas for Access to Care

It has been decades since the United States had a national conversation about universal access to child care, and the nation is just barely beginning a national conversation on elder care and caring for ailing family members. In 1971, Congress passed the nation's first and only comprehensive child-care legislation. The Comprehensive Child Development Act provided every child with access to child care, with a priority given to those with the greatest economic or social need. The bill laid out federal standards for quality control, staff training, and securing facilities. And it set child-care fees on a sliding scale according to income. President Richard Nixon, however, vetoed the bill, arguing that "federally-supported, institutional child care would undermine the family by encouraging mothers with young children to go out to work."[115] Despite the veto, however, women went to work. During the early 1970s, the participation of U.S. women in the labor force began a rapid rise. Today, forty years later, that national child-care conversation has still not resumed, even though most American adults are now employed outside the home.

States are experimenting with universal prekindergarten programs, which help families manage work-family conflict by offering safe, enriching, and affordable— and most often free—care for pre-K children, typically aged three and four. The state programs take a variety of forms. For example, half (53 percent) of Georgia's four-year-olds participate in state-funded pre-K, at a cost of $4,234 for each child, supported through a state lottery. Oklahoma enrolls 71 percent of its four-year-olds, the highest share in the nation, in publicly funded pre-K; as of 2008, 99 percent of its school districts offered pre-K programs. Research at Georgetown University found that "Tulsa's pre-K program produced substantial academic benefits for all children in the program, regardless of race or ethnicity."[116] Oklahoma funds its program through a state aid formula that provides grants to school districts regardless of income. West Virginia folds its pre-K funding into its public schools funding formula and has seen a 65 percent increase in four-year-olds' participation since 2002.[117] The National Institute for Early Education

Research, however, has found that only sixteen of the thirty-eight statewide universal pre-K programs have sufficient funding to meet all of their benchmarks for quality standards.[118]

In the areas of elder care, the federal government has been working to make it easier for families to acquire long-term-care insurance to defray costs for services that traditional medical insurance does not cover, such as help with activities of daily living or institutional care. The 2010 Patient Protection and Affordable Care Act included provisions from the Community Living Assistance Services and Support Act, a consumer-financed program administered by the government that allows people to purchase insurance for community living assistance and supports. The insurance is explicitly designed to help alleviate the burden on friends and family who have been acting as caregivers.[119] Although Medicaid and Medicare benefits often do not pay for long-term care in people's homes, the Community Living Assistance Services and Support Act provides a daily cash benefit to those who need support in activities of daily living, which can help family caregivers.[120]

The Way Forward

Crafting a comprehensive government policy to ease work-family conflict requires rethinking the basic labor standards and social insurance models that the United States has had in place since the 1930s, when Frances Perkins presented President Franklin Roosevelt with the ideas that became the Fair Labor Standards Act and the Social Security Act. Her dual vision for workers included ensuring fair treatment for workers at work and ensuring income support, based on insurance principles, for workers when they could not work or find work.[121] In developing these cornerstone pieces of legislation, Perkins did not foresee that just over half a century later, most American mothers would be either breadwinners or cobreadwinners and that most American families would need income support and flexibility when a family member needed to provide care. Updating the nation's basic labor standards and social insurance to address conflicts that arise between work and family today is the next step.

Endnotes

1. The term "workplace flexibility" has been used to encompass a wide array of policies that address work-family conflict. See Workplace Flexibility 2010: Georgetown Law (www.workplaceflexibility2010.org).

2. Author's analysis of Internal Revenue Service, "Table 1: Individual Income Tax, All Returns: Sources of Incomes and Adjustments," Department of Commerce (www.irs.gov/pub/irs-soi/07in01ar.xls).

3. Heather Boushey and Ann O'Leary, eds., *The Shriver Report: A Woman's Nation Changes Everything* (Washington: Center for American Progress, 2009).

4. Christian Weller and Amanda Logan, *America's Middle Class Still Losing Ground* (Washington: Center for American Progress, 2008).

5. Teresa Amott and Julie Matthaei, *Race, Gender, and Work: A Multicultural Economic History of Women in the United States* (Boston: South End Press, 1991).

6. Sherwin Rosen, "The Theory of Equalizing Differences," in *Handbook of Labor Economics,* vol. 1, edited by Orley Ashenfelter and Richard Layard (Amsterdam: Elsevier, 1986), pp. 642–92.

7. Elaine McCrate, *Working Mothers in a Double Bind: Working Moms, Minorities Have the Most Rigid Schedules, and Are Paid Less for the Sacrifice* (Washington: Economic Policy Institute, 2002); Robert Drago, Mark Wooden, and David Black, "Who Wants and Gets Flexibility? Changing Work Hours Preferences and Life Events," *Industrial & Labor Relations Review* 62, no. 3 (2009); Lonnie Golden, "Flexible Daily Work Schedules in U.S. Jobs: Formal Introductions Needed? " *Industrial Relations* 48, no. 1 (2009): 27–54.

8. Michelle J. Budig and Paula England, "The Wage Penalty for Motherhood," *American Sociological Review* 66, no. 2 (2001): 204–25; Jennifer Glass, "Blessing or Curse? Work-Family Policies and Mother's Wage Growth," *Work and Occupations* 31, no. 3 (2004): 367–94.

9. Nicola Dones and Netsy Firestein, *Labor's Participation in Work/Family Issues: Successes and Obstacles* (Berkeley: Labor Project for Working Families, 2002); Bureau of Labor Statistics, "Union Members Summary," U.S. Department of Labor (www.bls.gov/news.release/union2.nr0.htm).

10. John Schmitt and Ben Zipperer, *Dropping the Ax: Illegal Firings during Union Election Campaigns* (Washington: Center for Economic and Policy Research, 2007); Bureau of Labor Statistics, "Union Members Summary" (see note 9).

11. Claudia Goldin, "Marriage Bars: Discrimination against Married Women Workers 1920s to 1950s," Working Paper 2747 (Cambridge, Mass.: National Bureau of Economic Research, 1988): 1–46.

12. Rebecca Ray, Janet C. Gornick, and John Schmitt, *Parental Leave Policies in 21 Countries: Assessing Generosity and Gender Equality* (Washington: Center for Economic and Policy Research, 2008). In Australia, starting on January 1, 2011, parents who meet work and income requirements are eligible for eighteen weeks of paid parental leave at minimum wage, to be funded by the government. Families who do not take this leave can get a lump sum payment, which was given for all births and adoptions before the paid parental leave existed, and do not receive tax benefits that were formerly available. See: Commonwealth of Australia, *Australia's Paid Parental Leave Scheme: Supporting Working Australian Families* (Canberra: Australian Government, 2009), p. 29.

13. Joan C. Williams and Heather Boushey, *The Three Faces of Work-Family Conflict: The Poor, the Privileged, and the Missing Middle* (Washington: Center for American Progress and the Center for WorkLife Law, University of California, Hastings College of the Law, 2010).

14. Ellen Galinsky, Kerstin Aumann, and James T. Bond, *NCSW 2008: Times Are Changing: Gender and Generation at Work and Home* (New York: Families and Work Institute, 2009); Kerstin Aumann and others, *The Elder Care Study: Everyday Realities and Wishes for Change* (New York: Families and Work Institute, 2010), p. 45.

15. Williams and Boushey, *The Three Faces of Work-Family Conflict* (see note 13).

16. Jerry A. Jacobs and Kathleen Gerson, *The Time Divide: Work, Family, and Gender Inequality* (Harvard University Press, 2005), p. 272; Jennifer E. Swanberg, *Workplace Structure and Its Impact on Hourly Workers and Their Families* (Washington: Working for Change: A Conversation on Workplace Flexibility, 2008).

17. Heather Boushey, *It's Time for Policies to Match Family Needs: New Polling Data Show Widespread Support for an Agenda to Address Work-Family Conflict* (Washington: Center for American Progress, 2010).

18. Ed Reilly and Brent McGoldrick, "Heartland Monitor V: Millennial Experience," Allstate-National Journal Heartland Monitor Poll (www.allstate.com/Allstate/content/refresh-attachments/Heartland-5-Millennial-National-Topline.pdf).

19. Aumann and others, *The Elder Care Study* (see note 14).

20. Howard D. Samuel, "Troubled Passage: The Labor Movement and the Fair Labor Standards Act," *Monthly Labor Review* 123, no. 12 (2000): 32–37.

21. Department of Labor: U.S. Wage and Hour Division, "Fact Sheet #25: The Home Health Care Industry under the Fair Labor Standards Act (FLSA)" (www.dol.gov/whd/regs/compliance/whdfs25.pdf); Employment Standards Administration: Wage and Hour Division, "History of Changes to the Minimum Wage Law," Department of Labor (www.dol.gov/whd/minwage/coverage.htm).

22. There are no available data from the Department of Labor on the share of workers covered by the FLSA, and this estimate is based only on whether individuals reported being paid hourly or on salary. Author's analysis of Bureau of Labor Statistics, "Characteristics of Minimum Wage Workers 2009, table 10" (www.bls.gov/cps/minwage2009tbls.htm#10).

23. Exempt job duties include high-level management roles, professional occupations, outside sales positions, or operational positions. See: Code of Federal Regulations, "29 CFR Part 541: Defining and Delimiting the Exemptions for Executive, Administrative, Professional, Computer, and Outside Sales Employees" (http://ecfr.gpoaccess.gov/cgi/t/text/text-idx?c=ecfr&sid=cfb344dae2db85c15fc55b68376f32c5&rgn=div5&view=text&node=29:3.1.1.1.22&idno=29).

24. Ross Eisenbrey and Jared Bernstein, *Eliminating the Right to Overtime Pay* (Washington: Economic Policy Institute, 2003).

25. Williams and Boushey, *The Three Faces of Work-Family Conflict* (see note 13).

26. Susan J. Lambert and Julia R. Henley, *Scheduling in Hourly Jobs: Promising Practices for the Twenty-First Century Economy* (Washington: The Mobility Agenda, 2009).

27. State laws, as in California, can be more stringent.

28. David Walsh, "The FLSA Comp Time Controversy: Fostering Flexibility or Diminishing Worker Rights?" *Journal of Employment and Law* 20, no. 1 (1999): 74–137.

29. Brad Harrington and Jamie J. Ladge, "Got Talent? It Isn't Hard to Find," in *The Shriver Report: A Woman's Nation Changes Everything*, edited by Boushey and O'Leary (see note 3).

30. Lonnie Golden, "Flexibility Gaps: Differential Access to Flexible Work Schedules and Location in the U.S.," *Flexibility in Workplaces: Effects on Workers, Work Environment and the Unions* (2005): 38–56; Ellen Galinsky, James T. Bond, and E. Jeffrey Hill, "When Work Works: A Status Report on Workplace Flexibility," Families and Work Institute (www.law.georgetown.edu/workplaceflexibility2010/definition/documents/Lower-WageWorkersandFWAs.pdf); Cathleen Benko and Anne Weisberg, *Mass Career Customization* (Boston: Harvard Business School Press, 2007).

31. Heather Boushey and Ann O'Leary, *Our Working Nation: How Working Women Are Reshaping America's Families and Economy and What It Means for Policymakers* (Washington: Center for American Progress, 2010).

32. James T. Bond and Ellen Galinsky, *What Workplace Flexibility Is Available to Entry-Level, Hourly Employees?* (New York: Families and Work Institute, 2006), table 1; Ellen Galinsky, Kelly Sakai, and Tyler Wigton, *Workplace Flexibility among Small Employers* (New York: Families and Work Institute, 2010), p. 46.

33. Council of Economic Advisers, *Work-Life Balance and the Economics of Workplace Flexibility* (Washington: The White House, 2010), p. 1.

34. Harrington and Ladge, "Got Talent? It Isn't Hard to Find" (see note 29).

35. Under the flexible work schedule, employees must work certain core hours and days. Beyond these designated times, employees may structure their schedule to accommodate their personal needs. Under a compressed work schedule, an employee's basic biweekly eighty-hour work requirement is scheduled within less than the traditional ten workdays. Federal employees are not exempt from the FLSA, although individuals may still be exempt based on whether they have a managerial or other exempt job. With respect to both programs, if employees are unionized, then the collective bargaining agreement must include language that allows the alternative work schedule program.

36. Cali Ressler and Jody Thompson, "OPM ROWE Pilot Update," CultureRx (http://gorowe.com/2011/01/24/opm-rowe-pilot-update); Jonathan Foley, "Statement of Jonathan Foley, Senior Advisor to the Director, U.S. Office of Personnel Management," Office of Personnel Management (www.opm.gov/News_Events/congress/testimony/111thCongress/05_04_2010.asp).

37. This order did not extend to police officers, prison guards, court employees, or public university workers. Michelle A. Travis, "What a Difference a Day Makes, or Does It? Work/Family Balance and the Four-Day Work Week," *Connecticut Law Review* 42, no. 4 (2010): 1223–66.

38. Rex L. Facer II and Lori Wadsworth, "Four-Day Work Weeks: Current Research and Practice," *Connecticut Law Review* 42, no. 4 (2010): 1031–46.

39. Webb Lyons, *Flex in the City: The Story of a Mayor and His Vision* (Washington: Center for Law and Social Policy, 2006); Flexworks, "Flex in the City" (www.flexworks.org/fitc/index.shtml).

40. Jodie Levin-Epstein, *Getting Punched: The Job and Family Clock—It's Time for Flexible Work for Workers of All Wages* (Washington: Center for Law and Social Policy, 2006); Karen Kornbluh, "The Joy of Flex," *Washington Monthly*, December 2005.

41. Boushey and O'Leary, *Our Working Nation* (see note 31).

42. Levin-Epstein, *Getting Punched* (see note 40); Kornbluh, "The Joy of Flex" (see note 40).

43. Jodie Levin-Epstein, *How to Exercise Flexible Work: Take Steps with a "Soft Touch" Law* (Washington: Center for Law and Social Policy), p. 8.

44. Local Government Employers, "Flexible Working" (www.lge.gov.uk/lge/core/page.do?pageId=120012).

45. For more on this, see Ariane Hegewisch and Janet Gornick, *Statutory Routes to Workplace Flexibility in Cross-National Perspective* (Washington: Institute for Women's Policy Research and Center for WorkLife Law, University of California: Hastings College of the Law, 2008); Boushey and O'Leary, *Our Working Nation* (see note 31).

46. Boushey and O'Leary, *Our Working Nation* (see note 31).

47. Ann O'Leary and Karen Kornbluh, "Family Friendly for All Families," in *The Shriver Report: A Woman's Nation Changes Everything*, edited by Boushey and O'Leary (see note 3), p. 88.

48. Saranna Thornton, "Pregnancy Discrimination Act (2005)," Sloan Work and Family Research Network (wfnetwork.bc.edu/encyclopedia_entry.php?id=272).

49. O'Leary and Kornbluh, "Family Friendly for All Families" (see note 47).

50. Thomas H. Barnard and Adrienne L. Rapp, "The Impact of the Pregnancy Discrimination Act on the Workplace—From a Legal and Social Perspective," *University of Memphis Law Review* 36 (2005): 93–144.

51. Employees must be given time and a private place that is not a bathroom to express breast milk for up to one year after they have given birth. Employers with fewer than fifty employees do not have to provide time and space for women to pump milk if it would cause "undue hardship." See Patient Protection and Affordable Care Act, H. R. 3590, 111th Congress (2010); Department of Labor: U.S. Wage and Hour Division, "Fact Sheet #73: Break Time for Nursing Mothers under the FLSA" (www.dol.gov/whd/regs/compliance/whdfs73.pdf).

52. Workplace Flexibility 2010, "Americans with Disabilities Act" (http//:workplaceflexibility2010.org/index.php/laws_impacting_flexibility/ADA).

53. Center for WorkLife Law, "About FDR" (www.worklifelaw.org/AboutFDR.html).

54. Shelley J. Correll, Stephen Benard, and In Paik, "Getting a Job: Is There a Motherhood Penalty?" *American Journal of Sociology* 112, no. 5 (2007): 1297–1338.

55. Although all fifty states honor employment-at-will, all but four (Florida, Georgia, Louisiana, and Rhode Island) have statutory exceptions to the at-will doctrine. Jane Whitney Gibson and Lester Lindley, *The Evolution of Employment-at-Will: Past, Present, and Future Predictions* (Las Vegas: Ninth Annual Institute for Business and Economic Research and College Teaching & Learning Conference, 2009).

56. Equal Employment Opportunity Commission, "Enforcement Guidance: Unlawful Disparate Treatment of Workers with Caregiving Responsibilities" (www.eeoc.gov/policy/docs/caregiving.html).

57. Workplace Flexibility 2010, *The New South Wales Carers' Responsibilities Act* (Washington: Georgetown Law, 2006).

58. Boushey, *It's Time for Policies to Match Family Needs* (see note 17).

59. Tom W. Smith and Jibum Kim, *Paid Sick Days: Attitudes and Experiences* (Chicago: National Opinion Research Center, 2010), p. 44.

60. U.S. Social Security Administration, *SSI: History of Provisions* (Baltimore: Social Security Administration, 2007).

61. Shawn Fremstad, *Recent Welfare Reform Research Findings: Implications for TANF Reauthorization and State TANF Policies* (Washington: Center on Budget and Policy Priorities, 2004).

62. The contribution end of the system is regressive, because the tax only applies to earned income up to a fixed maximum, but the distribution end is progressive, repaying more to low earners relative to their contributions. See "Old and Enduring: Social Security Survives Conservative Attacks," *Dollars & Sense*, January/February 1988.

63. People born before 1929 need fewer credits.

64. Bureau of Labor Statistics, *National Compensation Survey: Employee Benefits in Private Industry in the United States, March 2007* (Washington: Department of Labor, 2007), ch. 7, table 7.2.

65. Heidi Hartmann, *The Importance of Social Security Benefits to Women: Testimony before the National Commission on Fiscal Responsibility and Reform* (Washington: Institute for Women's Policy Research, 2010), p. 6.

66. National Employment Law Project, *Implementing the Unemployment Insurance Modernization Provisions of the Recovery Act in the States* (New York: National Employment Law Project, 2010).

67. Family and Medical Leave Act, H.R.1, 103rd Congress (1993).

68. Committee on Labor and Human Resources, *Report on the Family and Medical Leave Act of 1993* (Washington: U.S. Senate, 1993).

69. Jane Waldfogel, "Family and Medical Leave: Evidence from the 2000 Surveys," *Monthly Labor Review* 124, no. 9 (2001): 17–23.

70. David Cantor and others, *Balancing the Needs of Families and Employers: Family and Medical Leave Surveys, 2000 Update* (Rockville, Md.: Westat, 2001).

71. Heather Boushey and John Schmitt, *Job Tenure and Firm Size Provisions Exclude Many Young Parents from Family and Medical Leave* (Washington: Center for Economic and Policy Research, 2007).

72. Ibid.

73. Bureau of Labor Statistics, "National Longitudinal Survey of Youth 1979 (NLSY79), Supplemental Table," Department of Labor (www.bls.gov/nls/nlsy79.htm).

74. The Employee Retirement Income Security Act of 1974 sets minimum standards for pension plans in private industry, requiring that an employer that provides a retirement plan to some employees must provide the same plan to employees generally.

75. In a study of the Fortune 100, the Joint Economic Committee found that "many firms responded with a minimum and maximum number of weeks of paid leave, depending on the employee's job category or tenure or other requirements and our analysis provides measures of both the minimum and the maximum weeks provided." See Joint Economic Committee, *Paid Family Leave at Fortune 100 Companies: A Basic Standard but Still Not the Gold Standard* (Washington: Joint Economic Committee of the U.S. Congress, 2008).

76. Ann O'Leary, "How Family Leave Laws Left Out Low-Income Workers," *Berkeley Journal of Employment and Labor Law* 28, no. 1 (2007): 1–62.

77. Tallese D. Johnson, *Maternity Leave and Employment Patterns of First-Time Mothers: 1961–2003* (Washington: U.S. Census Bureau, 2008).

78. Workplace Flexibility 2010 and Urban Institute, "Fact Sheet on Extended Time Off (EXTO)" (http://workplaceflexibility2010.org/images/uploads/EXTO_Fact_Sheet.pdf).

79. Janet C. Gornick and Marcia K. Meyers, *Families That Work: Policies for Reconciling Parenthood and Employment* (New York: Russell Sage Foundation, 2003); Ray, Gornick, and Schmitt, *Parental Leave Policies in 21 Countries* (see note 12). Australia funds its new paid parental leave program through general revenues.

80. State of California Employment Development Department, "Disability Insurance: Frequently Asked Questions" (www.edd.ca.gov/direp/difaq1.htm#Pregnancy).

81. Three other states (Hawaii, New York, and Rhode Island) have Temporary Disability Insurance programs, and across all five states (including California and New Jersey), mothers are granted a minimum of six weeks of leave to recover from childbirth. Hawaii, New York, and Rhode Island offer mothers longer leaves as necessary to recover from childbirth. In New York the length is capped at twenty-six weeks, and in Rhode Island the cap is thirty weeks.

82. Economic Opportunity Institute, "Our Successes: Family Leave" (www.eoionline.org/about/success_stories/paid_family_leave_success.htm); Government Accountability Office, *Women and Low-Skilled Workers: Other Countries' Policies and Practices That May Help These Workers Enter and Remain in the Labor Force* (Washington: Government Accountability Office, 2007).

83. Time to Care, "New York State Family Leave Coalition and the Time to Care Campaign" (www.timetocareny.org).

84. Eileen Appelbaum and Ruth Milkman, *Leaves That Pay: Employer and Worker Experiences with Paid Family Leave in California* (Washington: Center for Economic and Policy Research, 2011).

85. Heather Boushey, *Helping Breadwinners When It Can't Wait: A Progressive Program for Family Leave Insurance* (Washington: Center for American Progress, 2009).

86. Smith and Kim, *Paid Sick Days* (see note 59).

87. Iris S. Diaz and Richard Wallick, "Leisure and Illness Leave: Estimating Benefits in Combination," *Monthly Labor Review* 132, no. 2 (2009): 28–34.

88. Vicky Lovell, *No Time to Be Sick: Who Suffers When Workers Don't Have Sick Leave* (Washington: Institute for Women's Policy Research, 2004).

89. Ibid.

90. U.S. Census Bureau, *2008 American Community Survey 1-Year Estimates* (Washington: U.S. Census Bureau, 2008); U.S. Department of Health and Human Services, "Long-Term Care" (www.medicare.gov/longTermCare/static/home.asp).

91. Ann O'Leary, "What's the Workplace Impact?" in *A Women's Nation Takes on Alzheimer's,* edited by Angela Timashenka Geiger and others (Chicago: Alzheimer's Association and The Shriver Report, 2010), pp. 183–200.

92. Boushey, *It's Time for Policies to Match Family Needs* (see note 17).

93. Aumann and others, *The Elder Care Study* (see note 14).

94. Williams and Boushey, *The Three Faces of Work-Family Conflict* (see note 13).

95. U.S. Department of Health and Human Services, "Long-Term Care" (see note 90).

96. Aumann and others, *The Elder Care Study* (see note 14).

97. Rosemary Kendall and Michael Agosta, *Parents and the High Cost of Child Care: 2010 Update* (Arlington, Va.: National Association of Child Care Resource and Referral Agencies, 2010).

98. Williams and Boushey, *The Three Faces of Work-Family Conflict* (see note 13).

99. Aumann and others, *The Elder Care Study* (see note 14).

100. Internal Revenue Service, "Top Ten Facts about the Child and Dependent Care Credit" (www.irs.gov/newsroom/article/0,,id=106189,00.html).

101. Internal Revenue Service, *Topics 602 Child and Dependent Care Credit* (Washington: Department of Treasury, 2010).

102. O'Leary and Kornbluh, "Family Friendly for All Families" (see note 47).

103. Tax Policy Center, *Taxation and the Family: How Does the Tax System Subsidize Child Care Expenses?* (Washington: Urban Institute and Brookings Institution, 2007).

104. U.S. Department of Health and Human Services: Administration for Children and Families, "About the Child Care and Development Fund" (www.acf.hhs.gov/programs/ccb/ccdf/index.htm).

105. Administration for Children and Families, U.S. Department of Health and Human Services, "Fiscal Year 2009 Federal Child Care and Related Appropriations" (www.acf.hhs.gov/programs/ccb/ccdf/approp_2009.htm).

106. Randy Albelda and others, *Bridging the Gaps: A Picture of How Work Supports Work in Ten States* (Washington: Center for Economic and Policy Research, 2007).

107. Ibid.

108. Williams and Boushey, *The Three Faces of Work-Family Conflict* (see note 13).

109. Aumann and others, *The Elder Care Study* (see note 14).

110. Centers for Medicare and Medicaid Services, *2010 Annual Report of the Boards of Trustees of the Federal Hospital Insurance and Federal Supplementary Medical Insurance Trust Funds* (Baltimore: Department of Health and Human Services, 2010); Centers for Medicare and Medicaid Services, "Medicare and Home Health Care" (www.medicare.gov/publications/pubs/pdf/10969.pdf); Centers for Medicare and Medicaid Services, "Medicare Coverage of Skilled Nursing Facility Care" (www.medicare.gov/publications/pubs/pdf/10153.pdf).

111. Center for Medicare and Medicaid Series, "Nursing Homes: Paying For Care," Department of Health and Human Services (www.medicare.gov/nursing/payment.asp).

112. Aumann and others, *The Elder Care Study* (see note 14).

113. T. Alan Lacey and Benjamin Wright, "Occupational Employment Projections to 2018," *Monthly Labor Review* 132, no. 11 (2010).

114. Ibid.; Domestic Workers United (www.domesticworkersunited.org); Direct Care Alliance Inc., "Direct Care Workers United for Change" (www.directcarealliance.org).

115. Edward Zigler and Susan Muenchow, *Head Start: The Inside Story of America's Most Successful Educational Experiment* (New York: Basic Books, 1992).

116. William Gormley Jr. and others, *The Effects of Oklahoma's Universal Pre-Kindergarten Program on School Readiness* (Washington: Georgetown University Center for Research on Children in the U.S., 2004); W. Steven Barnett and others, *The State of Preschool 2009* (New Brunswick, N.J.: National Institute for Early Education Research, 2009).

117. Pre-K Now, "State Profiles," Pew Center on the States (www.preknow.org/resource/profiles).

118. Barnett and others, *The State of Preschool 2009* (see note 116).

119. Nevada Department of Health and Human Services, "CLASS Act" (http://dhhs.nv.gov/HealthCare/Docs/NVPolicyPapers/Section_8001_CLASS_Act_Survey.pdf).

120. Paul N. Van de Water, "CLASS: A New Voluntary Long-Term Care Insurance Program," Center on Budget and Policy Priorities (www.cbpp.org/cms/index.cfm?fa=view&id=3156).

121. Kirstin Downey, *The Woman behind the New Deal: The Life of Frances Perkins, FDR's Secretary of Labor and His Moral Conscience* (New York: Nan A. Talese, 2009).

International Perspectives on Work-Family Policies: Lessons from the World's Most Competitive Economies

Alison Earle, Zitha Mokomane, and Jody Heymann

Summary

The United States does not guarantee families a wide range of supportive workplace policies such as paid maternity and paternity leave or paid leave to care for sick children. Proposals to provide such benefits are invariably met with the complaint that the costs would reduce employment and undermine the international competitiveness of American businesses. In this article, Alison Earle, Zitha Mokomane, and Jody Heymann explore whether paid leave and other work-family policies that support children's development exist in countries that are economically competitive and have low unemployment rates. Their data show that the answer is yes.

Using indicators of competitiveness gathered by the World Economic Forum, the authors identify fifteen countries, including the United States, that have been among the top twenty countries in competitiveness rankings for at least eight of ten years. To this group they add China and India, both rising competitors in the global economy. They find that every one of these countries, except the United States, guarantees some form of paid leave for new mothers as well as annual leave. And all but Switzerland and the United States guarantee paid leave for new fathers.

The authors perform a similar exercise to identify thirteen advanced countries with consistently low unemployment rates, again including the United States. The majority of these countries provide paid leave for new mothers, paid leave for new fathers, paid leave to care for children's health care needs, breast-feeding breaks, paid vacation leave, and a weekly day of rest. Of these, the United States guarantees only breast-feeding breaks (part of the recently passed health care legislation).

The authors' global examination of the most competitive economies as well as the economies with low unemployment rates makes clear that ensuring that all parents are available to care for their children's healthy development does not preclude a country from being highly competitive economically.

www.futureofchildren.org

Alison Earle is a principal research scientist at Northeastern University. Zitha Mokomane is a senior research specialist at the Human Sciences Research Council of South Africa. Jody Heymann is the founding director of the Institute for Health and Social Policy at McGill University.

Alison Earle, Zitha Mokomane, and Jody Heymann

In the majority of American families with children today, all parents are employed. In 67 percent of families with school-age children, 64 percent of families with preschool-age children, and 60 percent of families with children age three and younger, the parents are working for pay.[1] As a result, the workplace policies that parents face—such as how many hours they need to be away from home, the leave they can take to care for a sick child, and the work schedules that determine whether and when they are able to visit a son's or daughter's school—shape not only their income but also the time they have available for childrearing.

U.S. policies on parental leave, sick leave, vacation days, and days of rest are often in sharp contrast to other developed and developing countries, but those who want to make these policies more supportive of parents and their children face stiff opposition from those who say such policies will harm the United States' ability to compete economically with other countries. This article takes an international perspective to evaluate whether having workplace policies that support parents' ability to be available to meet their children's needs is compatible with economic competitiveness and low unemployment. We analyze a unique global database of labor legislation, focusing specifically on those measures dealing with parental availability in the first year of life, when caregiving needs are particularly intensive; parental availability to meet children's health needs; and their availability to meet their children's developmental needs.

We first review the evidence on the relationship of parental working conditions to children's outcomes. Second, we discuss the claims made in the public debates regarding the potential costs and benefits of family-supportive labor policies to individual employers and national economies, and review the academic literature on this topic. We then use new cross-national data to examine the extent to which highly competitive countries and countries with low unemployment rates do or do not provide these policies. Finally, we summarize the implications of our findings for U.S. policy.

Relationship of Parental Working Conditions to Children's Outcomes

Research in the United States and in other developed as well as developing countries suggests that workplace policies that support parents' ability to be available for their children at crucial periods of their lives have measurable effects on children's outcomes.

Paid Parental Leave. Research shows that the availability of paid leave following childbirth has the potential to improve infant and child health by making it affordable and feasible for parents to stay home and provide the intensive care newborns and infants need, including breast feeding and a high caregiver-to-infant ratio that most child-care centers are unable to match.[2] Parental leave can have substantial benefits for child health. Christopher Ruhm's examination of more than two decades of data from sixteen European countries found that paid parental leave policies were associated with lower rates of infant and child mortality after taking into account per capita income, the availability of health services and technology, and other factors linked with child health. Ruhm found that a ten-week paid maternity leave was associated with a reduction in infant mortality rates of 1–2 percent; a twenty-week leave, with a 2–4 percent reduction; and a thirty-week leave, with a 7–9 percent reduction.[3]

Sasiko Tanaka reaffirmed these findings in a study that analyzed data from Ruhm's sixteen European countries plus the United States and Japan. The data covered the thirty years between 1969 and 2000 including the period between 1995 and 2000 when several significant changes were made in parental leave policies.[4] Tanaka found that a ten-week extension in paid leave was associated with a 2.6 percent decrease in infant mortality rates and a 3.0 percent decrease in child mortality rates. Maternity leave without pay or a guarantee of a job at the end of the leave had no significant effect on infant or child mortality rates in either study.

One of the most important mechanisms through which paid parental leave can benefit infants is by increasing a mother's ability to initiate and sustain breast feeding, which a wealth of research has shown to be associated with a markedly lower risk of gastrointestinal, respiratory tract, skin, ear, and other infections; sudden infant death syndrome; and overall mortality.[5] Health benefits of breast feeding have also been reported for mothers, including reduced risk of premenopausal breast cancer and potentially reduced risks of ovarian cancer and osteoporosis.[6]

Generous maternity leave benefits available across European countries make it possible for mothers to breast feed their infants for a lengthy period of time without having to supplement feedings with formula. In some cases the leave is long enough that mothers can exclusively breast feed for at least six months, as recommended by the World Health Organization; and in countries with more than half a year of leave, mothers can continue breast feeding (while also adding appropriate solid foods).[7] In contrast, in countries with less generous maternity leave, such as the United States, working women are less

likely to start breast feeding their babies, and those who do breast feed stop sooner, on average, than mothers in countries with these supportive policies.[8] Lacking paid maternity leave, American mothers also return to work earlier than mothers in most other advanced countries, and research has found that early return to work is associated with lower rates of breast feeding and immunizations.[9]

While far less research has been conducted on the impact of paternity leave policies, there is ample reason to believe that paternal leave can support children's healthy development in ways parallel to maternal leave, with the obvious exception of breast feeding. Although fathers can take time off under parental leave policies that can be used by one or both parents, they are more likely to stay at home to care for a new child when paternity leave is available.[10]

The longer the period of leave allowed, the more involved with their infants and families fathers are.[11] Moreover, longer leaves increase the probability that fathers will continue their involvement and share in child care even after the leave ends.[12] The benefits of fathers' engagement for children's social, psychological, behavioral, emotional, and cognitive functioning are significant.[13] In short, paternity leave policies are associated with greater gender equity at home and, through fathers' increased involvement with their infants, with positive cognitive and social development of young children.

Leave for Children's Health Needs. Four decades of research have documented that children's health outcomes improve when parents participate in their children's health care, whether it is a treatment for an acute illness or injury or management of a chronic condition.[14] As Mark Schuster, Paul Chung, and Katherine Vestal discuss in this volume, children heal faster and have shorter hospital stays when parents are present and involved during inpatient surgeries and treatments as well as during outpatient medical procedures.[15] Parents' assistance is especially important for children with chronic conditions such as diabetes and asthma, among others.[16] Parents can help improve children's health outcomes in many ways including by maintaining daily medical routines, administering medication, and providing emotional support as children adjust to having a chronic physical or mental health problem.[17]

If children are sick and parents do not have any schedule flexibility or paid leave that can be used to address a family member's health issue, children may be left home alone, unable to get themselves to a doctor or pharmacy for medication or to a hospital if a crisis occurs. Alternatively, parents may have no choice but to send a sick child to school or day care. The contact with other children and teachers contributes to the rapid spread and thus high incidence of infectious diseases in day-care centers, including respiratory infections, otitis media, and gastrointestinal infections.[18]

Research has also documented how significantly parental availability influences the level of preventive care children receive. Getting a child to a clinic or doctor's office for a physical exam or immunizations usually requires parents or other caregivers to take time off work. Working parents in a range of countries have cited schedule conflicts and workplace inflexibility as important obstacles to getting their children immunized against preventable childhood diseases.[19] One study of a large company in the United States found that employees who faced difficulties taking time off from work were far more

Despite substantial evidence that children gain when parents have adequate paid leave and work flexibility, the economic costs and benefits of providing this leave and flexibility are still the subject of great contention.

likely to report that their children were not fully immunized.[20]

In contrast to the vast majority of countries around the globe, the United States has no federal policy requiring employers to provide paid leave for personal illness, let alone to address family members' health issues. (The Family and Medical Leave Act covers only serious health issues of immediate family members and is unpaid.) Only 30 percent of Americans report that their employer voluntarily offers paid sick leave that can be used for family members' care.[21] As a result, many parents are unable to be present to attend to their children's health needs. Parents whose employers provide paid sick days are more than five times as likely to be able to personally provide care to their sick children as parents whose employers do not offer paid sick days.[22] Working adults with no paid leave who take time off to care for ill family members are at risk of losing wages or even their job.[23] The risk of job loss is even greater for parents whose child has a chronic health problem, which typically involves more visits to the doctor or the hospital and more days of illness. In a longitudinal study of working poor families in the United States, we found that having a child with health problems was associated with a 36 percent increase in job loss.[24]

Leave and Availability for Children's Educational and Developmental Needs. When parents are involved in their children's education, whether at the preschool, elementary, or secondary level, children perform better in school.[25] Parental involvement has been linked with children's improved test scores in language and math, fewer emotional and behavioral problems, lower dropout rates, and better planning for and transitions into adulthood.[26] Greater parental involvement in schools appears to improve the quality of the education received by all students in the school.[27] Research has found that fathers' involvement, like that of mothers, is associated with significantly better exam scores, higher educational expectations, and higher grades.[28]

Parental participation and assistance can improve school outcomes for at-risk children.[29] Educational outcomes for children with learning disabilities improve when parents are involved in their education both at school and helping at home with homework in math as well as reading.[30] Low-income children can also benefit markedly when their parents are involved in their classrooms and with their teachers at school.[31] Studies suggest that low-income children benefit as much or more when their parents also spend time assisting their children in learning skills and material outside the classroom; training or instructing parents in providing this assistance further boosts the gains of time spent together.[32]

Parents' working conditions can markedly affect their ability to play an active role in their children's education. Active parental involvement often requires the flexibility to meet with teachers or consult with specialists during the workday. To be able to help with homework, parents need to have a work schedule that allows them time with their children after school and before children go to sleep. Our national research on the availability of paid leave and schedule flexibility among parents of school-age children in the United States shows that parents whose children were struggling academically and most needed parental support were at a significant disadvantage. More than half of parents who had a child scoring in the bottom quartile on math assessments did not have consistent access to any kind of paid leave, and nearly three-fourths could not count on schedule flexibility. One in six of these parents worked during evening hours, and more than one in ten worked nights, making it impossible to help their children routinely. Families in which a child scored in the bottom quartile in reading had equally challenging working conditions.[33]

Economic Feasibility of Workplace Policies Supporting Parents

Despite substantial evidence that children gain when parents have adequate paid leave and work flexibility, the economic costs and benefits of providing this leave and flexibility are still the subject of great contention in the United States. Each time legislation to guarantee parental leave, family medical leave, and related policies has been brought to Congress, the debate has revolved around questions of financial feasibility. In particular, legislators and others have questioned whether the United States can provide these benefits and still remain economically competitive.

For example, the proposed Healthy Families Act would guarantee a minimum of seven paid sick days—a small number by international standards—to American workers so they could stay home when they or family members fall ill. At a hearing in 2007 on the legislation, G. Roger King, a partner at the Jones Day corporate law firm, summarized the general argument raised against the legislation, saying that the Healthy Families Act, or any similar "regulations" to protect employees, would diminish U.S. competitiveness in the global economy. "Employers in this country are already burdened by numerous federal, state and local regulations which result in millions of dollars in compliance costs," King stated in his written testimony. "These mandated and largely unfunded 'cost of doing business' requirements in certain instances not only hinder and impede the creation of new jobs, but also inhibit our nation's employers from competing globally."[34]

We report findings from our recent research that examines the relationship between work-family legislation and national competitiveness and unemployment rates. First, however, we briefly summarize some of the evidence on costs and benefits to employers from policies that support families.

A series of studies including data from the United States, Japan, and the United Kingdom show that women who receive paid maternity leave are significantly more likely to return to the same employer after giving birth.[35] Increased employee retention reduces hiring and training costs, which can be significant (and include the costs of publicizing the job opening, conducting job interviews, training new employees, and suboptimal productivity among newly hired workers during the period just after they start).

There is no research known to us about the costs or benefits to individual American employers related to paid leave for children's health issues, most likely because this type of leave is uncommon in the United States. To the extent that the leave allows parents to ensure their children have time to rest and recuperate and avoid exacerbating health problems that could result in additional lost workdays in the future, parents' productivity could increase and absenteeism be reduced.

Similarly, while we are not aware of any studies that examine the costs and benefits to employers of legislation guaranteeing time off for employees to be with children, recent studies showing that long hours are associated with lower productivity suggest that similar productivity losses may exist for employees who work for long periods of time without a substantial block of time away from work or, in the shorter term, for those who work without a weekly day of rest. A study of eighteen manufacturing industries in the United States over a thirty-five-year period found that for every 10 percent increase in overtime hours, productivity declined 2–4 percent.[36] Although small in absolute size, in the context of a forty-hour workweek, these productivity losses suggest that employers may be able to increase productivity by guaranteeing regular time off.

A study of highly "effective" employers by the Families and Work Institute found that many report a series of economic benefits resulting from their flexibility policies that include paid leave for new mothers and time off for caregiving among other scheduling and training policies.[37] Benefits cited by employers include "increasing employee engagement and retention; reducing turnover; reducing absenteeism and sick days; increasing customer satisfaction; reducing business costs; increasing productivity and profitability; improving staffing coverage to meet business demands; [and] enhancing innovation and creativity."[38]

The centrality of the economic arguments in policy debates calls for further examination of the empirical evidence on workplace policies important to parents and their children. We examine two important indicators of economic performance. The first is a measure of global economic competitiveness, a concept encompassing productivity, a country's capacity for growth, and the level of prosperity or income that can be attained. This indicator is of particular salience to businesses and is used by international organizations such as the World Economic Forum (WEF). The second is the national unemployment rate, the indicator more often cited as being of high concern in the public's mind.

To evaluate the claim that nationally mandating paid leave would cause a reduction in jobs or loss of competitiveness, one ideally would have evidence from a randomized or natural experiment where the policy in place is not associated with other country or state characteristics that could influence the outcome. That approach is not possible, because there have been no such experiments. However, to test whether policies supporting working families inevitably lead countries to be uncompetitive or to have high unemployment, it is sufficient to find counterexamples. To that end, we ask a straightforward question: Are paid leave and other work-family policies that support children's development economically feasible?

To answer this question, we developed a global database of national labor policies and global economic data on competitiveness and unemployment in all countries that belong to the United Nations. The database includes information from original legislation, labor codes, and relevant amendments in 175 countries, as well as summaries of legislation for these and additional countries. The vast majority of the legislation was gathered from NATLEX, the International Labour

Organization's (ILO) global database of legislation pertaining to labor, social security, and human rights from 189 countries. Additional sources included global databases that compile and summarize national legislation.[39]

Public Policies Supporting Working Families in Highly Competitive Countries

Using our global labor policy database, we set out to assess whether the countries that have consistently been at the top of the rankings in economic competitiveness provide working conditions that give employed parents the ability to support their children's healthy development. To identify these "highly competitive" countries, we use data from the business-led WEF.[40] Its annual Global Competitiveness Report includes country "competitiveness" rankings based on dozens of indicators of institutions, policies, and other factors that WEF members judge to be the key drivers of economic competitiveness. These factors include, among others, the efficiency of the goods market, efficiency of the labor market, financial market development, technological readiness, market size, business sophistication, innovation, infrastructure, and the macroeconomic environment.[41] We define "highly competitive" countries to be those that were ranked among the top twenty countries in competitiveness in at least eight of the ten years between 1999 and 2008. Fifteen countries meet this definition: Australia, Austria, Canada, Denmark, Finland, Germany, Iceland, Japan, the Netherlands, Norway, Singapore, Sweden, Switzerland, the United Kingdom, and the United States. Although India and China are not among the fifteen, we also present data on their family-supportive policies for two reasons. First, the press and laypersons often single out China and India as U.S. "competitors," and second, they have the two largest labor forces in the world.[42]

Table 1. Parental Leave Policies in Highly Competitive Countries

Country	Paid leave for mothers			Paid leave for fathers		
	Availability	Duration (weeks)	Wage replacement rate (%)	Availability	Duration (weeks)	Wage replacement rate (%)
Australia	Yes	18	flat rate	Yes	18	flat rate
Austria	Yes	81–146	100, flat rate	Yes	65–130	flat rate
Canada	Yes	50	55	Yes	35	55
Denmark	Yes	50–58	80–100	Yes	34–42	80–100
Finland	Yes	164	25–90	Yes	154	25–70
Germany	Yes	66–118	33–100	Yes	52–104	33–67
Iceland	Yes	26	80	Yes	26	80
Japan	Yes	58	30–60	Yes	44	30–40
Netherlands	Yes	16	100	Yes	0.4	100
Norway	Yes	90–100	80–100, flat rate	Yes	87–97	80–100, flat rate
Singapore	Yes	14	100	Yes	2	100
Sweden	Yes	69*	80, flat rate	Yes	67*	80, flat rate
Switzerland	Yes	14	80	No	n.a.	n.a.
United Kingdom	Yes	39	90	Yes	2	90
United States	No	n.a.	n.a.	No	n.a.	n.a.

Source: Based on updated data from Jody Heymann and Alison Earle, *Raising the Global Floor: Dismantling the Myth That We Can't Afford Good Working Conditions for Everyone* (Stanford University Press, 2010).
Notes: In the database and all tables, data reflect national policy. Coverage conditions such as firm size, sector, and duration of employment vary by country. Paid leave for mothers includes paid leave for women only (maternity leave) and parental leave that is available to women. Paid leave for fathers includes paid leave for men only (paternity leave) and parental leave that is available to men. The table presents data on the maximum amount of leave available to the mother if she takes all of the maternity leave available to mothers and all of the parental leave available to either parent. Parallel data are presented for fathers. The minimum and maximum (as a range) are presented to reflect that country's policy of providing parents with a choice between a shorter leave at a higher benefit level (percentage of wages or flat rate) and a longer leave at a lower benefit.
n.a. = Not applicable.
*Sweden's parental leave policy also allows parents to take part-time leave with partial benefits for a longer duration.

Paid Parental Leave. Paid leave for new mothers is guaranteed in all but one of the fifteen most competitive countries (table 1). The exception is the United States, which has no federal policy providing paid leave for new parents. (As noted, leave provided under the federal Family and Medical Leave Act is unpaid.) Australia's paid leave policy took effect starting in January 2011; under the Paid Parental Leave Act, all workers—full time, part time, or casual—who are primary caregivers and earn $150,000 or less a year are guaranteed eighteen weeks of leave paid at the federal minimum wage. All of the most competitive countries with paid leave for new mothers provide at least fourteen weeks of leave, counting both maternity and parental

leave, as recommended by the ILO. The norm of six months or more far exceeds the recommended minimum. China offers eighteen weeks (ninety working days) of leave for new mothers at full pay; India offers twelve weeks.

Table 1 also shows that although the duration of paid leave for new fathers is far less than for mothers, almost all highly competitive countries provide this type of leave. Switzerland is the lone top-ranked nation that provides paid leave to new mothers but not to new fathers. Neither India nor China has paid leave for new fathers.[43]

Breast-Feeding Breaks. Guaranteeing new mothers a breast-feeding break during the

Table 2. Leave Policies to Attend to Children's Health Care in Highly Competitive Countries

Country	Breast-feeding breaks	Age of child when breast-feeding breaks end	Break time of at least one hour a day	Leave to care for children's health needs	Leave is paid
Australia	No	n.a.	n.a.	Yes	Yes
Austria	Yes	For duration	Yes	Yes	Yes
Canada	No	n.a.	n.a.	Yes	Yes
Denmark	No	n.a.	n.a.	Yes	Yes
Finland	No	n.a.	n.a.	Yes	No
Germany	Yes	For duration	Yes	Yes	Yes
Iceland	No	n.a.	n.a.	Yes	Yes
Japan	Yes	1 year	Yes	Yes	Yes
Netherlands	Yes	9 months	Yes	Yes	Yes
Norway	Yes	For duration	Yes	Yes	Yes
Singapore	No	n.a.	n.a.	Yes	Yes
Sweden	Yes	For duration	Yes	Yes	Yes
Switzerland	Yes	1 year	Yes	Yes	No
United Kingdom	No	n.a.	n.a.	Yes	No
United States	Yes	1 year	Yes	Yes	No

Source: See table 1.
n.a. = Not applicable.

workday is the law in about half of the highly competitive countries, including Austria, Germany, Japan, the Netherlands, Norway, Sweden, Switzerland, and the United States (table 2). India mandates two breaks a day in the child's first fifteen months. China guarantees new mothers breast-feeding breaks totaling an hour a day for the baby's first year.

Leave for Children's Health Needs. Unpaid leave from work to address children's health needs is ensured in every highly competitive nation (see table 2). All but four of the fifteen most competitive countries provide paid leave for this purpose; the exceptions are Finland, Switzerland, the United Kingdom, and the United States.

Leave and Availability for Children's Developmental and Educational Needs. Neither paid vacation leave nor a day off each week is designed specifically for parents; these

rest periods benefit all working adults. Yet weekly time off and vacations do provide an important assurance that working parents can spend time with their children and be available to support their educational, social, and emotional development. All of the most highly competitive countries except the United States guarantee paid annual or vacation leave (table 3). The vast majority of these countries provide generous amounts of leave at full pay. Half provide more than four weeks a year: Austria, Denmark, Finland, Germany, Iceland, Norway, Sweden, and the United Kingdom. China's labor laws guarantee five days of paid leave after one year of service, ten days after ten years on the job, and fifteen days after twenty years. In India workers are provided one day of paid leave for every twenty days worked during the previous year.

Virtually all highly competitive nations also guarantee at least one day of rest a week.

Table 3. Policies on Paid Annual Leave, a Day of Rest, and Night Work in Highly Competitive Countries

Country	Availability of paid annual leave	Duration of paid annual leave (weeks)	Weekly day of rest	Premium for night work	Ban or broad restrictions on night work	Ban or restriction for children, pregnant or nursing women, or medical reasons
Australia	Yes	4.0	No	No	No	No
Austria	Yes	5.0	Yes	No	No	Yes
Canada	Yes	2.0	Yes	No	No	Yes
Denmark	Yes	5.5	Yes	No	No	Yes
Finland	Yes	4.4	Yes	No	Yes	No
Germany	Yes	4.4	Yes	After 11 p.m.	No	Yes
Iceland	Yes	4.4	Yes	No	No	No
Japan	Yes	1.8	Yes	After 10 p.m.	No	Yes
Netherlands	Yes	4.0	Yes	No	No	Yes
Norway	Yes	4.2	Yes	No	Yes	Yes
Singapore	Yes	1.3	Yes	No	No	No
Sweden	Yes	5.0	Yes	No	Yes	No
Switzerland	Yes	4.0	Yes	After 11 p.m.	No	Yes
United Kingdom	Yes	5.1	Yes	No	No	Yes
United States	No	n.a.	No	No	No	No

Source: See table 1.
n.a. = Not applicable.

The exceptions are the United States and Australia (see table 3). Both China and India guarantee workers a day of rest a week.

Labor legislation is relatively less common around a small number of issues that are receiving attention as a result of recent economic and technological developments. Countries are still adjusting their labor policies in response to the rise of the "24/7" schedule that has come about as global trade, communications, and sourcing of products have increased. Policies either to restrict or compensate for work at times when school-age children in particular benefit from a parent's presence—evenings and nights—exist in many highly competitive countries. Guaranteeing a wage premium increases the likelihood that a wide range of workers will volunteer for night work and decreases the likelihood that parents will need to work at night merely because of limited seniority. Finland, Norway, and

Sweden have passed laws placing broad restrictions on night work for all workers. Germany, Japan, and Switzerland instead guarantee a wage premium for those who are required to work at night. Over half of the highly competitive nations allow night work but restrict or ban it for workers who might be harmed by it: children, pregnant or nursing women, or employees with medical conditions that make them unable to work at night (see table 3). China bans night work for pregnant women. Although India bans night work for all women, some states have lifted it for women working in information technology and telecommunications.

Not new to parents but to some policy makers is the need for adults to occasionally take time off during the day to address a child's academic, social, or behavioral issue, or to attend a school event. Although leave during the day to meet with a teacher or attend an event typically does not involve a great deal of the employee's time in any given period, only four of the fifteen countries provide leave explicitly for such purposes. Labor laws in Denmark and Sweden require employers to provide leave to attend to "children's needs" including educational issues. Switzerland takes a different approach, requiring employers to structure work schedules and rest periods keeping in mind employees' family responsibilities including attending to the educational needs of children up to age fifteen. In addition, Switzerland also requires employers to provide a lunch break of at least an hour and a half to parents if requested. Parents in Singapore can take leave for their children's educational needs under the country's family leave law. Neither India nor China provides paid leave for general family needs and issues or for children's education.

Public Policies Supporting Working Families in Low Unemployment Countries

As an additional check, we also examined whether it was possible to have relatively low unemployment rates while guaranteeing a floor of working conditions that help parents care for children. We looked specifically at members of the Organization for Economic Cooperation and Development (OECD). The OECD definition of unemployment is comprehensive, including employment in formal and informal jobs.[44] We defined low unemployment countries as those OECD members ranked in the better half of countries in terms of unemployment at least 80 percent of the time in the decade between 1998 and 2007. Thirteen countries fit these criteria: Austria, Denmark, Iceland, Ireland, Japan, Republic of Korea (South Korea), Luxembourg, Mexico, the Netherlands, Norway, Switzerland, the United Kingdom, and the United States. Overall, do these

countries provide working conditions that can help parents support children's healthy development? In short, yes.

Paid Parental Leave. Every low unemployment country but one, the United States, has national legislation guaranteeing paid leave for new mothers. The length of the leaves ranges from twelve weeks in Mexico to more than a year in Austria, Japan, Norway, and South Korea. In the middle are Iceland and Ireland, where new mothers receive six months, and Luxembourg and the United Kingdom, with nine months. All but one of those with paid leave replace 80 percent or more of wages, and seven guarantee 100 percent.

Paid leave for new fathers, whether in the form of leave for fathers only or leave that can be used by either parent, is not universally available but is provided in nine of the thirteen low unemployment countries. Ireland, Mexico, Switzerland, and the United States do not provide this type of leave. New fathers are entitled to take between six months and a year in Denmark, Iceland, Japan, and Luxembourg, and more than a year in Austria, Norway, and South Korea.

Breast-Feeding Breaks. Ten of the thirteen countries ensure that new mothers can continue breast feeding for at least six months after they return to work, and eight of those ten ensure this right for a year or until the mother chooses to stop.

Leave for Children's Health Needs. Guaranteed leave to address children's health needs is the norm; all but two low unemployment countries—Mexico and South Korea—provide either paid or unpaid leave of this type. The leave is paid in Austria, Denmark, Iceland, Ireland, Japan, Luxembourg, the Netherlands, and Norway and unpaid in

Switzerland, the United Kingdom, and the United States.

Leave and Availability for Children's Developmental and Educational Needs. Every low unemployment country except the United States guarantees workers a weekly day of rest and a period of paid vacation leave once a year. Mexico and Japan guarantee from one to two weeks while nine of the thirteen guarantee four weeks or more. As noted earlier, labor laws in Denmark and Switzerland also require employers to provide leave to address "children's needs," which in the Swiss legislation explicitly include educational issues.

These findings show that mandating workplace policies that support parents' ability to ensure their children's healthy development does not inevitably lead to high job loss or high unemployment rates. As this discussion shows, many OECD countries kept unemployment rates relatively low while passing and enforcing legislation that supports parents. In fact, the majority of consistently low unemployment countries have adopted nearly all the policies shown to be important for children's health and well-being. Whether these nations would have had somewhat lower or higher unemployment in the absence of family support policies is not known. But our research clearly shows that it is possible for a nation to guarantee paid leave and other policies that provide parents with time to address their children's needs and at the same time maintain relatively low unemployment.

Summary of Findings

Longitudinal data are not available that would enable researchers to determine conclusively the immediate and long-term impact on national economic outcomes of changing

guarantees of parental leave and other family-support policies. However, an examination of the most competitive economies as well as the economies with low unemployment rates makes clear that ensuring that all parents are available to care for their children's healthy development does not preclude a country from being highly competitive economically. Moreover, as noted, evidence from decades of research on parents' roles during children's infancy and in caring for children's health and education makes clear that policies enabling working fathers and mothers to provide that care are likely to have substantial positive effects on the health and developmental outcomes of American children.

Few of the policies that would help working parents raise healthy children are guaranteed in the United States. As noted, the federal Family and Medical Leave Act allows new parents to take unpaid time off without fear of job loss when they adopt or give birth, or to attend to a parent or child suffering from a serious illness. Half of Americans are not covered by the act because of the size of the firms in which they work, the number of hours they have worked, or a recent job change, and many of those who are covered cannot afford to take all the leave they are entitled to because it is unpaid. Only in 2010 did the United States pass federal legislation requiring employers to provide breast-feeding breaks and facilities for breast feeding (as part of the health care reform bill and without much public awareness). Paid parental leave and child health care leave policies are the norm in the countries that have been highly competitive and those that have maintained low unemployment for a decade. The analysis of global data presented here suggests that guaranteeing paid parental leave as well as paid leave when a child is sick would be feasible for the United States without jeopardizing its highly competitive economy or low unemployment rates in the future.

The overwhelming majority of countries guarantee paid parental leave through a social insurance system. While many countries provide some kind of tax credit or stipend at the birth of a child, next to none rely only on this for paid parental leave. A critical step that European countries have increasingly followed is to guarantee that a percentage of the leave is dedicated to fathers as well as some dedicated solely to mothers. This approach ensures that men have in practice, and not just on paper, an equal chance of using the leave.

The countries that guarantee paid sick leave finance it through a variety of means ranging from requiring employers to pay employees benefits (that is, continue to pay salary or wages during the leave) to establishing a social security system whereby some combination of employees, employers, and government pay into a fund out of which payments are made to individuals while they are unable to work. One two-stage model requires employers to pay wages for short periods of illness but provides benefits from the social insurance system for longer leaves associated with major illnesses. Reasonably short employer liability periods—seven to ten days a year—make it feasible for the employer to reimburse wages at a high rate and keeps administrative costs low, while ensuring that paid leave covers most common illnessess that adults and children suffer. Covering longer illnesses through social insurance ensures that employers will not be overburdened with long-term payments.

The overwhelming majority of countries around the world guarantee all working women and men some paid annual leave and a weekly day of rest. In these nations the right to reasonable work hours is built into employers' labor costs and is often seen as a sensible, basic human right that also enhances productivity.

Considering policy change is always difficult, and recommending programs with public and private sector budgetary implications is particularly difficult when the United States is only now recovering from the Great Recession. That said, many of the country's most important social and labor policies date from the Great Depression. While periods of economic duress raise understandable questions about the feasibility of change, they also naturally focus attention on how critical safety nets are to American of all ages. As articles throughout this issue of the *Future of Children* demonstrate, guaranteeing a floor of decent working conditions and social supports is essential not only to working parents but also to the healthy development of their children. We believe that evidence is equally compelling that such guarantees are economically feasible for the United States.

Endnotes

1. U.S. Bureau of Labor Statistics, "Employment Characteristics of Families, Table 4: Families with Own Children: Employment Status of Parents by Age of Youngest Child and Family Type, 2008-09 Annual Averages" (www.bls.gov/news.release/archives/famee_05272010.htm); U.S. Bureau of the Census, "Women in the Labor Force: A Databook" (2009 ed.), Table 7, "Employment Status of Women by Presence and Age of Youngest Child" (March) (www.bls.gov/cps/wlftable7.htm).

2. Lawrence Berger, Jennifer Hill, and Jane Waldfogel, "Maternity Leave, Early Maternal Employment and Child Health and Development in the U.S.," *Economic Journal* 115, no. 501 (2005): F29–F47; Sheila B. Kamerman, "Maternity, Paternity, and Parental Leave Policies: The Potential Impacts on Children and Their Families (rev. ed.)," in *Encyclopedia on Early Childhood Development (online)*, edited by R. E. Tremlay, R. G. Barr, and R. D. Peters (Montreal: Centre of Excellence for Early Childhood Development, 2005) (www.child-encyclopedia.com/documents/KamermanANGxp_rev-Parental.pdf).

3. Christopher J. Ruhm, "Parental Leave and Child Health," *Journal of Health Economics* 19, no. 6 (2000): 931–60.

4. Sasiko Tanaka, "Parental Leave and Child Health across OECD Countries," *Economic Journal* 115, no. 501 (2005): F7–F28.

5. Richard G. Feachem and Marge A. Koblinsky, "Interventions for the Control of Diarrhoeal Diseases among Young Children: Promotion of Breast-Feeding," *Bulletin of World Health Organization* 62, no. 2 (1984): 271–91; Kathryn G. Dewey, M. Jane Heinig, and Laurie A. Nommsen-Rivers, "Differences in Morbidity between Breastfed and Formula-Fed Infants. Part 1," *Journal of Pediatrics* 126, no. 5 (1995): 696–702; Peter W. Howie, and others, "Protective Effect of Breast Feeding against Infection," *British Medical Journal* 300, no. 6716 (1990): 11–16; Philippe Lepage, Christophe Munyakazi, and Philippe Hennart, "Breastfeeding and Hospital Mortality in Children in Rwanda," *Lancet* 319, no. 8268 (1982): 403; M. Cristina Cerqueriro and others, "Epidemiologic Risk Factors for Children with Acute Lower Respiratory Tract Infection in Buenos Aires, Argentina: A Matched Case-Control Study," *Reviews of Infectious Diseases,* suppl. 8, no. 12 (1990): S1021–28; Christopher J. Watkins, Stephen R. Leeder, and Richard T. Corkhill, "The Relationship between Breast and Bottle Feeding and Respiratory Illness in the First Year of Life," *Journal of Epidemiology and Community Health* 33, no. 3 (1979): 180–82; Anne L. Wright and others, "Breast Feeding and Lower Respiratory Tract Illness in the First Year of Life," *British Medical Journal* 299, no. 6705 (1989): 946–49; Michael Gdalevich and others, "Breast-Feeding and the Onset of Atopic Dermatitis in Childhood: A Systematic Review and Meta-Analysis of Prospective Studies," *Journal of American Academy of Dermatology* 45, no. 4 (2001): 487–647; Jennifer Baxter, "Breastfeeding, Employment and Leave: An Analysis of Mothers Growing Up in Australia," *Family Matters* no. 80 (2008): 17–26; Amanda R. Cooklin, Susan M. Donath, and Lisa H. Amir, "Maternal Employment and Breastfeeding: Results from the Longitudinal Study of Australian Children," *Acta Paediatrica* 97, no. 5 (2008): 620–23; Gustaf Aniansson and others, "A Prospective Cohort Study on Breast-Feeding and Otitis Media in Swedish Infants," *Pediatric Infectious Disease Journal* 13, no. 3 (1994): 183–88; Burris Duncan and others, "Exclusive Breast-Feeding for at Least 4 Months Protects against Otitis Media," *Pediatrics* 91, no. 5 (1993): 867–72; Cody Arnold, Susan Makintube, and Gregory Istre, "Daycare Attendance and Other Risk Factors for Invasive Haemophilus Influenzae Type B Disease," *American Journal of Epidemiology* 138, no. 5 (1993): 333–40; Stanley Ip and others, "Breastfeeding and Maternal and Infant Health Outcomes in Developed Countries," Agency for Healthcare Research and Quality, AHRQ Publication 07-E007 (April 2007).

6. Ip and others. "Breastfeeding and Maternal and Infant Health Outcomes in Developed Countries" (see note 5).

7. Adriano Cattaneo and others, "Protection, Promotion and Support of Breast-Feeding in Europe: Current Situation," *Public Health Nutrition* 8, no. 1 (2005): 39–46.

8. Sylvia Guendelman and others, "Juggling Work and Breastfeeding: Effects of Maternity Leave and Occupational Characteristics," *Pediatrics* 123, no. 1 (2010): e38–46; Baxter, "Breastfeeding, Employment and Leave" (see note 5); Cooklin, Donath, and Amir, "Maternal Employment and Breastfeeding" (see note 5).

9. Berger, Hill, and Waldfogel, "Maternity Leave, Early Maternal Employment and Child Health and Development in the U.S." (see note 2).

10. Berit Brandth and Elin Kvande, "Flexible Work and Flexible Fathers," *Work, Employment and Society* 15 no. 2 (2001): 251–67.

11. Ruth Feldman, Amy L. Sussman, and Edward Zigler, "Parental Leave and Work Adaptation at the Transition to Parenthood: Individual, Marital and Social Correlates," *Applied Developmental Psychology* 25, no. 4 (2004): 459–79; Rudy Ray Seward, Dale E. Yeatts, and Lisa K. Zottarelli, "Parental Leave and Father Involvement in Child Care: Sweden and the United States," *Journal of Comparative Family Studies* 33, no. 3 (2002): 387–99.

12. Linda Haas and Phillip Hwang, "The Impact of Taking Parental Leave on Fathers' Participation in Childcare and Relationships with Children: Lessons from Sweden," *Community, Work and Family* 11, no. 1 (2008): 85–104; Lindy Fursman and Paul Callister, *Men's Participation in Unpaid Care: A Review of the Literature* (Wellington: New Zealand Department of Labour 2009) (www.dol.govt.nz/publication-view. asp?ID=289).

13. According to Catherine S. Tamis-LeMonda and others, "Fathers and Mothers at Play with Their 2- and 3-Year-Olds: Contributions to Language and Cognitive Development," *Child Development* 75, no. 6 (2004): 1806–20, one example is resident fathers who engage their children in more cognitive stimulation have children with higher mental development (that is, memory skills, problem-solving skills, vocalization, language skills) at twenty-four months (as measured by the Bayley Scales of Infant Development, Second Edition Mental Development Index). For a brief summary of this research, see Andrew Kang and Julie Weber, "Opportunities for Policy Leadership on Fathers," Policy Briefing Series 20 (Sloan Work and Family Research Network, Chestnut Hill, Mass., 2009) (www.wfnetwork.bc.edu). See also Ann M. Taubenheim, "Paternal-Infant Bonding in the First-Time Father," *Journal of Obstetric, Gynecologic, and Neonatal Nursing* 10, no. 4 (1981): 261–4; Per Nettelbladt, "Father/Son Relationship during the Preschool Years: An Integrative Review with Special Reference to Recent Swedish Findings," *Acta Psychiatrica Scandinavica* 68, no. 6 (1983): 399–407. Although the bulk of the literature has focused on the bonds between mothers and infants, no evidence exists to suggest that bonding with fathers is any less significant to children.

14. Inger Kristensson-Hallstron, Gunnel Elander, and Gerhard Malmfors, "Increased Parental Participation in a Pediatric Surgical Daycare Unit," *Journal of Clinical Nursing* 6, no. 4 (1997): 297–302; Mervyn R. H. Taylor and Peter O'Connor, "Resident Parents and Shorter Hospital Stay," *Archives of Disease in Childhood* 64, no. 2 (1989): 274–76; Patricia A. LaRosa-Nash and Jane M. Murphy, "An Approach to Pediatric Perioperative Care: Parent-Present Induction," *Nursing Clinics of North America* 32,

no. 1 (1997): 183–99; Alan George and Janice Hancock, "Reducing Pediatric Burn Pain with Parent Participation," *Journal of Burn Care and Rehabilitation* 14, no. 1 (1993): 104–07; Sarah J. Palmer, "Care of Sick Children by Parents: A Meaningful Role," *Journal of Advanced Nursing* 18, no. 2 (1993): 185; Perry Mahaffy, "The Effects of Hospitalization on Children Admitted for Tonsillectomy and Adenoidectomy," *Nursing Review* 14 (1965): 12–19; John Bowlby, *Child Care and the Growth of Love* (London: Pelican, 1964); James Robertson, *Young Children in Hospital* (London: Tavistock, 1970).

15. See also Taylor and O'Connor, "Resident Parents and Shorter Hospital Stay" (see note 14); Kristensson-Hallstron, Elander, and Malmfors, "Increased Parental Participation in a Pediatric Surgical Daycare Unit" (see note 14).

16. Annete M. LaGreca and others, "I Get By with a Little Help from My Family and Friends: Adolescents' Support for Diabetes Care," *Journal of Pediatric Psychology* 20, no. 4 (1995): 449–76; Barbara J. Anderson and others, "Family Characteristics of Diabetic Adolescents: Relationship to Metabolic Control," *Diabetes Care* 4, no. 6 (1981): 586–94; Kim W. Hamlett, David S. Pellegrini, and Kathy S. Katz, "Childhood Chronic Illness as a Family Stressor," *Journal of Pediatric Psychology* 17, no. 1 (1992): 33–47; Clara Wolman and others, "Emotional Well-Being among Adolescents with and without Chronic Conditions," *Adolescent Medicine* 15, no. 3 (1994): 199–204; Cindy L. Hanson and others, "Comparing Social Learning and Family Systems Correlates of Adaptation in Youths with IDDM," *Journal of Pediatric Psychology* 17, no. 5 (1992): 555–72.

17. LaGreca and others, "I Get By with a Little Help from My Family and Friends" (see note 16); Wolman and others, "Emotional Well-Being among Adolescents with and without Chronic Conditions" (see note 16); Hamlett, Pellegrini, and Katz, "Childhood Chronic Illness as a Family Stressor" (see note 16); Stuart T. Hauser and others, "Adherence among Children and Adolescents with Insulin-Dependent Diabetes Mellitus over a Four-Year Longitudinal Follow-Up: II. Immediate and Long-Term Linkages with the Family Milieu," *Journal of Pediatric Psychology* 15, no. 4 (1990): 527–42; E. Wayne Holden and others, "Controlling for General and Disease-Specific Effects in Child and Family Adjustment to Chronic Childhood Illness," *Journal of Pediatric Psychology* 22, no. 1 (1997): 15–27; Katrina Johnson, "Children with Special Health Needs: Ensuring Appropriate Coverage and Care under Health Care Reform," *Health Policy and Child Health* 1, no. 3 (1994): 1–5; Timothy A. Waugh and Diane L. Kjos, "Parental Involvement and the Effectiveness of an Adolescent Day Treatment Program," *Journal of Youth and Adolescence* 21 (1992): 487–97; J. Cleary and others, "Parental Involvement in the Lives of Children in Hospital," *Archives of Disease in Childhood* 61 (1986): 779–87; C. P. Sainsbury and others, "Care by Parents of Their Children in Hospital," *Archives of Disease in Childhood* 61, no. 6 (1986): 612–15; Michael W. L. Gauderer, June L. Lorig, and Douglas W. Eastwood, "Is There a Place for Parents in the Operating Room?" *Journal of Pediatric Surgery* 24, no. 7 (1989): 705–06.

18. Isabelle Diehl, "The Prevalence of Colds in Nursery School Children and Non-Nursery School Children," *Journal of Pediatrics* 34, no. 1 (1949): 52–61; Peggy Sullivan and others, "Longitudinal Study of Occurrence of Diarrheal Disease in Day Care Centers," *American Journal of Public Health* 74, no. 9 (1984): 987–991; Merja Möttönen and Matti Uhari, "Absences for Sickness among Children in Day Care," *Acta Paediatrica* 81, no. 11 (1992): 929. Frank A. Loda, W. Paul Glezen, and Wallace A. Clyde Jr., "Respiratory Disease in Group Day Care," *Pediatrics* 49, no. 3 (1972): 428–37; K. Strangert, "Respiratory Illness in Preschool Children with Different Forms of Day Care," *Pediatrics* 57, no. 2 (1976): 191; Anna-Beth Doyle, "Incidence of Illness in Early Group and Family Day-Care," *Pediatrics* 58, no. 4 (1976): 607; Ron Haskins

and Jonathan Kotch, "Day Care and Illness: Evidence, Costs, and Public Policy," *Pediatrics* 77, no. 6, (1986): 951–80; Muriel Oyediran and Anne Bamisaiye, "A Study of the Child-Care Arrangements and the Health Status of Pre-School Children of Employed Women in Lagos," *Public Health* 97, no. 5 (1983): 267; Susan D. Hillis and others, "Day Care Center Attendance and Diarrheal Morbidity in Colombia," *Pediatrics* 90, no. 4 (1992): 582; Centers for Disease Control and Prevention, "National Immunization Program: "Estimated Vaccination Coverage with Individual Vaccines and Selected Vaccination Series among Children Nineteen to Thirty-Five Months-of-Age by State" (Atlanta: 2001); World Health Organization (WHO), *WHO Vaccine Preventable Diseases: Monitoring System* (Geneva: WHO Department of Vaccines and Biologicals, 2000); Kim Streatfield and Masri Singarimbun, "Social Factors Affecting the Use of Immunization in Indonesia," *Social Science and Medicine* 27, no. 11 (1988): 1237–45.

19. Centers for Disease Control and Prevention, "National Immunization Program" (see note 18); World Health Organization, *WHO Vaccine Preventable Diseases* (see note 18).

20. J. E. Fielding, W. G. Cumberland, and L. Pettitt, "Immunization Status of Children of Employees in a Large Corporation," *Journal of the American Medical Association* 271, no. 7 (1994): 525–30.

21. Vicky Lovell. *No Time to Be Sick: Why Everyone Suffers When Workers Don't Have Paid Sick Leave* (Washington: Institute for Women's Policy Research, 2004) (www.iwpr.org/pdf/B242.pdf).

22. S. Jody Heymann, Sara Toomey, and Frank Furstenberg, "Working Parents: What Factors Are Involved in Their Ability to Take Time Off from Work When Their Children Are Sick?" *Archives of Pediatrics and Adolescent Medicine* 153, no. 8 (1999): 870–74; Jody Heymann, *The Widening Gap: Why America's Working Families Are in Jeopardy and What Can Be Done about It* (New York: Basic Books, 2000).

23. National Alliance for Caregiving and American Association of Retired People, "Caregiving in the U.S." (Bethesda: 2004); Heymann, *The Widening Gap* (see note 22).

24. Alison Earle and S. Jody Heymann, "What Causes Job Loss among Former Welfare Recipients? The Role of Family Health Problems," *Journal of the American Medical Women's Association* 57 (2002): 5–10.

25. Charles Desforges and Alberto Abouchaar, "The Impact of Parental Involvement, Parental Support, and Family Education on Pupil Achievement and Adjustment: A Literature Review," *DfES Research Report* 433 (Chelsea: Department for Education and Skills, 2003) (http://publications.dcsf.gov.uk/eOrderingDownload/RR433.pdf); Arthur Reynolds, "Early Schooling of Children at Risk," *American Educational Research Journal* 28, no. 2 (1991): 392–422; Kevin Callahan, Joyce A. Rademacher, and Bertina A. Hildreth, "The Effect of Parent Participation in Strategies to Improve the Homework Performance of Students Who Are at Risk," *Remedial and Special Education* 19, no. 3 (1998): 131–41; Timothy Z. Keith and others, "Does Parental Involvement Affect Eighth-Grade Student Achievement? Structural Analysis of National Data," *School Psychology Review* 22, no. 3 (1993): 474–76; Paul G. Fehrmann, Timothy Z. Keith, and Thomas M. Reimers, "Home Influences on School Learning: Direct and Indirect Effects of Parental Involvement on High School Grades," *Journal of Educational Research* 80, no. 6 (1987): 330–37.

26. Leon Feinstein and James Symons, "Attainment in Secondary School," *Oxford Economics Papers* 51, no. 2 (1999): 300–21. This study found that parental interest had a much stronger effect than either in-school factors such as teacher-student ratios or social factors such as the family's socioeconomic status and parental educational attainment. See also Arthur J. Reynolds, "Comparing Measures of Parental Involvement and Their Effects on Academic Achievement," *Early Childhood Research Quarterly* 7, no. 3 (1992):

441–62; James Griffith, "Relation of Parental Involvement, Empowerment, and School Traits to Student Academic Performance," *Journal of Educational Research* 90, no. 1 (1996): 33–41; Sandra L. Christenson, Theresa Rounds, and Deborah Gorney, "Family Factors and Student Achievement: An Avenue to Increase Students' Success," *School Psychology Quarterly* 7, no. 3 (1992): 178–206; Deborah L. Miller and Mary L. Kelley, "Interventions for Improving Homework Performance: A Critical Review," *School Psychology Quarterly* 6, no. 3 (1991): 174–85; James P. Comer, "Home-School Relationships as They Affect the Academic Success of Children," *Education and Urban Society* 16, no. 3 (1984): 323–37; John W. Fantuzzo, Gwendolyn Y. Davis, and Marika D. Ginsburg, "Effects of Parental Involvement in Isolation or in Combination with Peer Tutoring on Student Self-Concept and Mathematics Achievement," *Journal of Educational Psychology* 87, no. 2 (1995): 272–81; Tracey Frigo and others, "Australian Young People, Their Families, and Post-School Plans" (Melbourne: Australian Council for Educational Research, 2007).

27. James P. Comer and Norris M. Haynes. "Parent Involvement in Schools: An Ecological Approach," *Elementary School Journal* 91, no. 3 (1991): 271–77; Griffith, "Relation of Parental Involvement, Empowerment, and School Traits to Student Academic Performance" (see note 26); Arthur J. Reynolds and others, "Cognitive and Family-Support Mediators of Preschool Effectiveness: A Confirmatory Analysis," *Child Development* 67, no. 3 (1996): 1119–40.

28. National Center for Education Statistics, "Father's Involvement in the Children's Schools," NCES 98-091 (U.S. Department of Education, 1997); Christine Winquist Nord, DeeAnn Brimhall, and Jerry West, "Dads' Involvement in Their Kids' Schools," *Education Digest* 63, no. 7 (March 1998): 29–35; Michael E. Lamb, "The Emergent American Father," in *The Father's Role: Cross-Cultural Perspectives,* edited by Michael E. Lamb (Hillsdale, NY: Lawrence Erlbaum Associates Publishers, 1987); Rebecca Goldman, *Fathers' Involvement in Their Children's Education* (London: National Family and Parenting Institute, 2005).

29. Desforges and Abouchaar, "The Impact of Parental Involvement, Parental Support, and Family Education on Pupil Achievement and Adjustment" (see note 25); Reynolds, "Early Schooling of Children at Risk" (see note 25); Callahan, Rademacher, and Hildreth, "The Effect of Parent Participation in Strategies to Improve the Homework Performance of Students Who Are at Risk" (see note 25).

30. F. Davis, "Understanding Underachievers," *American Education* 20, no. 10 (1984): 12–14; M. Gajria and S. Salend, "Homework Practices of Students with and without Learning Disabilities: A Comparison," *Journal of Learning Disabilities* 28 (1995): 291–96; S. Salend and J. Schliff, "An Examination of the Homework Practices of Teachers of Students with Learning Disabilities," *Journal of Learning Disabilities* 22, no. 10 (1989): 621–23; H. Cooper and B. Nye, "Homework for Students with Learning Disabilities: The Implications of Research for Policy and Practice," *Journal of Learning Disabilities* 27, no. 8 (1994): 470–79; S. Salend and M. Gajria, "Increasing the Homework Completion Rates of Students with Mild Disabilities," *Remedial and Special Education* 16, no. 5 (1995): 271–78.

31. Arthur J. Reynolds, "A Structural Model of First Grade Outcomes for an Urban, Low Socioeconomic Status, Minority Population," *Journal of Educational Psychology* 81, no. 4 (1989): 594–603; C. S. Benson, E. A. Medrich, and S. Buckley, "The New View of School Efficiency: Household Time Contributions to School Achievement," in *School Finance Policies and Practices: 1980's Decade of Conflict,* edited by James W. Guthrie (Cambridge, Mass.: Ballinger Publishers, 2005); Reginald M. Clark, "Why Disadvantaged Students Succeed: What Happens Outside Schools' Critical Period," *Public Welfare* (Spring 1990): 17–23.

32. Joyce L. Epstein, "Parent Involvement: What Research Says to Administrators," *Education in Urban Society* 19, no. 2 (1987): 119–36; Ray T. J. Wilks and Valerie A. Clarke, "Training versus Non-Training of Mothers as Home Reading Tutors," *Perceptual and Motor Skills* 67 (1988): 135–42; United Nations Children's Fund (UNICEF), *The State of the World's Children 2001* (New York: 2001); R. Myers, *The Twelve Who Survive: Strengthening Programmes of Early Childhood Development in the Third World* (London and New York: Routledge in cooperation with UNESCO for the Consultative Group on Early Childhood Care and Development, 1992); Linda P. Thurston and Kathy Dasta, "An Analysis of In-Home Parent Tutoring Procedures: Effects on Children's Academic Behavior at Home and in School and on Parents' Tutoring Behaviors," *Remedial and Special Education* 11, no. 4 (1990): 41–52.

33. Heymann, Toomey, and Furstenberg, "Working Parents" (see note 22); Heymann, *The Widening Gap* (see note 22).

34. G. Roger King, "The Healthy Families Act: Safeguarding Americans' Livelihood, Families and Health with Paid Sick Days," Testimony before the U.S. Senate Committee on Health, Education, Labor, and Pensions, February 13, 2007.

35. Berger, Hill, and Waldfogel, "Maternity Leave, Early Maternal Employment and Child Health and Development in the U.S." (see note 2); Susan Macran, Heather Joshi, and Shirley Dex, "Employment after Childbearing: A Survival Analysis," *Work, Employment, and Society* 10, no. 2 (1996): 273–96.

36. Edward Shepard and Thomas Clifton, "Are Longer Hours Reducing Productivity in Manufacturing?" *International Journal of Manpower* 21, no. 7 (2000): 540–52.

37. Defined as meeting six criteria: job autonomy, learning opportunities, decision making, involvement, coworker/supervisor support, and flexibility.

38. Ellen Galinksy, Sheila Eby, and Shanny Peer, "2008 Guilde to Bold New Ideas for Making Work Work from the 2007 Winners of the Alfred P. Sloan Awards for Business Excellence in Workplace Flexibility" (New York: Families and Work Institute, 2008) (http://familiesandwork.org/3w/boldideas.pdf).

39. For a full description of the adult labor database, see Jody Heymann and Alison Earle, *Raising the Global Floor: Dismantling the Myth That We Can't Afford Good Working Conditions for Everyone* (Stanford: Stanford University Press, 2010).

40. The World Economic Forum (WEF) is an international organization made up primarily of business leaders, as well as government officials and academic researchers. Its aims are to be "the foremost organization which builds and energizes leading global communities; the creative force shaping global, regional and industry strategies; [and] the catalyst of choice for its communities when undertaking global initiatives to improve the state the world." WEF primarily gathers together business leaders at summits, conferences, and meetings to discuss and develop solutions to global issues (www.weforum.org).

41. From 1987 to 2005 the WEF published the Growth Competitiveness Index, which ranked each nation according to its score on thirty-five variables that represent three conceptual areas: the macroeconomic environment, the quality of public institutions, and technology. Beginning with the 2006 report, this report was renamed the Global Competitiveness Index. The WEF reported rankings based on each nation's scores on more than ninety competitiveness indicators organized into nine areas: institutions; infrastructure; macroeconomy; health and primary education; higher education and training; market efficiency; technological

readiness; business sophistication; and innovation. Many of the data used in the competitiveness reports are obtained through a global network of 104 research institutions and academics that partner and collaborate with WEF, as well as from a survey of 11,000 business leaders in 131 nations. The categories are weighted to account more accurately for levels of development in measuring each indicator's impact on competitiveness.

42. World Bank, World Development Indicators, "Labor Force, Total, 2009" (http://data.worldbank.org/indicator/SL.TLF.TOTL.IN?order=wbapi_data_value_2009+wbapi_data_value+wbapi_data_value-last&sort=asc).

43. China has no national standard, but leave is available in certain circumstances in some provinces.

44. The agreed definition of "unemployed" is working-age individuals who are not working and are available for and actively seeking work. The unemployment rate is then equal to the number of unemployed persons as a percentage of civilian employees, the self-employed, unpaid family workers, and the unemployed. For further information on the selection and development of this unemployment definition, see Eurostat Internet site (http://europa.eu.int/comm/eurostat). The original data from each individual country that are merged to create the OECD unemployment database are either "registered" unemployment from administrative data sources or are from national household surveys (for example, the U.S. Census Bureau's Current Population Survey). In the early 1990s almost all OECD nations agreed to use a common set of criteria for classifying individuals as "unemployed" based on common household survey information. The only variations that still exist are the age group included in the calculation of the unemployment rate and the definition of an "active" job search. Over the past two decades (the time period from which our data come), the consistency, quality, and comparability of the OECD data have increased. In addition to consensus on the definitions, data collection and processing methods have converged.

DATE DUE